More praise for

PULL ME UP

"There is love of family, of location, of song, of learning, and of language itself. There is illness and despair and money worries, but what else is there to do but have a beer, listen to and sing with Johnny Cash, fall back on Irish ballads, and to hell with the begrudges? You won't soon forget this book."   —Frank McCourt, author of *Angela's Ashes*

"*Pull Me Up* is a vivid record of a time and a place, a culture and a people whose likes we will not see again, as well as a lyrical meditation on faith, love, mortality, and the redemptive power of storytelling. It's a marvelous piece of reporting, an elegy, a love song, a gift."
                    —Alice McDermott, author of *Charming Billy*

"After the current crop of memoir devoted to bizarre navel-gazing, this is that most marvelous of things, a book so specific we can see it all in our mind's eye and yet so redolent of an era that the details are our own."
                                  —Anna Quindlen

"Unlike other recollections of that period, Dan Barry's memoir of life in suburban Long Island is neither retro nor campy. In the flat world of parking lots, tract homes, yellow school buses and Little League, Barry has managed to find the richness of heart of a now oddly distant America. . . . It's rare to come across a contemporary personal memoir that was not written to be cried about on 'The Oprah Winfrey Show' or 'Jerry Springer.' Though the story of *Pull Me Up* involves all the familiar elements of cancer, alcohol and a sensitive young writer, Barry, through his skilled prose and deft storytelling, has made it fresh again."
                        —Wendy Wasserstein, *New York Times*

"I hope we can always celebrate a writer who, trying to make intelligent sense of life's confusions, gives us a memoir that is witty, self-aware and peopled with strong characters. That's the case with *Pull Me Up*, by Dan Barry. . . . What drives us to read his book is the veracity of local details, the charm of his sentences and his sympathetic engagement with everyday life. . . . It is indeed a familiar story, and you want to cheer because Barry tells it with such a likable, frank air. . . . The gratitude he registers at the end for the grace that permitted him to live a little longer seems not pious so much as well earned. He has become one who appreciates and expresses the sacramental miracle of everyday life."

—Phillip Lopate, *New York Times Book Review*

"This affectionate, tough-edged, expressive tale of that life will move readers already fans of his writing and offers an inviting introduction to a remarkable writer's work for those who do not yet know him. . . . A thoroughly notable American voice, speaking a thoroughly American personal saga."   —Michael Pakenham, *Baltimore Sun*

"Barry's story, told in clear, clean language, feels both idiosyncratic and paradigmatic. This is the tale of a particular lower-middle-class, Long Island, Catholic struggle, and at the same time it is every boy's suburban idyll."   —Barbara Fisher, *Boston Globe*

"There is much to mine here, starting with Barry's evocation of the other side of suburbia, of the daily struggle to survive rather than the Cheeveresque anomie that often characterizes the 'suburban novel.' . . . Indeed, Barry himself is an inspiring messenger, whether he intends it or not. . . . This is much more than another Irish-Catholic kitchen-sink drama in which religion and tradition are merely handy devices to advance the plot but bear little weight of their own. Nor is it a reflexive embrace of the faith of one's fathers, the idealization of heritage. Barry goes deeper than that, and perhaps begins to limn a new narrative for a new generation of Catholics. Rather than railing at, and rejecting, the church—and taking satisfaction in recounting such a meager victory—he wrestles with God and learns from the struggle, and by doing so seems to find strength, or at least a way to move ahead."   —David Gibson, *Commonweal Magazine*

"After reading *Pull Me Up*, Dan Barry's incandescent memoir about growing up in an Irish Catholic family on Long Island, we can forgive him for going to a certain Times Square broadsheet after interning at the *Daily News*. Barry writes, 'I chase stories the way a child chases fireflies with a glass jar.' He's the first person to make mid-Island seem poetic since Walt Whitman."

—George Rush and Joanna Molloy, *New York Daily News*

"A memoir that looks fondly, yet unsparingly, at the eccentricities and internal pathologies that bound his family together."

—Matt Burgard, *Hartford Courant*

"A poetic personal memoir, a kind of 'portrait of the journalist as a young man,' it's full of eloquently restored memories and often rueful reminiscences."

—John Anderson, *Newsday*

"Barry figured out 'that you want to capture what you see with words . . . to preserve moments and then turn them upside down to see what truth lies beneath. You want to entertain, inform, engage, enrage. You want epiphany through words.' This delicious memoir does all of that. And more."

—Sam Cole, *Providence Journal*

"A lyrically written memoir that carries the flavor and richness that somehow seems to grow on the Emerald Isle of Barry's ancestors . . . the American version of *Angela's Ashes*, a poignant tale of hardship, laughter, drinking, enlightenment, suffering and death. . . . His uncanny ability to find just the right word, just the right phrase, makes *Pull Me Up* a special read, almost a book-length poem."

—Lee Coppola, *Buffalo News*

"*Pull Me Up* combines all of the elements that raise a book to the level of classic: universal themes, deeply personal experiences, incisive observations. Barry's writing is lyrical, even poetic at times. . . . *Pull Me Up* is achingly funny, hilariously sad, and beautifully expressed—like a rollicking, satisfying Irish drinking song."

—Eileen Murphy, *The Irish Echo*

"Barry's moving and often hilariously detailed book reads much like the conversational stories Barry weaves from fertile territory for the *New York Times*. But the Long Island of his youth is also fertile ground for Barry, who conveys the small moments in life with poetic phrasing and ironic humor. His stories aren't flashy dramatic diamonds as much as poignant little gems."

—Christina Mitchell, *Cherry Hill Courier-Post*

"Dan Barry's pitch-perfect blend of journalistic detail, penetrating insight, and luminescent prose makes *Pull Me Up* a rare and wonderful achievement—funny, unflinching, poignant, and true. A masterful reporter and a skilled stylist, Barry gives us the portrait of an artist who has come into full possession of his art. *Pull Me Up* is a book to remember." —Peter Quinn, author of *Banished Children of Eve*

"Here is that rare book that will touch your heart, a memoir that you will never forget. Dan Barry is a wonderful writer who brings to life people and places you'll recognize, because his story is so profoundly human."

—Terry Golway, author and editor of *The Irish in America*

"The term 'a must read' has become hackneyed, but when the book is *Pull Me Up*, by Dan Barry, the phrase is right on. Barry's memoir of growing up Irish-Catholic on Long Island and beyond is nothing short of riveting." —Peter F. Stevens, *Boston Irish Reporter*

"Barry, who has shared a Pulitzer Prize and a George Polk Award, [has] become a Pete Hamill or Jimmy Breslin for a new generation. All in all, *Pull Me Up* is a unique spin on the Irish memoir, because he never takes the easy way out." —Tom Deignan, *Irish America Magazine*

"The experiences that Barry describes are compelling in themselves. But it is the quality of the writing that really lifts *Pull Me Up* far above the ranks of other memoirs. Vivid imagery abounds, yet none of it is overwrought. Mawkishness doesn't enter the picture; the book's most emotional moments are described with a kind of tender sparseness."

—Niall Stanage, *Sunday Business Post* (Ireland)

"Barry's story is woven out of ordinary people and things, and is sustained by anecdotes and quiet compassion—but most of all by the writing: alternately elegant, ironic, blunt and funny."

—Chris Powell, *Journal Inquirer*, Manchester, Connecticut

"While all peoples have storytelling traditions, the Irish are, arguably, the best storytellers. In his new memoir, *New York Times* columnist Dan Barry shows that he is a worthy bearer of that heritage. . . . The ultimate question we ask of any memoirist is this: Why should I care about this person's life story? It is, perhaps on the surface, easier to answer this question when we're talking about the lives of the rich and famous. But Dan Barry's story is worth hearing for exactly the opposite reason. He shows us that a man can rise from a far-from-certain start in life to well-earned success in his chosen field. He also shows us that, in their intimate inner workings, his life and all our lives have much in common."

—William C. Gibson, *New Orleans Times-Picayune*

"This is a beautiful book."   —*Publishers Weekly*

PULL ME UP

PULL ME UP

A MEMOIR

DAN BARRY

W. W. NORTON & COMPANY NEW YORK LONDON

This is a true story. I have changed some names because it seemed the right thing to do. Not everyone might welcome the association.

Grateful acknowledgment is made for the permission to reprint lines from: "Cocaine Blues" by T. J. Arnall © 1979 Unichappell Music, Inc. & Elvis Presley Music. All rights administered by Unichappell Music, Inc. All Rights Reserved. Used by Permission. Warner Bros. Publications U.S. Inc., Miami, FL 33014 (page 46); "Sons of God" by James Thiem © 1966 F.E.L. Assigned 1991 to the Lorenz Corporation. All rights reserved. International Copyright secured (pages 62–63); *We're Going on a Bear Hunt*, written by Michael Rosen and illustrated by Helen Oxenbury, reprinted with the permission of Margaret K. McElderry Books, an imprint of Simon & Schuster Children's Publishing Division and with the permission of Walker Books Ltd., London SE11 5HJ. Text © 1989 Michael Rosen (pages 269–70); "Let's Face the Music and Dance" by Irving Berlin, © 1935, 1936 by Irving Berlin © Copyright Renewed, International Copyright Secured, All Rights Reserved, Reprinted by Permission (page 285).

For information about permission to reproduce selections from this book, write to Permissions, W. W. Norton & Company, Inc., 500 Fifth Avenue, New York, NY 10110

Manufacturing by The Courier Companies, Inc.
Book design by Chris Welch
Production manager: Amanda Morrison

Library of Congress Cataloging-in-Publication Data

Barry, Dan.
  Pull me up : a memoir / by Dan Barry.—1st ed.
    p. cm.
  ISBN 0-393-04960-4
  1. Barry, Dan. 2. Journalists—United States—Biography. I. Title.
  PN4874.B328A3 2004
  070.92—dc22   2003027689

ISBN 0-393-32691-8 pbk.

W. W. Norton & Company, Inc.
500 Fifth Avenue, New York, N.Y. 10110
www.wwnorton.com

W. W. Norton & Company Ltd.
Castle House, 75/76 Wells Street, London W1T 3QT

1 2 3 4 5 6 7 8 9 0

To the Barrys, the Minogues, and those like them
to Nora and Grace
and, most of all, to Mary

PROLOGUE

Alive, alive o!
Alive, alive o!
Crying cockles and mussels
Alive, alive o!
—"Molly Malone"

DANNY, PULL ME UP. Pull me up, Danny.

So my mother said in her morphine dementia, in her dying days. She lay deep in the living room couch that had been her place all those years—where she had sat in maternal sentry, where she had told her stories. After every scene described, after every voice mimicked, there would come the vaporous blue exhalations, the smoke of spent words. She would take a sip of beer to douse the embers, or maybe to stir them, and then move on to the next image, and the next. With her cigarettes at hand and her glass forming rings on the beaten tabletop, she would conjure such vivid scenes that the television flickered in silence, a fire without heat.

Maybe her story that night would be about an encounter with an oddball neighbor—and who were we to call anyone odd?—so vividly rendered that you could smell the neighbor's coffee breath, feel the hem of her cotton housecoat, sense the depths of her quiet despair. Or maybe her story would take us back to her own childhood on a farm in the west of Ireland, no sentimental ity-dity-da there in her tough Galway days, with parents dying too young and she an orphan at fifteen, bound for some place called Brooklyn for a stretch of all-in-the-family servitude. Aah, still: the memories of cycling miles home in the pitch of midnight Ireland after a rousing dance, in country air charged with magic. Listen! Was that the wind rustling through the hedgerows? Or was it the whispers of a lady-ghost's gown? After all, her own learned father, a man who brooked no nonsense—he rarely took a drink, the family boasted, leaving unsaid that he just couldn't keep it down—once heard a banshee's wail. He told his children then, sipping his tea and smoking his pipe, as she was telling us now, sipping her beer and smoking her Parliament, with no hearth's glow upon her, just the television's electric blue.

But in these her last days, she had lost her thirst: cigarettes unlit, beers untouched, stories untold.

Pull me up, Danny, she called and locked those farmer's daughter's hands around my neck, those strong, plump-veined hands that once ran through my hair but now had me penned, like gates swung shut. And she said it again. But I could not pull her from that sensation of slipping away, of falling, falling. All I could do was assure her. Don't worry, Mom. I have you.

Oh Danny.

NOREEN BARRY, NEE Minogue, originally of Shanaglish parish, County Galway, and lately and sporadically of Sts. Cyril and Methodius parish, Deer Park, Long Island, died on a rainy morning in February; she was all of sixty-one. And that should have been that: another Irish mother dies and another brooding brood is less for it, weeping into its cups, unable to silence that awful old song about how you never miss a mother's love 'til she's buried beneath the clay.

But six months later it was my turn to begin slipping away. I lay on white linens in a cancer ward with a tumor in my trachea that had doctors whispering hospice, not hope. I was relegated to the forty-one-year-old nonsmoking tough-luck category, for which the recommended course of treatment was six months of kitchen-sink chemotherapy, one month of raise-me-up radiation, and incessant lip-trembling prayers, muttered skyward in the hope that something might stick. Oh Jesus, Oh Mary, Oh Mom. Pull me up.

One minute I had been the City Hall bureau chief of *The New York Times*, recording the Rudy rant of the day, blathering away on local television; in the self-involved political circles of New York City, I was a D-list celebrity. The next minute I was the bald guy with the oatmeal-colored complexion in the far corner of the newsroom, next to the vending machines, not knowing what he or the *Times* could do to ease his mind. I knew that I had to put things in perspective, but by this stage it seemed that too much perspective could be worse than too little.

Now, in the kitchen of my childhood, five steps down from the living room where she used to preside, my father sat with legs akimbo and a pale arm's reach from the refrigerator door. To his right teetered piles of *Newsday* and the *Times*; newspapers have always been the Barry wallpaper. After I've said good-bye, he will read every word, hunting for misspellings and misuses of language, scouring for hints of the conspiracies that he knows are at play in the world: the genetic engineering of crops, the pharmaceutical monopolies that allow millions in the Third World to die, the big-business bastards, the dogs of war, the sons of bitches. Then he will shrug again in defeat, a prophet ignored.

He lit another one of his daily eighty cigarettes—You don't mind, do you, Danny?—and asked me to crack the kitchen door a little. Why should I mind? Me, a cancer survivor, I hope, a nonsmoker who grew up swaddled in cigarette smoke, who could build an Empire State Building out of all the Marlboros and Parliaments and now the latest brand, Native—which are cheaper and, he thinks, healthier—that were sucked to stubs in my presence.

Ah, but what is the use of climbing my worn pedestal to lecture the man, a white-bearded widower now in a house alone, who jokes that coughing is the only exercise he gets, who listens only to news on the radio because the Irish music makes him sadder, makes him want to drink.

For the Barrys, stories have always provided illumination of life and distraction from it, and so I thought, Why don't I tell him a story now? So many stories took place in this house alone, this house with the grease-caked oven from all those hams cooked in celebration, with the pockmarked walls from all those fists thrown in anger. My mind flipped through the selections like one of those toaster-size jukeboxes that used to squat on the tables of that diner on Deer Park Avenue.

What if I talked about watching Mom dance with her vacuum cleaner to the music of Johnny Cash, sweeping the carpet while singing backup on songs about guns, cocaine, and Folsom? Or about how she used to keep a decorated artificial Christmas tree in the back of the garage, behind the lawn mower, and then cart it in each December, adding new tinsel to freshen the glitter of Christmases past? Who knows, maybe I could get him to talk about the UFOs. Like that night, one of many, when he and Mom loaded us four kids into the station wagon and drove two hours to Podunk, New Jersey, because his sources were telling him that flying saucers were frequenting a reservoir there, lining up as though it were some filling station for extraterrestrials. That was a great night, a glorious night.

There was no use to it. I couldn't pull him up now, so deep was his sorrow. But I had to pull myself up. I needed a fresh drink. Fresh air. Fresh stories.

And so we went in April's chill: Mary, my wife; our daughter, Nora, who was not yet three; and me. We packed Nora's slicker, the color of a bathtub rubber ducky. We packed the wild-blue fleece sweater that matches the light in Mary's eyes. We packed the frayed blazer that looks as though it had been woven from hay and twigs. It had belonged to my friend Bill's brother, a merchant marine who died alone, and, well, the ratty coat didn't quite fit Bill, so I got it.

Among the other necessities, the pants and skirts, the underwear and footsie pajamas, we packed pens and paper because I am naked without them. I have rustled through life with a notebook pressed against my chest and a pen bleeding in my pocket. They are the instruments I use to ease the low-grade panic born of the absurd sense that it is my mission to record moments. I chase stories with pen and paper the way a child chases fireflies with a glass jar and a hole-dappled lid. But when I capture those moments, those fireflies, I do not know what to do next. The light dies to leave shells of moments, just words, recorded on scraps of paper, bar napkins, and old reporter's notebooks that I keep in boxes.

Why did I linger along a fair's darkened midway to jot down a barker's prerecorded pitch, while a thin man of quiet menace sat in front of the canvas tent, studying this lanky Rube taking down notes like some wannabe Fed? Better yet: why do I still have those notes from a New England summer's night in 1987?

Ladies and gentlemen, your attention please. If you have come to see the rare and unusual, come right in and see Big Alfie, the giant pig. Big Alfie is twice the size of the average pig. He is over 1,000 pounds. He is eight feet long and four feet tall—that's the weight of the average horse. His jaws are so powerful that they could take a man's leg off in one bite. Come right in and see Big Alfie before you leave this area. He's one of a kind!

And why did I save my notes from yet another conversation with yet another caller to a newsroom, nearly twenty years ago? He said he was a computer analyst for a large insurance company, and he had an important story to tell. He seemed calm and reasoned enough, even as he described the fifteen-day hunger strike he had staged at a psychiatric facility—but that was not the purpose of this call, he assured me. Actually, it was because he had spent the last several weeks with his head covered by a paper bag, inside of which he had written various mathematical formulas designed to answer a central problem. And this is exactly what he confided next: "Sir, I've solved the brain."

Good on you, sir. But can you tell me, Why do I feel compelled to record life at the expense of living life? Why do I ignore the lessons learned from what I have been through? Why do I want to repair things that are beyond repair? Why am I nagged by the constant sensation that I should be somewhere else—standing there, not here; witnessing that, not this?

Sir, can you solve my brain?

———

THEN WE WERE there in Ireland, my family, my pens, and me. I reveled in the green of the place, ate the salmon of it, drank the black of it. I recorded it all in ink of blue. And when the nub of my mind's pen connected all the dots in all my notes, old and new, I realized that I had formed a circle. It could have been a Communion wafer; it could have been the mouth of a pint glass. But I saw it as a golden ring that, when grabbed, pulls you back and pulls you up.

PART ONE

I'll tell me ma when I get home
The boys won't leave the girls alone
Pulled me hair, stole me comb
But that's all right till I go home
—"I'll Tell Me Ma"

W E FLOATED UPON a cerulean sea of scattered Hardy
Boys books, bobbing alongside baseball cards and balled-
up socks, there beside the bunk beds. We hovered over
our compass, a cheap children's phonograph intended for sing-song
anthems, of jolly holidays and chim chim cherees. But Brian, my brother,
always with me, and I had other plans.

We pored over the album covers like cartographers, searching for
some Brigadoon-like portal through which to join the strapping men
portrayed on the covers, men with sweaters the color of sea foam and
smiles of Celtic confidence: the Clancy Brothers—Liam, Pat, and Tom—
and Tommy Makem. I placed the needle gently down to find the groove.
And then we sang, raising our young voices to join tenors and baritones
in the ballad of an inebriate, a song whose infinite sadness was masked
in a rousing defiance that beguiled us.

When I am dead and in my grave
No costly tombstone will I have
Just lay me down in my native peat
With a jug of punch at my head and feet.

We sang the rousing anthems of war:

I bear orders from the Captain, get you ready quick and soon
For the pikes must be together at the rising of the moon
At the rising of the moon, at the rising of the moon
For the pikes must be together at the rising of the moon.

And then echoed them with the dirges of war:

You're an armless, boneless, chickenless egg
You'll have to be put with a bowl to beg
Oh Johnny I hardly knew ye . . .

We played the songs over and over, leaning close to the phonograph so as to absorb every word, every note, every nick on the spinning vinyl disc; some Irish songs would never again sound right unless they included a skip or crackle, even if performed live. Then, once the lyrics were recorded in the grooves of our memory, we sang with open throats, emboldened by the belief that boys in bedrooms everywhere crooned about glistening bayonets, legless beggars, and infernal, magical moonshine.

You killed me old father but dare you try me . . .

But why did we sing them?

Was it for my mother, who returned to Ireland only once in her adulthood? Who never uttered an opinion on The Troubles, preferring instead to let her car's bumper sticker do the talking ("England Out of Ireland")? Who was more inclined to listen to "A Boy Named Sue" than "The Galway Shawl"? But who remained proudly, defiantly Irish?

Was it for my father, the grandson of Irish immigrants? Who learned early on the link between song and drink in the pubs of his New York City youth? Who as a troubled boy, just fifteen, joined his young buddies in touring those same bars, brashly singing out the ballads because they knew full well that on one of those stools, some crumpled man in his cups would look at the horror in the mirror, remember his own sainted mother, and send down a pitcher for the lads? Who, when the dark clouds that enveloped him briefly lifted, would whistle the Irish airs while slapping on Old Spice for the first, self-administered sting of the day?

Or was it for us, the children of Eugene and Noreen Barry—Brian, Brenda, Elizabeth, and me, the eldest? To help us in piecing together how we came to be, and how we came to be here on Long Island, in a place called Deer Park.

Our parents never told us too much about their own heritage, partly because they did not know that much. Distance, hardship, and alcohol had conspired to interrupt the chain of shared memories, leaving us with unlinked bits of genealogical gossip and a prop or two. A black-and-white photograph of Mom as a child, the only photo from her youth, kept in a hatbox in the attic: she a wisp, surrounded by adults all looking so farm-scrabble old, and long dead by the time we came along. A green beer mug from my father, handed out when FDR became president and we Irish Democrats drank from its ceramic lip to seal the promise inscribed along its side: Happy Days Are Here Again.

Now and then on a rare afternoon, while both parents were at work, I invaded their bedroom to search for clues. Even in their absence, the room retained their presence. It smelled of them—of Old Spice and Chanel No. 5, of daybreak cigarettes smoked in silence and late-night cigarettes smoked amid whispers about children and bills and eternal love. I inhaled them as I burgled, searching for the handful of historic documents that I knew were tucked in the backs of nightstand tables, or hidden in the closet behind yellowed copies of *Argosy* and *Playboy*.

Look at this: a diploma from the Curtis Evening High School, certifying that in June 1950 my father had completed "the general course of study with a satisfactory record in scholarship, behavior, and citizenship." That's right; he told us that he was working full-time by the age of sixteen, and had to finish high school at night.

And this: his separation papers from the army in 1954, after three years of enlisted service during the Korean War. Says here he spent eight weeks in Fort Hood, Texas. That fits; he told us once that while in Texas he had wised off to another soldier, whose comeback was a punch that broke his jaw. Also says here that he spent more than two years in Tokyo. He never talked much about what happened in Japan, other than that he was a corporal in "Intelligence." Intelligence, we liked that.

And this: a clipped-out article from the old *New York Journal-American*, from 1957, about how a securities firm in Manhattan had just opened a new office on Wall Street ("One of the new features of the new office will be the 'Whiz' tube system which enables orders and messages to travel at the rate of 25 feet per second through a pneumatic tube"). The accompanying photograph depicted a dozen gray men at work, indistinguishable from one another except for a floating arrow, drawn on the clipping to point out one in particular. Small, in the background, working the phone, it is my father.

Reading these documents was only a misdemeanor, it seemed to me. I figured that I had some vague, constitutional right to see records that, in a roundabout way, were about me. Only when I reached again for that small brown book, stored in my mother's nightstand table, did I feel truly invasive and guilty of some familial felony. It was an autograph book that my mother kept in the years between her departure from Ireland in 1953 and her marriage in 1957, at the age of nineteen.

There were the scrawled good wishes of friends she had made when she first arrived in Brooklyn, office workers with names like Sheila and Millie. There were no notes from my father, but there was one from a man named Norman: "Knowing you has been a pleasure. I trust we'll meet again and soon."

My head throbbed in anger whenever I read those words, no matter that they had been written in 1955, three years before I was born. Who the heck was this Norman? And what did he mean that knowing my mother had been "a pleasure"? He trusted that "we'll meet again and soon"? Just try, Norman. Just try.

But other notes pushed dark thoughts of Norman from my mind and started me to wondering, again, what life must have been like for her before. There were sweet and innocent jottings from her younger brother Joe ("Dear Sister, best wishes always"), her sister Chrissie ("The higher up the mountain, the cooler the breeze, the younger the couple, the tighter the squeeze"), and her sister Mary, my godmother, who would die of Hodgkin's disease at the age of twenty-five ("Though the hills and vales divide us, and together we cannot be, whenever you think of old Ireland, always think of me").

And there was the farewell note, written with hurried pen at the old Shannon Airport by a protective aunt who felt compelled to speak for a young country that in the 1950s seemed a generation behind the rest of the western world and could not provide well enough for its children:

Tis nice to be young in this generation,
For Little Nora is leaving our Irish Nation.

There were these scraps of tucked-away paper, and little else—a footstool, a lamp, an old suitcase with nothing inside but the must of the past—as though my parents were suburban pioneers who had come to Long Island with little more than the clothes on their backs, the children in their arms, and a yearning to start anew. What they gave us instead were the snippets of stories, some that came readily, others that had to be pried from the cement of hard memory.

I knew that we were among the many mutts of America, barking from fenced-in, third-of-an-acre yards that were chockablock across the island. I also knew that a few other children in our neighborhood had distinctive backgrounds, ones that stood out among the squirming progeny of former Bronx and Brooklyn tenement dwellers. A few houses down, for example, a man who yelled at his sons in a strange language had numbers tattooed on his arm, and so there was that story. Our distinction was this: we were the children of an Irish farm girl who had grown up without running water, without an indoor toilet, without.

But oh the songs. They were songs of drinking and warring, of laughter and longing, of furtive sex and sex denied, of girls with nut-brown hair and boys who die too young—of regret. Old old songs that seemed written especially for me, there in Deer Park, at twelve.

> And all I've done for want of wit
> To memory now I can't recall
> So fill to me this parting glass
> Good night and joy be with you all

BECAUSE NEITHER KNEW how to drive, they arrived first by train, along the Long Island Rail Road's ancient Ronkonkoma line, east from Queens and bound for this promised land they had heard so much about, this place of unimpeded sunlight and lush grass. Where stand-alone houses smelled of fresh paint, and not whatever the old lady in 5B was cooking; where the empty rooms soon filled with the squeals and gaa-gaas of children. Him fatherhood proud, projecting that who-you-trying-to-kid confidence, born of a knock-around city childhood and three years' service in the army—enlisted, pal, not drafted. Her pregnant with her second, another boy, and seeing no room for four in their Jackson Heights walk-up. Through the train's window they watched the green Long Island blur.

As the train passed through Farmingdale, right at the Nassau-Suffolk border, my father's veil of Cagney confidence slipped, and of all things he began to cry, which was not among his repertoire of off-putting habits. It took some maternal coaxing, but finally my mother drew from him the cause. A flashback, he said, an awful flashback. Somewhere near here was the boys' home that he had been sent to when he was very young. He had been temporarily orphaned for a few months or maybe a year—he had shunned it from memory—while his parents used alcohol to anes-thetize themselves from the realization that the soup-line shuffle had replaced the Charleston. As bad as his childhood had been—burning bed-bugs with matches at night, wearing hand-me-down clothes that reeked of urine, finding the family's possessions piled on the sidewalk after an eviction—this abandonment was so traumatic that he would never discuss it with his own children, never.

But Gene Barry was twenty-seven now, a husband and a father. As my mother recalled, in the telling of another of her stories, he composed himself—the hell with the past—and they traveled on to search for a new home in this place that a friend had told them about, this village carved from scrub oak and pine, this Deer Park.

If my parents could have afforded an Andy Hardy, Primrose Lane, let's-go-down-to-the-malt-shop community, they would have made their way a few miles south to Babylon, on the Great South Bay. There, it seemed, all the houses were made of brick, all the streets were shaded by mature oaks and leafy maples, and all the residents could brag of their village's traditional link to fishing and the sea. Instead, my parents scraped up a down payment for a house in Babylon's landlocked country cousin. No hint of salt air there; no rich heritage. Just farmland, scrub, and ever-multiplying subdivisions.

For a lot of people, Deer Park is the place you pass on your way to someplace else: Exit 51 off the Long Island Expressway. The Hamptons, a community so different that it might as well be part of another country, is a good sixty miles to the east, and the gold coast of the North Shore lies about thirty miles to the northwest. Deer Park is that place between the extremes: Long Island's spiritual median.

Among the seminal moments recorded in a slim volume of Deer Park history that is kept at the Deer Park Public Library is the opening of the village's first McDonald's, in 1971. It is an apt entry, for the Deer Park of my youth had the look of a town built in haste, tailored for the harried and lacking in any sense of permanence. There was no downtown center; most of the old farms and roadhouse taverns had yielded to the disposable landmarks of our age, the gas stations and auto-part stores, the supermarkets and franchise restaurants. Businesses along an ancient Indian path called Deer Park Avenue appeared and vanished, like mirages in the sun-baked asphalt shimmer.

The builders of other towns chose fairy-tale street names like Sleepy Hollow Way or Songbird Lane, or relied on repetitions of a theme: the names of presidents, of states, of Ivy League colleges. But the developers of Deer Park's west side had many acres of woods to clear, with scant time to get cute about the rows of cookie-cutter houses they had cobbled. This is how the Barrys came to reside at 140 West 23rd Street—an address that sounded so much like one from the city they had just abandoned.

THE HOUSE, A mile from the nearest store, was a raised ranch with two stories and an attached garage—virtually identical to the houses at 135 West 23rd, 139 West 23rd, and 151 West 23rd. Less than five years old, it was already creaking with secrets. In the stuffy, cobwebbed attic, a half-filled bottle of whiskey hung from a string attached to a pipe overhead—an unintended gift from the previous owner, whose dedication to inspecting the crawlspace of his new home was legend. And it was years before those new tiles in the finished basement—the room that clinched the deal for my parents—buckled and popped, revealing their true purpose: to mask the water that was forever seeping through the poorly laid foundation.

Gene and Noreen Barry, with a baby boy named Danny and another named Brian on the way, joined Bobby and Millie down the block and Richie and Rosie up the block, and Jim and Gladys across the street, and Tommy and Connie, and Phil and Joanie, and others too numerous to name. Nearly everyone had migrated from Morningside Heights in Manhattan, Bensonhurst in Brooklyn, Kingsbridge in the Bronx, or some other corner of New York City brick. In explaining the reasons for their move, some genteelly referred to "changes" in the old neighborhood, or the growing presence of "new" people; others lacked such tact. All of them, though, wanted grass.

That's all: grass. Having grown up in tenements, many of the residents of West 23rd Street had experienced grass only through city parks and faraway stories told by immigrant parents and grandparents. Grass meant private property, where kids could do things that they never could before, like play a simple game of catch without hearing, "Car!"—the shout that interrupted so many games on city streets.

Grass meant mine, and mine alone. From the fence to the curb, mine. And so I will mow it, keep it neat against the curb with a wheeled device called an edger, remain vigilant for yellow spots, and if I find any, talk to the Barrys again about those damned dogs of theirs, wandering piss machines. After a long summer's day at work, I will sit in the cool of my opened garage and watch the mesmerizing sweeps of my sprinkler, whose water sprays cast rainbows upon my lawn. It's not much, nothing like what you see in Old Westbury. But it's mine.

People did what they could to distinguish their properties from those of their neighbors, to break up the sameness of it all and assert their individuality. This was usually done with lawn ornaments. One family placed the booty from a week-long excursion to Pennsylvania Dutch country on permanent public display, including a *Wilkum* sign above the door that probably confused the hell out of the mailman. Another family opted for year-round Christmas lights, another for an unintended, Calder-like display of junked cars. We Barrys went with seashells and smooth rocks that my mother routinely pilfered from Robert Moses beach—and, for some reason, a single ceramic troll with a red hat.

Still, the similarities among the neighbors often overshadowed the differences. The world view of nearly all the parents had been defined by the Great Depression, and at block parties they would try to top one another with strained jokes about childhood deprivation.

No one talked about the psychological damage done by abandonment, or alcoholism, or the embarrassment of wearing shabby, ill-fitting clothes to school. Childhood experiences like those of my father were, if not universally shared, routinely understood. If, while playing another game of penny poker with the guys at a metal kitchen table, he suddenly bid with the distant recollection of holding the soles of his shoes together with string, the other men would not say, could not say, Poor Gene, musta been tough. Instead, they would provide validation with long, Adam's apple–bobbing drinks from cans of Rheingold and glasses brimming with cheap red wine. They would check the cards in their hands, maybe stack the pennies strewn before them. Then someone would crack wise about my father's footwear of the moment—Hate to tell ya, Gene, but them shoes you got on now ain't much better—to launch a funny, insult-swapping scrum about shoes and suit jackets and boroughs of origin. It was group therapy for people who would rather kiss the oncoming 5:48 out of Jamaica than seek professional help.

With two devastating wars and the depression behind them, the neighbors on West 23rd Street thought they had it made. Leave it to others to smirk about the suburbs: the ticky-tacky houses, the stamp-sized lawns, the slapstick wrestling with hoses and sprinklers. Most of them did not realize that a genre of American literature was dedicated to the unflattering dissection of suburbs. They probably had never heard of Cheever or Roth, and if they had, most likely they would have threatened to pile into a station wagon to go kick some artsy-fartsy ass—though they would not have known where to go. Few from our neighborhood ever went to the North Shore, or to the Hamptons, unless it was to install a toilet or do some landscaping job.

There was that one afternoon, though, when our parents drove us in the family's Chevy Impala station wagon to the Hamptons. They had read in *Newsday* that a couple of women, relatives of Jackie Onassis, were living in a run-down mansion infested with cats. We packed some sandwiches, drove dozens of miles east to the land of the rich, and inched past what we thought must be the notorious mansion, straining to detect every detail of squalor. We discussed the lesson that money cannot buy happiness; we expressed pity; we basked in the fleeting moment of feeling superior. And then we drove dozens of miles west, back to where we belonged.

Our own neighbors—men with bloated bellies who could throw horseshoes without spilling their beer, women with marble-veined legs who could convey affection in their bellows to get the hell out, or get the hell in—were the giants of my world, a world of twenty-one houses along West 23rd Street, bounded by Grand Boulevard and Park Avenue. Some of its inhabitants said "terlit" instead of "toilet." Some told us to get lost by saying "scram" or by suggesting that we go play with broken glass on the railroad tracks. Some taught us the poor-kid games of their youth: johnny-on-the-pony, or stickball, or skelly, where the only equipment necessary was a bottle cap filled with melted crayon that could be flicked along the pavement, from one numbered box to the next. Some taught us obscure songs and ditties that would remain imbedded in our brains until we died.

My mother and your mother were hanging out the clothes
My mother punched your mother right in the nose
What color was the blood?

They were the secular chants of the street, echoing the time and place of other childhoods, those of our city-bred parents. But we would not pass these chants on to our own children; too violent, we would say, too racy. And so the words loop forever in our memory, with no place to go. Whatever happened, for example, to Miss Lucy? I remember she had a steamboat, and the steamboat had a bell. Then Miss Lucy went to heaven and the steamboat went to

Hello operator, give me number nine
And if you disconnect me, I'll kick you in the
Behind the 'frigerator, there was a piece of glass
Miss Lucy slipped upon it and broke her little
Ask me no more questions, tell me no more lies
The boys are in the bathroom pulling down their
Flies are in the meadow . . .

Amid all these songs and games, they also taught us how to glory in suburbia because, Kid, you don't know how good you got it. You don't know nothing, they'd say, and of course they were right.

In those early years, from the late 1950s to the dawn of the 1970s, the people of Deer Park's subdivided west side knew how good they had it. They celebrated their pioneering spirit with all-night block parties and costume get-togethers inspired by prime-time television fare. My mother once dressed up as the sit-com vampire Morticia Addams, my father as the nutty old-lady character created by Jonathan Winters. The workweek began with the women playing mah-jongg on Monday nights and ended on Fridays with games of canasta that devolved into drinking sessions before winners could be declared. On weekends, they drank mixed drinks and ran barefoot on grass, their grass.

Each household on our block possessed its own habits and manner of speech—its own color, in a way. But when blended together, by happenstance or intention, these colors created a new and distinct hue, one not to be found in Commack, or Massapequa, or even on West 22nd Street. It was peculiar to a moment and place in time, and was absent on the color charts at the paint store up on Deer Park Avenue. You had to be a part of it to see it, this color called West 23rd.

Some residents splashed more color on the canvas than others. Down the block lived Sharon Bernardi, who saw life through finger-smudged glasses. One summer she won the friendship of all the neighborhood children with a breathtaking generosity. Every time the Bungalow Bar ice cream truck—shaped like a cottage and sporting its own pitched roof— came tinkling down the street, Sharon bought toasted almond bars and ice pops for every grimy hand stretched out before her. We thanked her by singing the famous Bungalow Bar song of farewell ("Bungalow Bar tastes like tar, the more you eat, the sicker you are"), which never failed to elicit a parting Italian epithet from the discarded wrapper of a driver, an old man we knew only by the nickname of "Baciagaloop."

One black day on West 23rd Street, Mr. Bernardi discovered that his cherished collection of American silver coins had been depleted, and the local mystery of the source of his daughter's beneficence was sadly solved. What her father must have thought: dozens of Mercury dimes and Standing Liberty quarters, rare coins whose collective weight reflected his adult worth, exchanged for the most perishable of items. Items that melted if not eaten; items that left only sticky sticks of wood for posterity.

Across from where Sharon Bernardi gazed forlornly out her living-room window—the word on the street was that her parents had grounded her until Thanksgiving—there lived the Jorgenson family, whose father worked long hours doing work that darkened his blue collar with the damp of sweat. But he relaxed after-hours in the shade of an old BelAir's raised hood. He spent so much time hunched over the engine that my father remarked that he was breech-born from a Chevy. Meanwhile, his wife, wearing sunglasses, high heels, and Capri pants so tight that she dared not cough, would languish on the front lawn, rising now and then to water down the driveway with a garden hose. This odd form of yard work seemed designed to drive the neighborhood men crazy, which it did—a few with desire, more with mental calculations of what the Jorgensons' water bill must be.

The neighborhood judgment, reached by Star Chamber consensus over the greasy memory of an Entenmann's Danish ring, was that Mrs. Jorgenson had indeed acted upon a more liberal interpretation of her marriage vows. This was based on three damning pieces of evidence. First: men who were clearly not from the neighborhood occasionally visited the Jorgenson house in the middle of the afternoon, when Mr. Jorgenson was idling his engine somewhere in Long Island Expressway traffic. Second: one of these male visitors drove a Cadillac—enough said. And third: the week after the last of the Jorgenson children had graduated from high school, Mr. Jorgenson climbed into his fine-tuned BelAir and drove down West 23rd Street for the last time.

There were others who contributed to the neighborhood story: Young Ernest and Joseph, whose foreign-speaking father had those numbers tattooed on his arm; he could explode in rage at the squeak of a gate, the slam of a door, the sound of young laughter. The eccentric Mrs. Guilderland, who insisted on teaching cats to swim no matter how many perished in her backyard pool; the neighborhood children were forbidden to enter her home. The Palmers, whose children never left their front yard, whose obese mother never even left the house; all the neighborhood women sighed when recalling how beautiful Eleanor Palmer had been when she first came to West 23rd. The Simons, whose teenage daughter died in a car accident. Two days later, all her stuffed animals, the fluffy relics of birthdays and carnivals, were piled at the curb, droopy from rain, waiting for garbage pick-up. For weeks afterward, my mother could not bear to drive past their house.

So much rain has fallen since those stuffed animals wept at curbside; so many changes have come to West 23rd. Many of the neighbors, like the daughter-less Simons, have moved away. Others, like crazy Mrs. Guilderland, have died. But once, in the time of Tricky Dick, in the time of astronauts planting the American flag on the moon, they lived side by side in one of those subdivisions you drive past without noticing. They borrowed cups of sugar, they split six packs of beer, they worked, squabbled, laughed, hollered, and seared memories into the minds of the children all about them. The Bernardis, the Jorgensons, the Palmers. Oh. And the Barrys.

2

THIS IS HOW it was: My father, a tall, good-looking ringer for Nelson Eddy, hustling out at 6:30 every morning to catch the Long Island Rail Road, known in our house as the "goddam train," and often coming home later than other fathers, his noose of a tie loosened, his suit a cloth wipe for smoke and sweat. Many times his rumpled appearance was caused by the drudgery of it all, commuting two hours to work in an unreliable, rolling sardine can, hawking stocks and bonds all day on Wall Street, returning two hours back squeezed between strangers. But sometimes he looked the way he did because he had had a few too many, the result being a succession of train connections missed. This required my mother to pack her four young children into the station wagon and drive a mile to the Wyandanch train station every half hour or so. Together we would hunt for my father among the men disgorged into the night by the 6:38, the 7:08, or the 7:38 bound for Ronkonkoma. Kids, kids, pay attention. Keep an eye out for your father. Is that him? Coming down the stairs? No? Some nights we just sat at the train station in silence, listening for the clanging of crossing signals, waiting for a tiny dot of white to appear at the distant end of the track line. Now and then my mother would quiz us to pass the time. What is the capital of South Dakota? Of North Dakota? Of Oregon? But there are only fifty states; if it got too late, we would return home and wait for the call.

Gene? What do you mean you fell sleep?

Our mother's words cuffed our ears, sounded a warning.

And where are you now? Ronkonkoma?

Ronkonkoma?!?

That meant my mother had to bundle her brood into the family's one car once again and drive forty minutes east to the last stop on the line. Tension, like the smoke from my mother's cigarettes, filled our station wagon on those Ronkonkoma rescues. So much depended on his mood. If he climbed into the car with the latest edition of *Mad* magazine, or some Mexican dancing beans that he had picked up at a novelty store, then we knew everything was all right. Soon we would be eating in peace: invariably Swedish meatballs and noodles, followed by bowls of ShopRite-brand artificial vanilla ice cream, as we watched *The Merv Griffin Show* together, a family after all. But if the car's interior light revealed a certain wild look, and if his peppermint Lifesavers were not enough to mask the smell of alcohol, and if he slammed the passenger door shut, then we knew that the night, if not the next several days, was lost to shouting and slamming of doors and contrived reasons for sending us to our rooms. Our father was clearly not always at peace.

He infused our house with a defiant city atmosphere, idiosyncratically shaped by a harsh childhood and an insatiable thirst for the printed word—everything from the *Mad* magazines of the Harvey Kurtzman era to the *Encyclopedia Americana* volumes that he had bought at my birth. He sometimes explained himself by quoting Rafael Sabatini's description of his swashbuckling character, Scaramouche: "He was born with a gift of laughter and a sense that the world was mad." He rejected most of what our neighbors in the 1960s bought into—the American value system. He refused to let Brian and me join the Boy Scouts—"a little army," as he called it. He refused to let us play football—a blood sport and a risk to developing bone structures. But he also refused to let us listen to the Beatles, who he felt advocated drug use.

Gradually, our value judgments were shaped by what he hated, and loved.

He hated Bob Hope; he loved Bob and Ray.

He hated Nixon; he loved Kennedy.

He hated opera; he loved *A Night at the Opera.*

He hated "Strangers in the Night"; he loved "Wimoweh."

He hated Liberace; he loved W. C. Fields.

He hated red beets, which tasted of the depression, night after night, cheap red beets. But he loved red cabbage.

He hated John Wayne. The only battles that sonofabitch fought were on movie lots, while kids were dying in Normandy and Guadalcanal. And now he's got the goddamned gall to wrap himself in the flag and mouth off about Vietnam? Like he's some war hero? Like he actually went to Bataan?

My father seethed at the thought, his hands gripping the frayed arms of his living room chair, his eyes slits of contempt. *Sonofabitch* was too good a term for John Wayne. He was worse; he was a motherless bastard.

It seemed at times that my father hated more than he loved. But there was one thing he loved above all else, including his children. That was his wife, and everybody knew it; she was the final piece to the Gene Barry puzzle, the piece in the center of his chest. An attractive brunette, still slim after four children and two miscarriages, his Galway beauty worked as a clerk in some cellblock office on Route 110 in Farmingdale. At home she was the one who mowed the lawn, trimmed the hedges, painted the rooms, hung the wallpaper, did the laundry, bought and cooked the food. Maybe this was because my father couldn't have been bothered, or maybe because she was squeezing what she could from a way of life that she never could have imagined just fifteen years before, when she was living on a farm in Ireland, with few amenities and no mother.

My mother had her own distinct tastes, of course. She preferred Schmidt's beer to Budweiser, Scrabble to Monopoly. She hated the movie *Shane* because she thought the kid was a whiner, but loved to cry over the plight of the kids in *The Sound of Music.* She became furious with me one Easter night for cheering when the quisling boyfriend tells the Nazis where they might find the fleeing von Trapp family. She loved to play a silly game in which two people standing several feet apart tried to flip a quarter with carefully placed bounces of a Spalding; we would not know until years later that these contests, which had no name, were a variation of an old Irish street game called Pitch and Toss.

Generally, though, my mother did not define her world in terms of likes and dislikes. Her upbringing on a farm, it seemed, had taught her early on that life is not meant to be all bountiful harvest. The rain sometimes falls too much, or not enough; cows die in calving. This closeness to the ground, this acceptance of the impersonal natural order, endowed her with quiet command. My father would rail from his armchair, issuing edicts and delivering rants. But none carried the weight of law until my mother had separated the wisdom from his bombast, as though culling wheat from chaff.

A carefully maintained detachment from everything outside her family's walls further enhanced my mother's authority. The neighbors knew, for example, that she had been in the United States since 1953 but still refused to become a naturalized citizen. She preferred crossword puzzles to soap operas, yard work to getting her nails done. The resulting question of gossips—Who does she think she is?—really did not need to be answered, because it was obvious. By keeping her distance, albeit politely, from the suburban humdrum and hubbub, my mother made it clear that if you wanted a job done or a decision made at 140 West 23rd Street, she was the one to see, and the one who saw. She saw it all.

We could be driving to the Food Fair supermarket in the Sunset City shopping center, or maybe to the ShopRite, if they had a better sale on milk. Or we could be going to Sts. Cyril and Methodius Church, up on Deer Park Avenue. Wherever we went, whether to feed our stomachs or nourish our souls, my mother was always the one behind the wheel, eyes alert, taking it all in. And every five seconds, or so it seemed, she looked into the rearview mirror of the 1968 Chevy Impala station wagon to check on her gang of four, pen marks on their hands, peanut butter on their breath, reading books, teasing one another, staring out the window, waiting for what came next.

There was Brian, born in the Cold War year of 1959. Lanky and blond, he was so smart that the family transposed the vowels in his name to give him the nickname "The Brain." He played the guitar, the trumpet, the harmonica, and any other musical instrument placed before him, and he could do a dead-on imitation of Rex Harrison's solos on the original Broadway cast recording of *My Fair Lady*. Brian was the fearless one, the one who jumped from the ten-foot diving board at the town pool, the one who let garden snakes coil around his arms, the one who would strike a match just for the danger of holding a dancing blue flame. He played endless games of catch with me; he was my best friend.

There was Brenda, born in 1961, the year the country witnessed the inauguration of its first Roman Catholic president. Brenda was blond and cute and determined to collect stray animals the way her brothers amassed baseball cards. Her First Holy Communion portrait, with her mouth closed to conceal the tooth knocked out by an errant playground swing, was so beatific that our parents framed it in silver and set it in a place of honor—on top of the television. She worshiped Humphrey Bogart.

There was Elizabeth, born in 1964, the year after the assassination of that Roman Catholic president. Elizabeth was blond and cute as well, but with the toughness that comes from being the youngest of four. She was nicknamed "Lizbat," and she was the baby, and when she was very young she sang herself to sleep to the "yeah yeah" lyrics of "She Loves You." What could our father say about Beatles lyrics so innocuous? If Brenda loved Bogart, Elizabeth loved Cagney, and he was better because at least he was still alive.

And there, face pressed against the far window like a Labrador retriever out for a Sunday drive, her oldest, Daniel Francis. Born in 1958, he was named after a maternal grandfather who died years before Danny was born and a paternal grandfather who died three months after. Look at him there, she must have wondered. What's to become of him?

I was tall for my age, gawky, with a concave chest in which pools of water formed when I took a bath. I had straight brown hair with a cowlick in the back. I had the first tiny marks of acne flecking my chin, harbingers of roaring facial battles to come.

I had an overbite so pronounced that I could fit three fingers between my upper and lower teeth; it seemed that I needed two spoonfuls of oatmeal to consume just one. My parents had no choice but to take me to an orthodontist who shoved bits of metal, swabs of cement, some rubber bands, and anything else he could find around the office into my gaping mouth. When he finished, my lips became the gates to Erector Set City. I obviously needed the braces, but they limited my facial movements. A simple yawn might snap a rubber band and send it rocketing out of my mouth to clip the ear of the student in front of me.

My poor coordination as a young boy marked me for life. I had once fallen off my bicycle and banged my head hard on the pavement, imbedding a stone the size of a Rice Krispie into my forehead, about an inch above my eyebrows. My mother's Old World solution: dab the wound with hydrogen peroxide and leave the stone protruding from my head for about two weeks. It was there when I went to school, when I went to church, when I sat in the living room watching Bugs Bunny cartoons. Then, one day, my mother gently picked the stone out, leaving a much smaller mark than if she had pried it loose on the first day.

I loved reading about gangsters: Dillinger, Capone, Vincent "Mad Dog" Coll. I loved the Dead End Kids, the Marx Brothers, the Little Rascals, and all the horror films produced by Universal Pictures. I reveled in knowing that L.S.M.F.T. stood for "Lucky Strike Means Fine Tobacco"; that W. C. Fields used to threaten to sic a woodpecker on Charlie McCarthy; that Bing Crosby won an Academy Award for *Going My Way*. I loved all these things because they evoked the 1930s and 1940s, the period of my father's mysterious childhood, and I could run to him and say, Daddy, Daddy, come to the living room, Billy Gilbert just showed up in a Laurel and Hardy short. And he and I would smile because we were probably the only father and son who knew who Billy Gilbert was—a character actor known for his magnificent sneezing fits—or at least were the only ones talking about him at that very moment.

Like my father, I came to crave Entenmann's: the chocolate layer cakes, the cupcakes, those raspberry pastries with white "drizzle" frosting. That's how he would describe them as my mother left for Food Fair—and get an Entenmann's, the raspberry drizzle. The white Entenmann's boxes, adorned with that elegant blue script, were as essential as the oven to a Long Island kitchen. They were removed from their places of honor, usually on top of the refrigerator, and presented for every occasion: weddings, wakes, mah-jongg, breakfast, midmorning coffee breaks, lunch, dessert, and that late-night something that goes so well with *The Honeymooners*. For us, Entenmann's was the bread of life.

I shared a bunk bed of Western, wagon-wheel design in a room with Brian, who was eighteen months younger but already stronger than me. This was our haven. We decorated the walls with the covers of *Mad* magazine. We collected the blue-covered Hardy Boy books—*The Tower Treasure, The Missing Chums, The Mystery of the Chinese Junk*—and secretly wished for some dastardly crime to be committed in our neighborhood so that, like Frank and Joe Hardy, we too could do some brotherly sleuthing. At night, we turned on a transistor radio and listened to the cackles and confidences of Jean Shepherd on his nightly broadcast. He would begin spinning a yarn about his childhood in the Midwest, pause to rant against some obnoxious television commercial or to sing a chorus of "The Sheik of Araby," and then return seamlessly to complete that wondrous and wistful tale.

Sometimes we fought in our sanctum. During one brawl, one of us kicked a heel through the wall. It was hardly the last hole to be punched through the walls and doors of that house, but this particular hole became the hellgate of nightmares. More than once I awakened in a sweat from having dreamed that trolls were crawling out of it to take me away, like those child-snatching fairies of my mother's Ireland.

Most of the time, though, my brother and I comforted each other. When our father barreled out of the house and sped away, pressing the gas pedal so that the engine roared in final exclamation to his last furious point. When there was nothing for us to do except wait, sometimes for hours, until we heard the reluctant grumble of tire upon gravel, meaning that he had returned; he always returned. Or just when there was something a boy could not even articulate to his brother: the embarrassment of wearing braces, or the hurt of a parent's unwarranted cuff to the back of the head. That was when we climbed together into the bottom bunk and took turns caressing each other's back in a gentle tickle.

First came the argument over who would tickle whose back first, for it was always best to be tickled last; that way you could drift toward sleep with the sensation of fingers sliding across your back and the knowledge that all your obligations had been met. Then came the argument over the length of tickle time, which was measured by the one doing the tickling:

Onetwothreefourfive . . .

You're counting too fast! Go slower, like I did.

Then came the argument over technique:

You're doing it too hard! Do it softer.

You're a real jerk, you know that?

Silence came next, with two tired young bodies taut with the anger of the wronged. Then the anger faded, and the desire to reassure—and be reassured—returned:

Okay, let's tickle in words. What word am I writing on your back now?

Fork?

No.

What's the first letter?

J.

Pause.

Jerk?

A snort turned into a giggle, which turned into two giggles, which encouraged outright laughter that shook the bed despite the shooshes from one brother and then the other, and the two young bodies were now shaking in silliness, and—

Go to sleep goddammit!

Our father's command seemed to fly up the stairs, as we knew he would at the sound of the next peep. We knew that things could quickly escalate, so we traded shooshes and composed ourselves. Then one boy's forefinger returned to his brother's back, looping figure-eights until, finally, it skated off the map of consciousness.

THE BARRYS TRIED to blend in as best they could. My father joined the other neighborhood men in posing as leaders of small tribes; they stood together around backyard barbecue grills, drinking the beer they deserved and feeling the heat on their crotches as blood-red beef patties turned to black. My mother took her turn as hostess of the weekly mah-jongg games, a singular treat for us children. In addition to inheriting the leftover eclairs from the Cream Puff Bakery, we got to watch Mrs. Spitz drink so many grasshoppers that her eyes would close and her head would fall back, as though toppled by the weight of her glorious bouffant. The boys played Little League, the girls played softball. We went to church on Sundays.

In many ways, though, we were the family from another planet. Like other Roman Catholic households, we kept *This Is the Mass* and other works by Archbishop Fulton J. Sheen on our bookshelves. But our Sheen books cracked when they were opened. My father had acquired the works of the good bishop years earlier to prove that he had set aside his wise-ass atheist ways and was therefore worthy of joining this virginal Irish farm girl in the blessed sacrament of Holy Matrimony. These few volumes exploring the mysteries of faith were also surrounded, even overshadowed, by dozens of books about the mysteries of the universe: UFOs, extrasensory perception, alien encounters, government conspiracies, reincarnation, secular prophets, and other subjects that subverted the Sunday homilies we endured at St. Cyril's.

My father was an avid student of the paranormal and pursued the possibility of alien life with all the determination and considerable brain power he could muster. He established contacts with other conspiracy theorists around the country, collected photographs of the most plausible sightings, and developed such a reputation among the UFO cognoscenti of Long Island that a professor at Hofstra University in Hempstead invited him to participate in a panel on the subject of extraterrestrial life. We children sat in the back of the auditorium, eating French fries and basking in the reflected glory of a father finally being recognized for his mastery of such a narrow and potentially world-shaking discipline.

UFOs—or, rather, the pursuit of them—became integral to our family life. In our pockets we carried blue business cards identifying us as officials of a new organization called AIR: Aerial Investigation and Research. We also joined in the occasional research missions that my father conducted on behalf of an information clearinghouse called MUFON, the Mutual UFO Network. One weekend afternoon, we accompanied him to Plainview to interview a man who lived on a hill and had seen something in the nighttime sky—something curious. A case, perhaps, for the Hardy Boys of West 23rd Street.

There were late-night phone calls from mysterious men, strange packages arriving in the mail, and loud, unsettling discussions that lasted into early dawn. Wisps of those alcohol-fueled conversations rose like heat from the living room, up to the bedroom where Brian and I lay, too scared to sleep and too enthralled to close our door. Other children may have nodded off with the strains of soothing lullabies in their heads; we tossed and turned, our minds veering from one heart-stopping image to another. That photograph of ectoplasm dripping from a woman's mouth like a warmed-over Charleston Chew. Those breathless reports of alien abductions and ghostly encounters. Among the many stories overheard, one in particular rattled my little world. A farmer is walking across a field while his wife and a local judge are chatting on the farmhouse porch, gazing after him. Suddenly, the farmer vanishes—swallowed, my father theorized, by a breach in the limited dimensions of our world, a wrinkle in time. For years afterward, the wife would go to the spot and hear her husband calling for help, but she never saw him again.

If a fissure in time could form on a farm, I reasoned, one could just as easily develop somewhere in Deer Park. And with my luck, I'd be the one to stumble through, my pleas for help too low to be heard above the everyday suburban clatter: the summer roars of lawn mowers, the winter moans of cold car engines, the shouts of children, the rustles of weeping willows. Whenever I walked alone down my street at night, I thought of the disappearing farmer and quickened my step.

Other families went on traditional outings to the bowling alley or the miniature golf course; we went in search of UFOs. One summer evening, our parents had us dress in pajamas and piled us into the gray Chevy station wagon for a "very special" eighty-mile trip to a place called Wanaque, New Jersey, where alien spaceships supposedly had been spotted hovering over a local reservoir.

As the oldest, I always got a window seat, a privilege that suddenly grew in importance, given the evening's special mission. I stuck my hand out the window, letting it rise and fall with the warm slices of air as our car traveled west along the Long Island Expressway. By the time we made it to the George Washington Bridge, its necklace of lights was twinkling against the dusk of night with extraterrestrial possibility. It never dawned on me that at this hour, Joey Boyle, Todd Jorgenson, and all our other friends in the neighborhood were preparing for bed. I never thought how strange this mission was, how odd that every member of my family half expected to see an alien spaceship that night. We had been weaned on our father's stories and on the general premise that it was supremely arrogant to imagine we were the only intelligent beings in God's universe. My father was convincing because of his command of the material and because he was our father.

On this night we became the Addams Family of Long Island, happy within ourselves, oblivious to the odd looks and whispers of others. On this night we were the Barrys, and we were a family.

Somewhere deep in New Jersey, my parents stopped at a delicatessen to buy a couple of cups of coffee and a bag full of sugar-powdered Linzer tarts. Then, with my mother driving and my father wielding a pair of binoculars, we ventured on. We parked at the edge of the dark void that we took to be the Wanaque Reservoir and began our surveillance. In the back seat, the two boys stared out the windows, while the two girls, sandwiched in the middle, fought off the sleepiness brought on by the late hour and the cozy blanket draped across their legs. In the front, my father leaned out the window to hunt the clear skies like some hypervigilant air-raid warden. My mother calmly sipped her coffee, as though she had been conducting UFO stakeouts all her life.

Nearby there were several parked cars containing silhouettes in clutches. Word of the UFO sightings had clearly leaked out, we reasoned: others were keeping watch as well, holding one another to ward off the fear.

Brenda and Elizabeth fell asleep. The oldies radio station played Dean Martin, Rosemary Clooney, and others who sang "the music of your life." Each time an airplane passed overhead, Brian and I shouted, Is that one? Is that one? And each time, my father obligingly aimed his binoculars in the general direction of where we were pointing, just to double-check that it wasn't something other than a plane. He had a small camera waiting at his feet. He was a hunter, looking to bag the extraterrestrial tiger that would change his life, and all others.

The UFOs never did come to the Wanaque Reservoir. At least not that night. At least as far as I know. After a while, Brian fell asleep, and then so did I. But before I closed my eyes, I took in the wonder of it all: the taste of powdered sugar around my lips, the warmth of my siblings beside me, and the sight of my parents gazing out into the Jersey darkness, peering with hope, peering up.

ONE WEEKNIGHT DURING this period of paranormal pursuit—a time when we children would descend the stairs in the morning to find a living room of empty beer bottles, crumpled cigarette packs, and scattered photographs of alien mug shots—there came a knock on the door.

My father jerked his head slightly sideways. Danny, the gesture said, see who's at the door.

I did not want to leave the couch. The television's glow covered my family like a comforting, black-and-white quilt. No missed train this night, no arguments, no alcohol. Just wholesome mindlessness: Merv modeling his blazer, Merv bantering with Arthur Treacher, Merv promising to be right back after this commercial break. Merv Griffin interested me because he interested my parents; I savored these calm conversations with Merv and Arthur, Gene and Noreen. Still, I was the oldest. It was my duty to answer the door.

I turned the knob, pulled—and jumped back. The front lawn was ablaze! A dozen sizzling road flares, protruding from the grass and looking like sticks of dynamite, were shooting flames that cast our house in the candy-corn colors of Halloween.

Framed by the light of this front-lawn inferno was its proud creator, Peter McGonigle, an imp of a man in his early thirties whose wispy grin suggested the joy of not having been caught at his greatest imposture, that of being an adult. He lived by a rule that my parents were drawn to but could not fully embrace: fun first, then fun. While my mother put her faith in God and my father questioned the existence of God, Peter McGonigle prayed only that God allow him to pull as many pranks as possible before summoning him to that fun house in the sky.

How yah doin', yah little shit? he cracked. Where's yer old man?

As I reveled in the thrill of having been called a little shit, he brushed past me to interrupt the familial peace that had temporarily settled over the Barry living room. My sisters and brother cheered with delight: McGonigle was a man-child, a Pied Piper who cast spells of irresponsibility upon my parents. The television was clicked off: good night, Merv; good night, Arthur. My father bounded toward the refrigerator for a couple of beers, while my mother rushed outside to douse the front lawn with the garden hose before one of the neighbors called the fire department.

My parents had gotten to know McGonigle through the mysterious social network that had developed among New Yorkers who believed in UFOs. Beyond his devotion to the cause, though, we knew precious little about who McGonigle was, or where he came from—except for the offhand references he made to a Barnumesque lifestyle. A typical day in the life of McGonigle, apparently, was to dress in a priest's collar and cadge a meal down at the local Howard Johnson's. This sounded about right, given what we witnessed during his hell-bent visits to West 23rd Street, when he howled and brayed and ranted at any indication that a neighbor was tired, or relaxed, or just not interested in another drink. It was as though he feared the onset of a communal coma. He flirted with the women in front of their husbands, taught the children how to curse properly, and needled the men right up to the point where one more wisecrack would elicit a fist-to-the-jaw comeback.

Morning dawned one summer's day on the wreckage of an unusually raucous block party, whose epicenter had been our now-trashed backyard. A plastic garbage can brimmed with the stagnant water of melted ice, the last soldier in its hold being a soda, not a beer. The white dust of spent charcoal briquettes coated the grass around the cold grill. And there on the patio, sitting on the one picnic bench still upright, was McGonigle, bug-eyed awake and plotting his next prank. He raced upstairs, roused my brother, and demanded that he hand over his grade-school trumpet. Then he was gone.

Soon the bleat of a trumpet sounded to violate a Sunday morning's peace. It was McGonigle, of course, marching up to each doorstep on West 23rd Street to blow a fair approximation of reveille. Through their groggy hangover fog, neighbors realized that the only way to silence this intoxicated Gabriel was to open their doors and share with him a breakfast beer. He knew they could not resist: he was as crazy as they wished they could be, and one disrupted morning was worth the lifetime memory of having said one Sabbath morn, Ah, the hell with it.

Pete McGonigle was a flame as impermanent as the flares he had planted in our front lawn. He was there, and then he wasn't. We heard later that he was back upstate, that he had moved out West, that he was living on a mountaintop somewhere to be that much closer to the space aliens he hoped someday to meet. We could never figure out whether those reports of his whereabouts were part of another elaborate McGonigle scam, or whether his greatest ruse of all was the feint of sanity. For years afterward, though, a late-night knock on the door of 140 West 23rd Street raised the remote hope that our front lawn was again on fire.

THE FRUITLESS SEARCH for UFOs, the lawn set afire, McGonigle—they all blended into the everyday family tumult. They helped to illuminate the larger lesson being imparted by our parents: life is fragile; take nothing for granted; everything can change in the bat of an eye. You could be called in from the fields to be told that your young mother has died on the operating table in Dublin. You could turn a city corner and find your mother sitting on her living room sofa, there by the curbside, the family evicted again. Your father could be on the 6:38, the 7:38, or the 9:38. You could be abducted by aliens.

Of course, we were already living with a resident alien: our mother, who reveled in the distinction.

With a milk moustache rimming my lip and the remains of a Scooter Pie knockoff lodged in my molars, I once watched an exhibition of the intense psychic connection that had developed between Johnny Cash, balladeer forever in black, and Noreen Barry, housewife forever in sneakers bought for ninety-nine cents from John's Bargain Store.

My mother placed the first of two Johnny Cash albums onto the turntable of the high-fidelity stereo near the clothes dryer. Not just any Johnny Cash record, but the live recordings he made from San Quentin and Folsom prisons. She turned the volume knob to ten. Then, as the applause of felons faded and that famous train-rumble of a voice rose, she began to polish the furniture. Soon she was doing a roadhouse twist with the vacuum cleaner and providing backup vocals to songs about drugs and liquor, guns and violence:

> *I took a shot of cocaine and I shot my woman down*
> *I went right home and I went to bed*
> *I stuck that lovin' .44 beneath my head.*

Nearly two hours later, the needle lifted and the stereo arm returned for the last time to its place of rest. My mother was worn out, her brow damp, her voice hoarse from singing about mournful train whistles, hanging judges, and a boy named Sue. The house was redolent of Lemon Pledge.

I was sure that other mothers did not clean their houses this way, and I suspected that it had something to do with my own mother's background. She had not grown up being groomed to fit the American housewife mold, of course, but there was something more than that. It was her farm girl's practicality too, her quiet eagerness to point out the absurdities in the everyday suburban life of her adopted country.

Take Christmas, for example. With each passing year, my mother removed herself one degree more from the commerce-driven frenzy that surrounded her favorite holiday. The same gift-wrapped boxes were used year after year; only the presents inside were different. The live Christmas tree gave way early on to an artificial tree. Then the artificial tree lost its branches, one by one, until one year it was little more than a hole-dappled aluminum pole.

Still, that bent and scraggly make-believe tree became a central component of a proper Barry Christmas Eve. We turned on Channel 11 and felt the virtual warmth of its annual Yule log broadcast. We got out our stack of scratched Christmas albums and played favored selections, including Marlene Dietrich's torch-song rendition of "The Little Drummer Boy." We ate Ritz Crackers slathered in peanut butter or deviled ham, and washed them down with vanilla-charged eggnog whipped up by Elizabeth. Then we gave out gifts. Dad might get another Old Spice deodorant and after-shave set that his sons had chipped in for at the Bay Shore mall. Mom might get a statuette of a seagull; her daughters had bought it at Ha-Cha Stationers because they knew how much she loved the beach.

These were cherished moments, because we all remembered the time my father, enraged over something or other, picked up the Christmas tree and was ready to toss it out the front door when, in deference to my mother, he paused a few moments while she hurriedly removed all the fragile ornaments. That was years ago, when our Christmas trees were real.

With the passing of New Year's Day, there was one final ritual to the season. At my mother's direction, the artificial tree, still decorated, would be picked up by its stand, taken outside, and placed in the back of the garage, behind the lawn mower and the rakes. There it would stay, through spring, summer, and fall, until mid-December, when it would be lifted—tinsel, ornaments, and all—and returned to its place of honor in the living room, where a quick dusting would remove any cobwebs.

My mother's quiet resolve to challenge the societal boundaries of her adopted country came at the oddest times, it seemed. One day Bonnie, our Shetland sheepdog, gave birth to seven puppies—the result of having been sniffed and charmed a few months earlier by a local gigolo who had wiggled his way under our chain-link fence. The thought of six people living in a house with eight dogs forced my mother to convene a family meeting for an important announcement: the runt, a gray squish that came to be called Pixie, could stay, but the rest had to go.

Go where? we asked, our eyes the size of Oreos, our noses already sniffling. The p-p-p-ound?

My mother ended the meeting, reached for her cigarettes, and before long had devised a plan. She invited a couple of the neighborhood kids to accompany the Barrys and six puppies to the TSS department store on Montauk Highway. She laid out her scheme as she drove her Chevy wagon along the back roads of Long Island's South Shore. Each child was to conceal one of the puppies inside his jacket, nonchalantly walk into the store, and head straight to the pet department. Understood?

Although the purpose of this plan remained unclear, the six children in the back eagerly nodded yes. This was better than any of the contrived plots we had seen on *The Brady Bunch* or *The Partridge Family*. This was adventurous, faintly naughty, and real, all scripted by a mysterious brunette with an intriguing foreign accent. What's more, none of us knew how it would end.

My mother pulled into the department store's parking lot. She gathered her own litter about her and went over the plan once more. Each child grabbed a puppy from the box in the back of the station wagon and lovingly tucked it inside the folds of a jacket. Then, straining to look like just another obedient brood tailing after their mother, we followed her past the security guard and into the store's harsh lights.

A few steps from the pet department's dog cage, my mother gave the nod—the signal for the start of Phase Two. We took our places in front of the cage, removed the puppies from our coats, and began to play with them, giggling as they climbed our shoulders and licked our faces. Before long, a harried-looking man with a name tag hanging limply from his rumpled shirt marched over and instructed us to put those puppies *back* in the cage and leave the pet department—*immediately!* We obeyed.

Candy bars were our reward, a cigarette hers. Just another day.

SOME DAYS, THOUGH, my mother was someplace else. Some days she would stay curled on the couch in that sweatshirt and those paint-stained pants. She would not go to bed. She'd top off the beer in her glass and call up, Good night, sleep well, to her worried children on the landing. Leave me be, she was really saying. I'm going home.

And so she would, there on the couch. She would scamper across the fields, past Topsy Hartigan's orchards, and, panting with joy, dip her hands in the font of blessed water at Shanaglish Church, there above the cemetery. She would linger outside Whelan's, the village's only pub, breathing in the thick air that smelled of hops and sweat and spilled stories. She would see the people, her people, the ghosts; she'd tell us so.

There's miserly Katherine Grogan, legs pumping the pedals of a black bicycle from under a black dress. If you ask Katherine would she like a biscuit with her tea, she'd say yes, bury the cookie in one of many pockets, and bring it home. When she died, her husband found twenty-pound notes stitched throughout the folds of her clothing, and so led the town in a toast to her posthumous generosity. There too is himself, Topsy, not the most learned of men. One time your man caught him holding a newspaper upside down and told him you can't read it that way. His answer: Any eejit can read it the other way. But he was a damned fine fruitier, raising gooseberries and blackberries and apples, and wasn't he mad that time they caught young Nora and her sister Mary stealing apples from his stone shed. Mad for only so long, though.

And there is the family: Aunt Maggie, with child and without a husband and so had to leave Shanaglish, and is that how she came to be a whiskey breath in Washington? Aunt Nora, who spent her life polishing the silver of the rich in Old Westbury and Newport, then sending the money back to the family, so poor they couldn't afford a First Communion dress for any of the girls. One time she mailed a dress from the States but it didn't arrive in time, or so it seemed, until Aunt Nora came home and, nice as you please, asked for a closer look at that lovely First Communion photograph of a postal worker's daughter. In the dress, of course, and Aunt Nora screamed blue murder. Blue. Murder.

MOST OF ALL, there are the parents. Agnes, the mother, who went to Dublin for a routine gallstone operation and died, simple as that. Sweet-smelling, warm hands, but gone before Noreen was ten, gone before they could talk about boys and life and what to wear to the dance in town. What was she like again? What would she have said of her own arranged marriage to the wiry buck from Scariff in Clare, this boy on the run, this Daniel Minogue.

He was like a lot of other lads during The Troubles, taking the occasional shot at the peelers. They got his name anyways, and when they came to the door he was already gone, hidden somewhere between Gort and Peterswell, working as just another hand on the farm of some friends, his proud surname now a secret. The friends knew the Hartigans down in Shanaglish, and so a marriage was arranged, with him coming down to live with Agnes on the Hartigan farm. He was a good worker, not one for the drink: if he tried to keep up with the other men, he'd soon be hunched in the grass by the side of the road. No, his vice was his pipe, and the ancient set of encyclopedias he read most nights by the light of the hearth fire.

They lived in Gortmugga, the smallest of places, where the hedges were kept clean and low so you could always tell what the neighbors were up to. Theirs was a small farmhouse, with a hen shed, a pig shed, a cow shed, and a shed for the single horse, not far from the outhouse. No running water, so the water was carried in wooden buckets from a well down the field, and sometimes the fragrance coming off Topsy's fruit trees made the air smell like a wedding.

At night the local men gathered to play cards, a thrupence a hand, with the wireless radio crackling in the corner and the tea strong and the bread brown and the gentle jousting sometimes turning serious. About the Loughnanes, of course, Patrick and Harry, working in the fields in 1920 when the Black and Tans found them, beat them, tied the two of them to the back of a lorry, and dragged them for miles, brothers burned and scraped of their Loughnane-ness. Their bodies wouldn't have been found but for a cousin's dream, and that was where they were, submerged in a muddy pond. The Loughnane brothers were buried in Shanaglish cemetery, in a spot now marked by a massive tombstone inscribed with three prominent letters: IRA. Every Easter Monday the rebel faithful come to Shanaglish to remember the boys.

Back then, though, no one could ever forget the Loughnanes; they loomed larger in death than in life. The farmers of Gortmugga, the men who knew Patrick and Harry, knew them well, would clutch their cards and tell the story again, examining it from every conceivable angle, asking questions of one another over and over until the time came for them too to be buried in Shanaglish soil. What would ye do? What would ye do if that lorry came your way that time? What would ye do?

The card-game conversations often veered from the political to the magical, which is what the eavesdropping children loved best. About the time Daniel heard the banshee. About why he trod so carefully around the ring forts in the fields. About how you can never bring to a boil any water taken from a holy well. About what to do if it's late at night, dark as pitch, and you don't know where you are: turn your coat inside out and put it back on, and you'll find your way. About Biddy Early, the auld one with the special powers up there in Feakle. The priests hated her but the people revered her. Daniel knew her—or so he said, even though she died years before he was born. One time he went to her for his seizures, and she gave him an elixir and some instructions: drink this for three days and then throw the bottle into the lake. He did as he was told, and never again did he have one of those fits. That is what he said, and the children loved it.

Imagine an elixir for pain. Not this beer, not alcohol, but a truly magical potion that takes away the hurt and sickness and ensures that we all live til ninety, that we all see our grandchildren grown. It wasn't the kick of a cow that struck Daniel Minogue down. That was just what they told the children—easier to say than cancer.

Nonie, they said, for that is what they called her. Nonie. It is time you go. You're fifteen now, and there is an aunt in a place called Brooklyn, in New York, to look after you. You're going to America, Nonie. Aren't you the lucky one.

THESE, THEN, WERE the ingredients of the Barry porridge simmering on the neighborhood stove, sending eruptions now and then until the flame was lowered, and then all was fine. You could never know with him—a smile one time, a glare the next. Her with her ways—did you hear what she did with them puppies? And those kids, always just a bit off.

For the most part, the rest of West 23rd Street accepted us, and we them. But there were times when we kept our distance, times when neighborly smiles were dropped to reveal bared teeth. One Fourth of July night, with the tart scent of exploded firecrackers thick in the still air, a couple of the fathers and a few of the older boys grabbed sticks and baseball bats and joined a mob that was running to confront some black men at the imagined boundary, a block from our house, that separated Deer Park from Wyandanch, white from black. I watched from my yard as they raced past, many of them brave from beer, a few of them known to me. Men who on other days would say, Danny, how ya doin'?

My father called me into the house, and for a minute we watched through the screen-door haze as the mob ran past.

There's nothing for you there, Danny, he said to me finally. Just racists and idiots.

Eejits. Then he closed the front door shut.

And there were times when the neighbors kept their distance from us, allowing the occasional outburst between my parents to reach its exhausted conclusion without interruption. The neighborhood children sometimes gathered along the curb across the street, as if waiting for the drive-in movie to begin, while their parents suddenly decided to take in some fresh air in those corners of their front yards where the acoustics were best. They might clip a leaf or two from a hedge, fiddle with an idle rake, then pick up a pebble and examine it as though it were Yorick's skull.

They were usually rewarded for their patience with some old-fashioned family entertainment: a kind of suburban vaudeville with something for everyone, from slapstick to melodrama.

One night my father came home very late and very drunk. But it wasn't his inebriated condition that upset my mother so much as the cig-arette that was smoldering in his hand. Just a week earlier, the two of them had sworn off cigarettes; they had even sealed their pact by agree-ing to put all the money that would have been spent on butts in a large glass jar placed prominently on the kitchen counter (We could pay for a week in the Catskills with what we save!). And now here was Gene Barry with a Marlboro, clearly savoring its forbidden taste.

How can I trust you anymore? God only knows how much you've been smoking in the city!

Noreen, what I do with my lungs is my own goddam business. And smoking is the only relief I get after slaving all day and then riding that goddam train.

Door slams kept the beat to the soaring skat of argument. He sent pots sailing out the kitchen door, pots weighed down with what she had cooked for that evening's meal. At some point there came my mother's quiet plea that my father lower his voice, and his thunderous, crowd-pleasing response: I don't give a good goddam what the neighbors think!

These arguments lasted anywhere from an hour to a week. They would eventually end, though, and our kind of normality would return. Once again the neighbors of West 23rd Street could count on the singsong of one of us Barry kids as we plaintively called for our wander-ing, meatloaf-shaped dogs, including Pixie's roly-poly addition to our clan:

Bonnie, Pixie, Gypsy! Bonnie, Pixie, Gypsy!

Our dog call became sort of an evening prayer, signaling that dusk was settling again over a corner of this endless suburban stretch. The garden hoses were rolled up, the garage doors pulled down. Dinner was eaten, the dishes done. A few houses away, two children of the Holocaust sat like statues, silent and still, fearing the creak a mere footstep might bring. Down the street, Mr. Boyle, the forever-weary truck driver who seemed to live in his blue work pants, grabbed a second Piel's and collapsed into the arms of his Barca lounger, where sleep was just a few sips away. Across the street, Mrs. Hopper searched her mirrored reflection for those signs of time passing, signs in need of camouflage. From most every house, there emanated the unifying blue light of television.

Then would come the noise of twelve little paws scurrying through overgrown grass: the sound of home rediscovered.

Bonnie, Pixie, Gypsy! Good girls.

3

ORNING CAME WITHOUT natural disaster; my prayers had not been answered. There had been no earthquake overnight, no typhoon or springtime blizzard, only the sun in all its mocking glory. God had forsaken me.

Music test.

I nudged Brian with my foot on the climb down from the top bunk.

Wake up, I said.

Mmmf, he said.

We could smell the blended aromas of cigarettes and coffee emanating from downstairs, the very smell of morning in our house, accompanied always by the very sounds of morning, the coughing hacks and the radio murmurs. This was true on weekday mornings only, for on weekends my parents sometimes did not rise until well after noon. On those Saturdays and Sundays, with the distant whine of lawn mowers reminding us that other families were in full embrace of the day, I would set the kitchen table, cut the grapefruit, place the carton of eggs on the counter, and practically will my parents to Get up, Get up, Oh please get up. But if you stay awake most of the night, drinking and smoking and solving the riddles of the universe—or just finding cozy, late-show comfort in *Curse of the Werewolf*—you are not going to greet the dawn.

Weekday mornings were different, though—regimented and not to be tinkered with. We listened to the news on 88 WCBS-AM, never 1010

WINS-AM. We ate boiled eggs, never poached; Corn Flakes, never Sugar Smacks. We read the blue-collar *Daily News* at breakfast, never the white-collar *Times*. And I wore a uniform—always, a uniform. Green pants with the black stripe down the sides. Green socks. Green belt with gold trim. Black loafers sold exclusively by the shoe store near Ha-Cha Stationers (A goddamned monopoly, my father called it. A Catholic shakedown). A gold shirt with the circular icon of the Holy Spirit stitched into the breast pocket. Once I clipped on my green tie, I looked like a waiter at a St. Patrick's Day party in Oz.

I walked toward the bus stop in a chain-gang trudge, lugging a book about the meaning of Jesus and a peanut butter ball of a sandwich lumped at the bottom of an old Wonder Bread bag. My eyes darted about for public school bullies who were practically duty bound to slap me as they wheeled past on their Stingray bicycles; in my green-and-gold uniform, I might as well have been wearing a sign that said, "Kick Me for Christ." All the while, my head throbbed in panic: Music test, music test, what will I sing for my music test?

Oh God—Oh Miss Doyle!—how could you two do this to me?

The school bus appeared, dashing my last hope for reprieve. I climbed aboard to join the similarly dressed and to complete this rolling study in green. We stared in silence as the bus lumbered toward the Sts. Cyril and Methodius church and school, the light-brick fortress shimmering at the horizon's lip, where children first witnessed the transubstantiation of mere bread and water into the body and blood of their Savior; where, through the sacrament of Holy Confirmation, fifth-grade cadets like me would soon be transformed into sixth-grade soldiers in Christ's army; and where young Catholic boys and girls were groomed to become the future leaders of the Rosary Altar Society, the Nocturnal Adoration Society, or, dare we say it, the next John F. Kennedy.

For years a small clapboard chapel had provided more than enough space for the Catholics in the area. Then came the New York City throngs of the 1950s: the Barrys and Bernardis and Boyles, buying houses, having babies, cramming into the chapel's pews with squirming, screaming offspring. The parish had no choice but to build. By the summer of 1963, the cement trucks and bricklayers and glaziers were gone from the parish lot on Deer Park Avenue, leaving in their wake a house in which God could dwell: a majestic cross-shaped church, with mosaic-tiled columns, terrazzo floors, and a magnificent stained-glass front that on sunny Sundays would shower the congregation in reflected raindrops of blue and red. This parish complex—with its convent, rectory, and school, directly across the street from the bakery where everyone got their cannolis—seemed to have a secular as well as a spiritual purpose. It gave concrete evidence to how dramatically one Long Island community had changed in a decade.

One glorious day that July, His Excellency, Walter P. Kellenberg, the Bishop of the Roman Catholic Diocese of Rockville Centre, appeared in all his finery to impart his blessings. He wore white shoes with gold buckles, a gold ring on one of his white-gloved fingers, a red-and-gold robe, and a gold miter that winked in the sunlight. The people of the parish blinked as the prelate flicked the blessed water into the polished pews. They dipped their fingers into whatever moisture they could find and made the sign of the cross. Men in dark suits with white shirts and narrow ties, and women in dresses the color of the Virgin Mary's powder-blue robes, their heads bowed in reverence, so that wherever the bishop looked, he saw bare heads with hair slick from Vitalis—and hats, many, many hats, some of them like flowery bird's nests, others more stylish and even worthy of the First Lady, Jacqueline herself.

It was a special morning, after all, a morning in which a young Catholic community had formally anchored itself to the Long Island soil. Up and down Deer Park Avenue, people rejoiced. Under the space-age hair dryers at Lucretia's Beauty Salon, which prided itself as being "for the budget wise woman who wants the best." In the bays at the Fairview service station, where plaid stamps were handed out with every oil change. At the counter of the Deer Park delicatessen, where Ernie made the best German potato salad this side of the Atlantic because he didn't skimp on the bacon. These entrepreneurs may have suspected that their businesses would not survive the century. That chemical whiff from Lucretia's perms, that faintly dangerous cigarette-and-gasoline bouquet in the Fairview's waiting room, that vanilla-like fragrance of Ernie's homemade rice pudding, so warm that it fogged up the display-case glass—by the millennium these aromas wafted only through the chambers of memory, recalled by Deer Park old-timers when trying to help one another navigate between past and present.

But this they knew: their new and holy place, their church, would loom over Deer Park Avenue for generations to come, its parish rolls forever inscribed with the names of the beauticians and car mechanics who financed its construction back in 1963. The *new* Sts. Cyril and Methodius generated so much community pride that when a formal dance was planned to celebrate the church's blessing and dedication, nearly two hundred people volunteered to be on the dance committee.

It took a few months for the excitement to subside. The bishop in all his finery returned to Rockville Centre, the smell of newness evaporated like holy water mist, and fifteen hundred miles away, in Texas, a man named Oswald assassinated the first Roman Catholic president. After the mourning, the suburban Catholic parish settled into the comforting and familiar routine of bingo nights and CYO games, of solicitations for the choir and reminders to enroll children in parochial school. By the mid-60s the Sts. Cyril and Methodius complex, a kind of office park of religious design, had become an accepted part of the Deer Park infrastructure—and a second home for kids like me.

Every morning I was confronted at the school's doors by the life-sized statues of St. Cyril and St. Methodius, their stone faces haggard with holiness. They must have been good men in their time; they were, after all, the patron saints of Czechoslovakia. But day in and day out, as we marched in single file and in size order past their mournful concrete visages, Cyril and his brother Methodius scared the bejesus out of me. The statues set the tone for what awaited inside: a mish-mash of tenderness and torment, of role models good and bad, of learning to see Our Lord Jesus Christ as someone to run to and run from.

There were the bathrooms, which in my home were considered to be sanctuaries, havens of contemplation. But into the boys' bathroom would come Mrs. Carnevale, her slightly shorter leg causing her block of a body to sway like unfastened cargo. She was a linebacker in a dress, and she would stand over us as we fumbled and flustered before the row of urinals. All right, gentlemen, do your business, she would bellow. I never could.

There were the school's corridors, forbidden passages to all but those in trouble or on some errand of Vatican-level urgency. The classrooms were brightly lit and warmed by the collective body heat of four-dozen fidgeting children, but the halls were cool, dark alleys of mystery. And because my surname began with a *B*, I usually sat near the front of the first row, which meant that when someone threw up his olive-loaf sandwich, I was invariably dispatched on the urgent mission to fetch Joe the Janitor.

Time was of the essence. If not addressed immediately, regurgitated luncheon meat could disrupt the delicate balance of power in a classroom; control of the students' behavior could suddenly shift from the teacher to the olive loaf.

Quickly, Mr. Barry! the teacher would say. Quickly!

But I had come to see these vital assignments as temporary furloughs, freeing me from my head-aching efforts to become invisible so that I would not be called upon to name all twelve of the apostles. I never seemed able to remember more than six, which I feared was particularly damning because I could name all seven dwarves.

When sent to find Joe the Janitor, I dallied.

After pausing to allow my eyes to adjust to the hallway darkness, I would slowly start on my mission, my black shoes clicking loud enough for the unseen but omniscient nuns to mark my progress. Sometimes I imagined that behind certain locked doors, especially those that were supposedly reserved for "supplies," a nun with corporal's rank was watching a bank of TV monitors, all flickering with images captured by tiny cameras that were hidden throughout the building: in the *R* of the

I.N.R.I. inscription above every crucifix, or one of the dark-rimmed, sleep-deprived eyes of the portrait of Pope Paul VI.

I would pause ever so briefly at the portal of each classroom to peer into other worlds: 6-1, 5-3, and the incomprehensible universes of the seventh and eighth grades—7-3, maybe, or 8-2—where the girls had begun to give shape to their plaid uniforms, and the boys reclined at their desks in sly contempt of order. I might catch Mrs. Quirk sneaking an Almond Joy from her top desk drawer as her students perspired over a surprise test (sometimes called a "Jap quiz" by kids who never connected the slur to Pearl Harbor). When I was in her fourth-grade class, Mrs. Quirk confiscated my *Mad* magazine—Inappropriate, she barked—and then sat at her desk reading it, trying not to laugh, while we toiled over a quiz about the New Testament. Or I might hear a group of second-graders practicing the offertory song to be sung at their First Holy Communion, when eight-year-old children are expected to understand the concept of transubstantiation. The wine is not a symbol of Christ's blood, students; it *is* Christ's blood.

Now and then I encountered a fellow sufferer, someone who had also identified the gulf between acceptance and ostracism much too early in life. His forehead would be pressed against the wall, a trademark punishment of some teachers. Hearing my tentative footsteps, he would swivel his head slightly against the brick to watch me, his face a teary blotch of red. I would nod in greeting and receive a sniffle in return.

Down the steel-tipped steps I would go, to the basement—a term that did no justice to the many purposes of the sprawling and chilly space that ran beneath the school and the church, its walls concrete blocks, its floors hard tile. Unblessed by natural light, this subterranean haven was the school cafeteria, the assembly room, the bingo hall, the gymnasium, and the setting for the lifeless 11:45 Sunday Mass, attended by those too late or too conservative for the popular 10:15 "folk Mass" in the main church upstairs. When our family made it to Mass, it was always barely and always down here, for the 11:45, which Brian and I resented because the timing came smack at the beginning of the weekly Abbott and

Costello feature on Channel 11. Arriving so late that we had to stand, we would slump against the cold wall and listen to a priest make the miracle of the loaves and fishes sound like a word problem on a math test. He'd be talking in a monotone, Jesus blah-blah, our faith calls us to blah-blah, while we'd be thinking about the movie we were missing, *Here Come the Coeds* or *Pardon My Sarong*, and—Bop!—a hard tap to the back of the head.

Stand up straight, would growl the grudging agnostic, my father.

In the stairwell I might pass a line of sixth-grade boys, reeking from bologna lunches and glistening in sweat from having spent the last half hour hurling a dodge ball around the basement. That red ball might boomerang off some goofy child's head, ping off the floor tiles and stacks of metal chairs, clatter about the pots in the stainless-steel kitchen, then bound up the stage to skirt behind the curtain, where various religious supplies were kept—some cassocks, some candles, a forgotten statue of an out-of-favor saint. Any kid sent to fetch the ball would return with enough images to haunt a week's worth of dreams.

There, in the basement, in the janitor's closet, I would find Joe the Janitor, sitting on an upturned wash bucket and studying the latticework formed by his own intertwined fingers. He was old and spent, a used sponge. He scared me more than statues, reducing my voice to squeaks.

Joe?

Goddam. Can't you kids hold your food?

He would exhale, take one last look at his hands, and wearily ask, What room?

5-1.

Goddam.

He would rise with a snap-crackle-pop and reach for his Can of Mystery, an item available only to school janitors, expressly developed to solidify the vomit of the young. Then, slowly, he would start wheeling his bucket and mop toward the stairs, Goddam, goddam.

FINALLY, THERE WERE the Sisters of St. Joseph, most of all and everywhere. At first they might have seemed indistinguishable in those black-and-white habits, gliding along the corridors as if perched on forklifts beneath their robes, but each woman was distinct in her manner and reputation. One sister might use her chalk-dusted hands to deliver face slaps hard enough to bring tears; another might use hers to gently wipe away tears. It seemed so arbitrary, so unfair; depending on your classroom assignment, your school life could be one of joy or one of dread.

Squatting there in the parking lot that served as our playground, flicking rocks along the mazelike patterns of the sewer grates, I pondered the nun. I did not know whether she ate, whether she drank, whether she used the bathroom, whether she even slept. Through personal sacrifice and denial, she seemed to have ascended to some higher level of being: she was a bride of Christ, professing her devotion to the Lord by dedicating her life to educating children, kids like me. I could feel the maternal pull of some of them, feel deep down inside me the desire to nestle my head in the folds of their black robes and have them tell me everything would be all right.

I particularly adored Sister Gladiola, whose devotion to the New York Mets approached idolatry. When something struck her funny, her massive body jiggled beneath her extra-large habit and her raucous laughter rang down the corridor, prying a smile from even the most withdrawn child. I admired Sister Hydrangea, a milquetoast with big, thick glasses who blithely allowed snakes to curl along her outstretched arm, and so became our adventuress, our guide to the wild kingdom of God. And every child loved Sister Poinsettia, always strumming her guitar, always encouraging students to sing folk hymns reflecting the Church's effort to make transubstantiation hip somehow:

Sons of God, hear His holy word
Gather round, the table of the Lord
Eat His body, drink His blood

And we'll sing a song of love
Allelu- Allelu- Allelu-u-u-u-ia

But for every three Sister Poinsettias, there seemed to be one Sister Tiresias, the dormouse of a librarian with a walleye cast in a honey-like glaze. She began each library hour by leading us in prayer for "our boys in Vietnam," then would turn on one of those box-sized phonographs to play a recording of "White Christmas" because Bing Crosby was a good Catholic. September or May, it did not matter. Surrounded by hundreds of tempting books, from the Matt Christopher series of sports adventures to Beverly Cleary's hilarious stories about Henry Huggins, we were not allowed to reach for a single volume until Der Bingle had finished warbling.

One day this absurd ritual of denial—enveloping us in books that we could not touch—led to a boy's inevitable giggle or burp, spoiling the sanctity of the moment. Sister Tiresias wheeled around, pointed a finger and screeched: You there! Stand up!

But because of her errant eye, the wrong boy stood up.

Not you! You!

Another innocent boy rose.

Not you! You, you devil! You know who you are!

Still another boy stood up. Sister Tiresias slapped all three. Then the bell rang and we shuffled out of the library without having read a single page, while Bing Crosby shared his wish that our days be merry and bright.

But Sister Tiresias was just a fun-loving biddy compared to Sister Delicatessa. With cheeks that sagged like deflated party balloons, she seemed to have dedicated her face to expressing the suffering of every unbaptized baby in limbo, every sinner in purgatory, every martyr, every saint, the Blessed Virgin who saw her only son die on the cross, and Jesus Christ Our Lord amen.

We sat before her with hands clutched, petrified that the mere scratch of a head might be in violation of one of her many classroom rules. All textbooks had to be tightly sheathed in book covers. All handwriting had to follow a one o'clock slant (a particular hardship on left-handers like me). The legs of each desk had to be lined up exactly with those of every other desk in its row, and the space between two rows had to be exactly four linoleum squares wide.

What caused me the greatest distress, though, was the psychological grenade that Sister Delicatessa lobbed into our unformed psyches one afternoon, when she confided in a low growl that Jesus calls on every one of us to join the religious life: boys to be priests or brothers, girls to be nuns. And we all have to be prepared—vigilant!—for the moment when Jesus makes that call. Those who hear and answer His call will be blessed for all eternity; those who are too busy with foolishness to know when He is calling them will have missed their chance.

I fretted for days afterward, terrified that I might miss His call. I was almost certain that I did not want to be a priest, but I did not want to be rude about it. I could not fathom what Jesus might think if He were to call on me—pierced hands outstretched, Sacred Heart shining like a badge from His chest—and I did not hear Him because I was intently reading the back of the Corn Flakes box. What if He called me while I sat mesmerized by the race of raindrops streaking down our station wagon's window? Or while I was lying on the couch with my head on my mother's lap, her fingers curling through my hair, as together we watched *The Lawrence Welk Show*? Imagine: missing the call of Jesus because of a Lennon Sisters serenade!

And what would I say about Danny Barry? How would I introduce myself? Then again, He would already know, wouldn't He? Worrisome little metal-mouth boy: fretting about alcohol and cigarettes and mutterings of divorce; fretting about the dinner table being set so there's one less thing for the neighbors to hear about; fretting about a music test of all things. Fretting, this one is—always fretting.

I saw three possibilities for my inevitable call from Jesus. One: Jesus had already called me, and I hadn't answered, in which case I had failed

Him. Two: Jesus was about to call me, which meant that I had to remain vigilant; in bed at night, I closed my eyes and then opened them quickly, as if to catch Him approaching. Did that brightness suddenly pouring through the cracks of my bedroom door mean that He had finally arrived—or had my mother merely turned on the hallway light?

I leaned toward the third possibility: that Jesus had decided not even to bother with me, reinforcing the aching sense that I was somehow separate from this Catholic school fraternity, that I was more apart than a part. And if the seeds of my insecurity were planted in the hurly-burly of my home life, they began to flower at St. Cyril's on one particular day in the fifth grade. The day of the music test.

Miss Doyle, my teacher, greeted us as always, with infectious cheer. She wore her frosted hair in a Jiffy Pop style, smelled faintly of cigarettes, and had a bit of a gun-moll strut that made the clipped movement of her backside almost mesmerizing. She was the anti-nun, and I liked her very much. Except she had one trait that frightened me even more than the cock of a nun's hand: a gleeful determination to have her students properly graded in music. The only musical instrument at St. Cyril's seemed to be the guitar attached to Sister Poinsettia's hip, and woe to anyone who tried to remove it. But Miss Doyle would not be dissuaded; she was a perky That Girl of a teacher, intent on freeing the musical talent trapped inside our green-and-gold uniforms.

She rejected the methods being used in other classrooms as uninspired. Let other teachers lead their students in a sing-along and then give every student a B in music; let other teachers lead a tepid discussion about the various instruments used in an orchestral recording. Miss Doyle thought that she had a better approach, one that used music as a vehicle to encourage public speaking and build self-esteem. Listen up, children, I have a wonderful idea! For our music test next week, each student will stand in front of the class and sing a song!

As the rest of the class erupted in joyful anticipation, I stared into the chalkboard's green abyss. Danny Barry, the kid with braces who can barely whisper yes or no to a direct question? Singing alone? In front of all his classmates? In front of Kathleen Cudahy, who never moaned "Ooh ooh" when wanting to answer a question but rather would coolly raise her hand the way a queen might summon a carriage? Who was so self-assured that she had somehow transformed her own braces into a fashion accessory? A girl with whom Danny Barry had never made direct eye contact? A girl he secretly loved?

Across the room, Kathleen Cudahy in the flesh chatted excitedly with her many friends about what song she might sing. I felt betrayed by her and everyone around me: Oh-so-perfect Lawrence Henderson, always bringing the perfect lunch—ham-and-Swiss sandwich without the crust, Twinkie, apple—in a crisply perfect brown bag with his name on it, and me with my peanut butter ball in a bag. Ooh-ooh-pick-me Margaret Mary Malone, waving her hand and wanting to answer a question the teacher hasn't even posed yet. And, yes, aren't-we-special Miss Doyle, with her plan to humiliate me. You don't know what it's like, Miss Doyle, you have no idea.

You don't know what it's like on those good Saturdays, when my father is feeling happy and one with his family and lets us know by singing in the commanding baritone that won him so many free drinks over the years. You don't know what it's like to have a brother who sings like one of the Cowsills. On long family trips, hunting for UFOs or just getting some air, the two of them singing so beautifully that even the suicidal contemplations of "Goodnight, Irene" sounded almost sweet. And me somewhere between them, chiming in only when they forget a line and then slipping back into silence. Singing was greatly valued in our house; it was a measure of worth as defined by the Gene Barry World Experience.

Miss Doyle, you don't know what it's like.

A snap of a cosmic finger and a week was gone, all those days and nights that I had hoped to spend selecting the most appropriate and least humiliating song—gone, lost in the blur of boy time. Where you take a moment to study the statistics on the back of Hank Aaron's baseball card, you start to imagine all those home runs hit on humid nights in Milwaukee, and suddenly an hour has passed. Where you decide to make a collage of all the Alfred E. Newmans you've cut from all the *Mad* magazines in your collection—a decision you will almost immediately regret—and before you know it your mother is calling for you to peel the dinner's potatoes. Where the last thing you remember is pausing to watch the frenzy of an ant colony thriving in the crack of your backyard patio, and suddenly the sun has dropped from view and another Saturday has melted away. Boy time.

Now it was the afternoon of the music test, and I still—still!—had not chosen a song to sing. What's more, every song that barreled into my head seemed inappropriate somehow, from Irish ditties ("Oh the Irish flag is a dirty old rag, but a damned sight better than the British") to old cowboy songs ("His wife got killed in a poolroom fight, But still he keeps singing from morning til night"). Soon these songs were blending into one confounding singsong taunt, about a moonshiner looking to quench his thirst on the streets of Laredo while spying a young cowboy all wrapped in white linen as cold as the clay and hearing a fishmonger and sure 'twas no wonder she was singing, Oh what a beautiful morning oh what a beautiful day.

Miss Doyle closed her religion book and said that the time had come for the music test. While everyone else smiled, I sensed the rising taste of peanut butter in the back of my throat. Maybe someone should fetch Joe the Janitor right now.

Before long, the music test had evolved into Child Prodigy Hour. Tiny Theresa Popko squeezed out a saddle shoe–tapping rendition of "Roll Out the Barrel" on an accordion that slowly seemed to be eating her. Brian McShane and Timothy Byrnes, the classroom's Smothers Brothers, harmonized nicely on "Snoopy vs. the Red Baron." And while Marialisa Simonetti sang in a foreign language to some kind of folk dance, I tried to melt into the classroom brickwork, the way the clay people in those old Flash Gordon movies always do.

Who's next, I wondered—the von Trapp children?

Daniel Barry?

The name didn't ring a bell. Miss Doyle called it out again.

Daniel Barry?

Snippets of musty lyrics continued to flood my mind, competing with one another for my attention, creating a maddening cacophony heard only by me. The theme from one of my favorite TV shows, *F Troop*, gave way to the "Whiffenpoof Song," which I knew from an old Bing Crosby album, followed by a hyperventilating medley from Christmas carols: silent night, dashing through the snow, hark the something something sing. Then came the complete recollection of one song above all others: the simple "My Country 'Tis of Thee."

As if just awakened, I stumbled to the front of the room and turned to see forty-five pairs of eyes blinking in judgment of me, including those of the lovely Kathleen Cudahy. I took a deep breath to calm myself, but it only fed more oxygen to my fear. And just as my lips were meeting to sound my first note, I noticed that among the eyes upon me were those of Billy Carew, crossed.

I started to laugh, *heh heh*, and so my classmates laughed too, in solidarity it seemed, not ridicule. But soon I was the only one laughing, emitting a nervous, quavering, uncontrollable bray that had taken over my very being. My stomach hurt, my head pounded, my cheeks burned, and yet I could not stop laughing. With my teacher and classmates and Kathleen Cudahy bearing witness, I had become a slight, round-shouldered vessel of hysteria.

It may have been a few seconds or it may have been the month of May, but at some point Miss Doyle came over to me, concern furrowing the brow beneath her mushroom-cloud bouffant. She got behind me, placed her hands on my shoulders, and guided me to the back of the classroom, almost as though she too expected me to vomit. The touch of her hands and the smell of her perfume, mingled with the faint whiff of her lunch-break cigarette, would normally be enough to make me grin all the way home. Now her closeness only deepened my mortification. Me, laughing when I feel like crying; I can't get anything right.

No one look at Daniel, she commanded, as she returned to her seat at the front of the room. Of course, she would be watching.

And then there I was, alone, staring at the backs of forty-five heads in Room 5-1 of a new school that was the pride of the community, laughing into heh-heh hoarseness.

Go ahead, Daniel, Miss Doyle said, her voice itself in a soothing lilt. Sing.

When I hit my first note, forty-five sets of shoulders flinched. But I soldiered on, no way was I stopping now, until I gasped the kindergarten-worthy finale, "le-et free-dom ring." Wasted, I found my way back to my desk and lived the rest of the afternoon as though underwater, with every sound coming to me in an echo, from a distance.

That night, face buried in my pillow, I exhausted myself to sleep by trying to imagine having a second chance some day with Kathleen Cudahy. Maybe we ride our bicycles up to the school, the streamers of her Huffy rippling in the breeze. We pause before those scowling statues of Cyril and Methodius, and I make a joke that has *her* laughing now instead, and somewhere within her laughter I find and reclaim my dignity. We pedal on, toward the railroad overpass, to the pane-glass door of our favorite Deer Park delicatessen, where I buy two cups of Ernie's homemade rice pudding. It's still warm, of course, and we take our time spooning away the sweetness, while together we watch the Long Island bustle of Deer Park Avenue.

As we cycle home, through a dusk that unites us, I begin to sing in a baritone as strong and clear as my father's. I sing for Kathleen and I sing for myself. I sing not about the glory of battle or the love of drink, but about the knot of longing in my chest. I sing about that.

4

THE DEAD STARED back at us from photographs taken in that time before color. Among the Great Depression's many hardships, it seemed, was the constant struggle to distinguish yourself in the pale, black-and-white world, maybe with polka dots on your tie, maybe with stripes on your dress. Here they were, my pasty Barry forebears, photographed for posterity with expressions betraying the ache of a simple smile.

They winced at us through silver frames arranged on old-lady furniture, the kind with marble tops and spindly legs and a sharp, brittle presence that said, Don't you dare bump into me, don't you dare touch. So we sat like Hummel figurines in old-lady chairs—the kind that breathed *tsk-tsk* as soon as you sat on the cushion—and clutched our glasses of tepid ginger ale. Slices of melba toast were splayed on a plate, undisturbed.

For the Barry children, this was Manhattan. True, there was that time we had gone to the St. Patrick's Day parade in the rain and posed for photographs in front of the Father Duffy statue in Times Square and got jostled about in some Blarney Stone bar while adults sprinkled us with stout. Usually, though, Manhattan was portrayed as the place from which my father could never quite escape no matter how hard he tried. The idea of returning to that hellhole on a weekend was anathema to him, unless it was to visit his father's beloved sister, Aunt Betty, in Stuyvesant Town.

That was Manhattan for us then: the Midtown Tunnel, an East Side complex of brown-brick apartment buildings built for white people, and
chairs that went *tsk-tsk* with every fidget.

Aunt Betty never married, having no time for that sort of tomfoolery.
She had devoted her life instead to teaching, coaxing the genius from
gifted children enrolled at the Hunter College Elementary School.
Retired now, she wore her white-and-gray hair in a symmetrical puff
with a breath of purple, and spoke with the assuredness of the learned.
There was, though, that slight speech impediment, which she described
with some difficulty as a "lateral emission of the *s* sound." It made her
sound like Sylvester the Cat. We children used to imitate her when
repeating certain Aunt Bettyisms—"I've had an elegant sufficiency," for
example—but we loved her dearly. She was about the closest we had to a
paternal grandmother; on our birthdays she always sent us cards with ten
dimes shoved into slots above a picture of a juggling clown.

Aunt Betty was generous in other ways as well, and duty bound beyond
what might be expected of a woman in her seventies. She allowed Ronnie,
another nephew who was slightly younger than my father, to live with her.
He was said to be brilliant, which in our family was sympathetic code
language for troubled, not quite right, unable to function *out there*. He used
to work as a Russian translator, but now, well, he needed rest, Ronnie did.

We sat there on this November day, glancing out the window at the
black squirrels and leafless trees of Stuyvesant Town, while my father and
Aunt Betty tried again to patch together some kind of Barry genealogy.
Their expedition into the past never traveled too far, though. About all
they knew was that Aunt Betty's father and my great-grandfather, Brian
Barry—or was it Bernard Barry?—had left County Cork—or was it
County Mayo?—under ambiguous circumstances.

Maybe he was a sheep stealer, my father said, joking.

Sheep stealer? An indignant Aunt Betty was laterally emitting her "s"
sounds all over the room. Never!

What they did know was that Great-grandfather Barry got a job as a
doorman at the old Waldorf, or maybe it was the Plaza. Being a doorman

at a high-class hotel was a good job in those days, they assured each other, especially when you considered the benefits: the leftovers of the swells—the curls of shrimp and nuggets of beef to be taken home to the family.

As they reminisced about the Barrys of before, tiptoeing with their silence around this drinking binge and that fragile marriage, and as we nursed our flat ginger ales, there walked into the room an unshaven specter in a rumpled trench coat. He was gripping a bag by the neck of the bottle inside, as if to choke it.

Say hello to Uncle Ronnie, children.

Only a vague recollection of social graces seemed to keep my father's first cousin in the parlor. With drink in hand, he sat mute during the talk of relatives out of touch or long dead, but snapped alert when my father told him a little bit about Danny: the kid's passion for baseball—especially the Yankees. Nodding toward me, he explained, It broke this kid's heart when Mantle retired, but he still can't get enough of the game. Even keeps track of the box scores from the grapefruit league.

It was true. In my innocence I thought that the practice games played by major league baseball teams during spring training actually mattered in some way, and so I cut out the box scores for safekeeping. I could never have imagined that my heroes—Mays, Aaron, and the ballplayer being touted as the next Mantle, another kid from Oklahoma named Bobby Murcer—saw the grapefruit league as little more than a six-week stretching exercise.

Ronnie looked at me as though he had just realized there were children in the room. He cleared the phlegm from his throat and, with a voice in a high-wire tremble, began to quiz me on the game I loved.

Who managed the 1927 Yankees?

Miller Huggins.

What's Yogi Berra's real name?

Lawrence Peter.

What number did Joe DiMaggio wear?

Five.

What number did Mantle wear before he wore number seven?

Six.

What team did the Yankees play in the 1951 World Series?

The Giants.

Who won?

The Yankees, I said. Of course.

Ronnie put his drink down on one of the old-lady tables and abruptly walked out of the room. As Aunt Betty slid a coaster beneath Ronnie's glass, I searched my father's face for an explanation. Had I offended this strange man in some way? He made a subtle hand gesture, a slight wave, to signal that everything was all right, not to worry. His gesture was like that of a baseball coach calming a rattled pitcher.

Ronnie returned a minute or two later with a baseball that fluttered like a knuckleball in his unsteady hand. Here, he said, presenting it to me.

The ball was covered with what appeared to be scuffs but upon closer examination proved to be dark pen scribbles. As I peered deeper into its hide, certain names came into focus like secrets revealed—Mays, Stanky, Dark, Durocher—and then I realized. This was an autographed baseball, signed by members of the 1951 New York Giants, the team that beat the Dodgers in the most famous game ever played, the game that ended when Bobby Thomson hit the "shot heard round the world" off sorrowful Ralph Branca. The Giants win the pennant! The Giants win the pennant!

My mind raced to construct the story of the ball. How had Ronnie come to own it? Had he been there that day at the Polo Grounds? Had he met the rookie Willie Mays? Was a drink to him then an egg cream, maybe, or a Pepsi, and nothing more? What stories could this baseball tell me about the game I loved, about Ronnie—about us?

I looked up to see Ronnie leaning over me, his vodka vapors hot upon my face, his rheumy eyes reading me for that glimmer of connection I sensed he found so elusive in life.

Keep it, he breathed, and I cradled the ball as though it were an egg.

———

THE NECESSITY OF baseball had come to me while studying the angry hackles along the back of my father's neat neck. He liked to keep clean, and every couple of weeks he returned from a barbershop on Deer Park Avenue with his dark-blond hair combed back from his forehead and tapered to prickly rows along the ridge of his shirt collar. Day after day, I stared at the back of his head from my seat in our station wagon, trying to figure out how to get past those bristles standing guard—how to connect with whatever was going on inside. All the while, the car radio was shouting out the answer in the play-by-play drone of another baseball game.

In its essence, my father's love for baseball was a love for the Yankees, whose constant success and easy sophistication appealed to a Depression-era kid who had neither. He bought into the mystique of the Yankees as a finely tuned corporate entity that happened to conduct business on grass. He saw DiMaggio and then Mantle as personifications of New York City class: guys who perspired and ached and grunted all day, and then at night tightened the double Windsor knots of their silk ties and went out for a few cocktails at the Stork Club, or the Copacabana. Marilyn Monroe didn't fall for Duke Snider, now did she?

So my brother and I studied the history of the Yankees for the path it might provide into the heart of this complex man who was our father. Perched in the back of the station wagon, we cast our lines into the front seat's murky waters, seeing what the bait of our Yankee trivia might catch. Hey Dad, what Yankee pitcher once won forty-one games? Hey Dad, what was the name of the first baseman that Lou Gehrig replaced? Hey Dad, guess how many stolen bases Jerry Kenney has this year? Hey Dad, who was the Dodger batter that Don Larsen struck out to win his perfect game?

Sometimes our lines tugged back: Dale Mitchell, of course. I told you: I was at that game. Other times, the lines stayed slack, or worse, we'd have to reel them in because of choppy waters: Not now, for Chrissake. Not now.

We identified a cosmic connection between our father and Mickey

Mantle. The man known as "the Mick" grew up in Commerce, Oklahoma, of course, a long way from the streets of New York; he was also a superhero, while Gene Barry was among the tens of millions of journeymen just getting by. But Mantle was blond and blue-eyed, like my father. Not quite six feet tall, like my father. And born on October 20, 1931, just ten days after my father's birth. What's more, the Mick hid his many pains and injuries beneath an ever-present uniform; my father hid pains too, I suspected, emotional ones from childhood that were tucked somewhere beneath his ever-present suit. What we did not know about our father's background was more than made up for by the Scholastic Books biography of Mickey Mantle. Maybe we had to pause before remembering that the name of our father's father was Francis, but we knew instantly that Mickey Mantle's father's name was Mutt. And, like Francis, Mutt had died much too young.

Mickey Mantle was years past his Most Valuable Player prime by the time Brian and I came of baseball age. Still, we thrilled to see that magical "7" stretched across his massive back; it cemented an association between man and number that would last the rest of our lives, creating a new kind of math: 7 = Mantle. We sucked in our breath as he peered from under his midnight-blue helmet, so relaxed that he could have been hailing a bus with those hi-there waves of his bat, a bat that in his hands seemed to be a natural wooden extension of his thigh-sized forearms. Sometimes he swung—from the left side or the right, it didn't matter to Mickey Mantle—and the baseball fled from his presence to find ricocheting refuge among the seats beyond the outfield wall. Other times he missed a pitch so badly that his body coiled in awkward torque, and he grimaced in such naked pain and humiliation that we ached for him.

Through the summers of 1967 and 1968, we saw those grimaces more than we saw his home-run hobble around the bases. And then Mickey Mantle vanished from our summer days. Once a year he reappeared at Yankee Stadium, but only to tip his hat along with Joe DiMaggio, Tommy Henrich, and the other old-timers who had made the ball club of my father's youth and young adulthood so dominant. Now, in their stead, was a hapless assembly of ballplayers for whom mediocrity was a goal. They were not lovable losers; they were just losers.

So, then, were Brian and I, because the two baseball teams in New York City had essentially swapped places in the time that it took us to become baseball aware. The Mets of the early '60s may have been among the worst teams ever to take the field, but at least Choo Choo Coleman and Marvelous Marv Throneberry brought ineffable charm to baseball haplessness. Now the Mets were World Series champions, and the sons of Brooklyn Dodgers and New York Giants fans avenged their fathers by harassing us: boys too young to have basked in past Yankee successes and who now were hitched to a team that was actually worse than the early Mets because it was so devoid of personality. No Marvelous Marv here. Just men who seemed ill at ease in pinstripes: center fielder Bill Robinson, so graceful in the on-deck circle, who had more strikeouts than hits in 1969; catcher Jake Gibbs, the erstwhile Mississippi golden boy who did not hit one homer all year; pitcher Stan Bahnsen, a former Rookie of the Year, who lost sixteen games and won but nine.

We were Yankee fans and there was nothing we could do about it. So we listened. On the Saturdays and Sundays of summer, we struggled to keep up with our father as he marched past blankets and umbrellas in search of an undeclared plot of sand at Robert Moses beach, a transistor radio in one hand and a Styrofoam cooler in the other, the swish of its ice loudly ordering everyone else to be quiet: *shish, shish, shish, shish*. He was easy to keep in sight, with his black socks stretched to his knobby knees and his blue flip-flops kicking up puffs of sand, and that determined, this-is-a-public-beach-mister face shadowed by a straw hat and mirrored sunglasses. Once we had staked our claim, and a can opener had punched holes in our beer and soda cans, my father flicked on his little radio and fiddled with the dial so that it screeched like a cat set aflame. When he finally found the station he desired, he turned up the radio as loud as it would go. Soon the despairing sounds of yet another Yankee loss were competing with the roars of waves beating against sand.

We cheered into the gray plastic grill of his transistor radio, trying to coax a hit from the bespectacled librarian of a Yankees second baseman, Horace Clarke, who seemed to disdain physical contact. Still, we rooted for him as though he were Ruth; "Hoss," we called him. We rooted too for Gene Michael, the lanky shortstop whose nickname, "the Stick," became an ironic reference to his weak hitting, and the two pitchers, Fritz Peterson and Mike Kekich, who provided distraction from the team's failures one year by swapping wives. And there were many failures back then, daily failures to just about every other team in the American League. But in my mind's eye, the Yankees are always, eternally, losing to the Baltimore Orioles and their leader, Frank Robinson, so good that he was scary. In his twenty-one-year, Hall of Fame career, Frank Robinson hit 586 home runs; I believe that 560 of those were hit against the Yankees on weekend afternoons in the late 1960s.

Still, we rooted and were rooted. There, at Robert Moses beach, with the August sun baking our fair skin to the color of cherry Froot Loops. With the announcer known as "the Scooter," Phil Rizzuto, prepping us for another loss, like a doctor standing at our sickbed. With our mother lost in another crossword puzzle, and our father rooting too, only with his hand in the cooler's icy waters for another beer. We slurped from our own cans and cheered, as Horace Clarke stepped into the batter's box to face the oncoming waves.

AS MUCH AS I loved the Yankees, it was the act of playing baseball that mattered most to me. The sensation of my bat meeting a pitched ball, and having that ball travel fair and true, was the electrifying feel of physical connection. Better yet was the sensation of a batted ball landing in the web of my outstretched glove; it felt complete, like the rightful return of a dove to its nest.

I was among the legion of young boys who slept with new baseball gloves beneath their beds. Beyond the psychic appeal of sleeping on the subject of your dreams, the arrangement had a certain practical purpose.

New gloves back then had nowhere near the malleability of the pre-treated baseball gloves of today; they were like frozen pieces of leather, serving more as a shield against a pelted ball than as something designed to catch one. So I participated in a ritual that was necessary for my new baseball glove to become responsive, flexible, a part of me. I do not recall how I learned the mechanics of this ritual. It could have been from my father, or from other kids on the block, or simply from a dream.

First, you locked your bedroom door. This was a sacred moment, after all, and the presence of parents would only spoil the spell, ensuring that the glove would drop more balls than it caught. You took a ballpoint pen and scrawled your name, address, telephone number, and the name of your Little League team—in my case, the Ducks—across the glove's thumb in letters so big and loopy that the glove's second and third fingers would also be required for this vital information. If, God forbid, you lost this precious piece of leather, you wanted to leave no doubt about its ownership should a stranger come upon it.

Then you soaked your new glove in so much neat's-foot oil that it left outlines of the mitt on your pants and bedcover. You kneaded the oil into the glove with your bare hands until your fingers were yellow enough to retain its pungent scent for days afterward. You dug up your brother's baseball that you had been hiding from him and placed it firmly in the glove's pocket. You closed the glove around the ball; given the stiffness of the leather, you might actually have to sit on the glove to make it close. Then, holding it shut, you wrapped several of your father's belts around the glove and cinched the buckles. True, you might have to deny knowing the whereabouts of these belts, but ultimately you knew that you could not be persecuted for practicing your American faith. Finally, you wedged this slimy, foul-smelling object between the mattress and bedspring of your bed, and you slept on it for several days, like a fidgeting hen warming an egg.

After a week, you released the glove from its restraints. It might remain so tightly shut that you would have to shuck it open like a clam. Every evening for the next week you opened and closed the glove, again,

and again, and again—while you studied, while you ate your macaroni-
and-cheese dinners, while you watched *Hogan's Heroes* repeats, while you
brushed your teeth before bed.

Then, one glorious day, your glove suddenly felt as though it was a
part of you—your actual hand, only branded with the name of Rocky
Colavito or Al Kaline. Now you were ready to test its magic. You raced
outside and threw the baseball high into the sky, reaching over curbs,
shrubs, and car windows to rob Frank Robinson of another home run.

These solitary test runs lasted so deep into the night—so deep into
autumn, in fact—that I often could only see the descent of one of Robinson's moon shots when it broached a street lamp's arc of light. He may
have been playing for the awesome Orioles, but I was playing for the
Ducks, who feared no one. In my baseball dreams, the massive Robinson
stands at the plate of a Little League field in Deer Park, his bat a plank
from the bleachers, his helmet scraping the top of the metal backstop.
The Duck pitcher, Timmy, launches a rainbow pitch so polite that it
pauses in deference at the plate. A swing, the clack of wood against ball,
and I start back, my baseball stirrups sagging against my black socks, my
Keds finding no traction in the grass, my hat tipped sideways. Back, back,
I run, just the ball and me now, the sounds of Little League—the shouts
of overinvested parents, the tinkling bells of ice cream trucks—gone
silent. There is only the *heh-heh* of my breathing. Back, back; *heh-heh,
heh-heh.* A leap, a crash through the fence, the catch—Frank Robinson
denied. The Ducks win the pennant! The Ducks win the pennant!

The Ducks. We lost twenty-one games and won three that summer,
taking our punishment every Tuesday and Thursday beginning at 6 P.M.,
the precise hour at which clouds of mosquitoes rose from sewers and
streams to mix with the kicked-up dust of plays at the plate. We were so
bad that the umpires sometimes ended the games early, for fear that the
drubbings-in-progress would cause lasting damage to our sense of self-
worth. We were so bad that opposing players—and their parents—used
to quack when we blundered onto the field. We were the Ducks, after all,
playing against teams named after aggressive birds of prey. After a

matchup between the Hawks and the Ducks, whose downy feathers would you expect to see fluttering across the empty infield?

Even so, I lived for Tuesdays and Thursdays at 5:15, when my weary and potbellied neighbor and coach, Mr. Perelman, lumbered out of his house, like some hibernating bear disrupted, and hoisted himself into the big red truck he drove for a Brooklyn bread company. On the dashboard, two small boxes containing unblemished baseballs wrapped in tissue: the game balls. On the passenger's side, his son, Greg, and his left-handed second baseman, Danny Barry, proud and vigilant guards from the Ducks Bread Security Company. In the back, aluminum shelves for bread, folded cardboard bread boxes, and two grimy duffel bags bulging with bats, balls, and helmets. As the truck rattled its way toward the Deer Park Little League field, the aroma of fresh-baked bread mingled with thoughts of baseball. Bread and baseball equal life: perfect.

I was an awful ballplayer those first few years, and I looked it: a scrawny apology of a boy with my green Ducks baseball cap adhered to my butch-style haircut, the bill pulled so low that I had to tilt my head up, as though compensating for a nosebleed, just to see straight ahead. But the game called to me, and I played as often as I could. Every afternoon I sat on the curb at the corner of West 23rd Street, watching a group of older boys play stickball and wishing the balls into foul territory, just so that I could fetch them. I chased after those foul balls like a loping golden retriever, and threw the balls back to the big boys with my tongue protruding and my body contorted in some pretzel-like windup. Once my throws sailed over the heads of my intended targets, I sat down, beaming, and waited intently for another ball to skip outside the lines of fair play.

Every child has his local hero, and mine was Raymond Liskowsky, the neighborhood's hulking giant. At fifteen years old, he was six foot two, with blue stubble on his chin and black-framed glasses clasped with rubber bands to his block of a head. He was an eternal child in a man's body who would later be sent away for shooting BBs into living room windows, including ours. Still, I never saw anyone hit a Spalding higher or farther. He seemed blessed without thought, and had a primal response to the pink ball thrown to him: a clean, instinctual swing of a bat that could just as easily have been aimed at a human head. I worshiped him.

The natural order of things followed course on West 23rd Street, and before long I was among the boys dominating the street. We painted an elongated baseball diamond on the narrow road, spelled out the Mets, the Yankees, and the names of our Little League teams right behind home plate, and then sketched out a lopsided hopscotch pattern to distract the girls and keep them from bothering us. Pavement graffiti was de rigueur then. A newly paved street meant that an oversized blackboard beckoned. It was a newsworthy event in my childhood, as important as when the bug truck drove slowly down our street on a muggy summer's evening, releasing clouds of pesticide that we would loop in and out of on our Stingray bicycles. For years afterward, driving on a repaved street filled me with the guilt of improper use, as though I were violating a black canvas intended for the idle chalk marks of children.

We played a baseball of indeterminate innings on those doubleheaders of summer days. Rather than break for lunch, we brought jugs of Kool-Aid and ice water to the corner, along with a bag of peanut butter sandwiches. We stopped only for passing cars, or for nightfall, or for the angry dinner calls of parents whose hunger blinded them to the charm of our obsession. And if there weren't enough kids around for a game, my brother and I played catch, trying and failing to throw each other curveballs and knuckleballs. And if Brian wasn't around, I threw a Spalding onto the roof of our house and tried to guess where it would bounce back into view. And if the Spalding got stuck in the gutter, I dug out an old baseball, its guts of yarn wrapped in black electrical tape, and tossed it skyward again and again, stretching, diving, catching, Frank Robinson denied.

I played first base and the outfield for so many teams that I can only recall some of their names: the Hawthorns, the Ducks, the Crows, the Expos, the Giants, the Friars. I played in Little League, the Babe Ruth League, and a senior traveling league; for my elementary school, my high school, and my town of Deer Park. One summer I played for two teams in separate leagues, and as Barry luck would have it, both teams were scheduled to play at the same time on the same ballfield complex. I chose the team for which I had a higher batting average, which was not saying much. I played outfield during a game in which a bird was nesting its eggs in the exact spot where I was supposed to be positioned. I played in a Great South Bay fog so thick and low that we outfielders had no choice but to wait for the fly balls to plop to the ground like discarded apples of the gods.

All those hundreds of games I played become one: a game one humid August night, on a bug-infested ballfield at a remote and wooded edge of Deer Park. Tire tracks rutted the outfield and pebbles pocked the infield, which meant that no pop fly was an easy jog to reach and no grounder was true; every hit ball had the potential to split your nose. Still, I loved playing there because of the beacon-bright lights atop soaring steel poles that allowed us to play at night. Baseball glows under the lights, especially when played on diamonds removed enough from house lights and street lamps to be their own sanctified grounds. The ball itself assumes a radiant, electric quality; it sparks off a swinging bat and skitters over dew-wet grass like some errant, white-hot ball of energy.

Mom, I'm going to the ballfield to be transported.

All right, Danny. Get a hit for me.

The two teams took batting practice and shagged fly balls, while our coaches and some of the parents sat in the stands, cutting the mugginess with a few bottles of Schmidt's beer. It was a given that people would bring a few coolers: one packed with Yoo-Hoo and Pepsi, the others packed with beer. Those squat amber bottles fit so snugly into the callused mitts of my coaches, Herb and Sal and Kenny, blue-collar guys who lived for those games. They'd grab a fungo bat, launch a few to their sons in the outfield, and then cut the dust with a cold one.

On this night, though, technology threatened to thwart the game. We had the bats, the gloves, the balls, and an opponent, a team from the neighboring town of Commack. We even had a couple of beer-drinking umpires. What we did not have was light. The maintenance man, who seemed to list from the weight of a thousand keys on a ring attached to his belt loop, had not shown up. After a consultation over the beer cooler, the adults of Deer Park decided to send Mrs. Feeley to find the maintenance man.

In the consuming dark and with Mrs. Feeley dutifully dispatched, our guardians gathered closer for the light to be found in bottles bobbing in ice water. We ballplayers hit grounders to one another until the ball could not be distinguished from the grass. Then we threw pop flies until it became too dark to discern even the shadow of the ball. Finally, we just sat in the dugout, a row of teenage boys slightly unnerved by the enveloping night. By 9:30 it was pitch black, but all the adults were lit.

Tree frogs peeped their summer serenades; the faint whiff of skunk hung in the air. Then, at about ten o'clock, we heard the approaching rattle of keys; Mrs. Feeley had found the maintenance man. A key inserted here, a flick of a switch there, and a ballfield magically appeared before us—a dreamlike vision with real bases and a real home plate. Boys cheered while parents squinted into the sudden glare.

The home-team players ran to their positions, the umpires tottered toward theirs, and the game began. The second batter hit a grounder to short. When the umpire correctly called him safe, on a play to first that wasn't even close, Kenny—or was it Herb? Or Sal?—charged the field and belly-bumped the umpire. A drunken scrum broke out between adults, and when it was cleared, one of our coaches was banished to the distant parking lot, from where he shouted half-hearted epithets between sips of another beer.

We played on, deep into the night and early into the morning. After a while, the tree frogs and the drunken coach fell silent, leaving the sounds of baseball to echo in suburban stillness: the thock of bat hitting ball, the thud of ball meeting glove, the umpire's call, the brief bursts of dugout chatter.

Now you're set, we said. Now you're set.

And we were.

KEEP IT, RONNIE said of the baseball. Keep it.

I could not believe his offer. Imagine owning a baseball that was once held by Willie Mays? That was signed by all those ballplayers, each one a participant in baseball history? The 1951 New York Giants, who won the pennant, who won the pennant.

Before my joy rose to the point of exclamation, I caught sight of my father, my coach, just over the sag of Ronnie's shoulder. He was shaking his head, slowly, solemnly. This is not open for debate, his gesture said. The reasons are beyond you, beyond the ball.

I took one last look, oh how I wanted that ball, and handed it back to Ronnie. It was too valuable to accept, I stammered, but thank you anyway thank you very much. Ronnie nodded a little too vigorously and left the room. He did not return.

He went back to killing himself, of course, slowly, with the cheap kind of vodka often bought in half-gallon bottles. It took another decade, first with those walks down to the liquor store on First Avenue, him in his trench coat, eyes averted, smarter than everyone else but what good was it, what good was anything. Then, when his equilibrium left him entirely, with the buzz at the door that meant the liquor store had come to him, and still no need to meet the deliveryman's knowing gaze.

In 1982, Aunt Betty, his protector and senior by more than thirty years, died first, which surprised everyone. Then it was Ronnie alone, in her apartment, surrounded by old-lady furniture and photographs of the dead. The aromas of steeping tea and lavender bathwater gave way to those of finger-yellowing cigarettes and despair.

A few months after Aunt Betty's funeral, I visited Ronnie in Bellevue Hospital, on the East Side. I was twenty-four, at my beginning. He was at his end, hands and legs strapped to a gurney, belly bloated from a distended liver, skin the palest of yellows, mind too addled to muster even fear. He had no idea who I was. An intern walked by and pointed to Ronnie's sticklike arm.

Better take your father's watch before it disappears, he said.

That's not my father, I said, in hindsight a little too quickly.

Ronnie died the next day; in actual years he was a mere forty-five. He was buried in a coffin so cheap that I could see the staples in the nickel-colored velveteen covering.

A few days later and for the last time, the Barrys returned to the apartment in Stuyvesant Town to remove the possessions of an old, refined lady and a brilliant, tortured inebriate. I went into his dank room and drew open the curtains heavy with dirt, inviting the long-forgotten guest of sunlight. There, piled about the rumpled and soiled mattress, were his effects: high school records documenting his intellectual prowess; books of Latin poetry; collections of Pogo comic strips; programs from the old Metropolitan Opera productions of the 1950s and 1960s; opera albums, as many as two hundred, stacked on top of one another: Puccini's *Turandot*, Bizet's *Carmen*, Bellini's *Norma*.

An image came to me: Ronnie hunched by the hi-fi, glass in hand, finding affirmation for all the sadnesses of his life in *La Boheme*, in the songs of lovestruck artists and a dying girl of the city.

Era buio, e il mio rossor
non si vedeva.
"Che gelida manina,
se la lasci riscaldar!"
Era buio, e la man
tu mi prendevi . . .

It was dark and you couldn't
see me blushing.
"What a frozen little hand,
let me warm it for you!"
It was dark, and you
took my hand . . .

I searched under his bed but saw only empty vodka bottles on their sides. Then, amid the clutter on his dusty dresser, I found it: the baseball. The smoke of countless cigarettes, smoldering in the sunless room, had gradually coated the signatures of heroes in a leathery brown glaze so dark that their names could no longer be deciphered.

It was a worthless Barry relic. One that I would keep.

5

WITH THE CHILDREN gone to bed and him moaning upstairs, she sat down at her wobbly kitchen table to write. She was not one for writing letters; rarely did she write home to Ireland or to her childhood friend now living in New England. But these were desperate times. My mother reached for a pen.

The three dogs, Bonnie, Pixie, and Gypsy, wheezed in sleep a few feet away, nuzzled so close together that their mottled coats of brown and black and gray rose and fell as one. The dish rack was empty; Danny had washed the plates and flatware, Brian had scoured the pots, Brenda and Elizabeth had cleaned off the table and put everything away. The washing machine next to the stove churned, occasionally bucking against the Formica counter before settling back into balance. Now and then the fluorescent light flickered above, as if in synchronicity with the off-and-on hum of the refrigerator and the sighs of the sleeping dogs. Outside, the October winds had come to Long Island. She lit another cigarette and pressed her pen against the clean piece of loose-leaf paper.

With a style of handwriting not often seen in the States, a script that reflected the tight loops and curls taught by the nuns of Gort, she wrote out her name and address in the upper right-hand corner of a kind of paper normally used for homework assignments. Now, how to begin a letter to Hollywood? Well, there was only one way to begin any letter, and that was with a salutation:

Dear Mr. Capra,

My husband has been a fan of yours for many years and some time ago he read your book, "The Name Above the Title." Well in this book you mention "Cluster Migraine." That's the reason for this letter.

"That's the reason for this letter," Noreen Barry wrote, so as to leave no doubt. Mr. Frank Capra, this is not another fan letter affirming your exalted status as the director of a series of movie classics. This is not "I saw *Mr. Smith Goes to Washington* last night and I wanted to tell you how much . . ."; this is not "Would you be so kind as to send an autographed photograph? . . ." This is not about *It's a Wonderful Life.*

No. This is about "cluster migraine" headaches, like the ones that once tortured you: attacks that in your autobiography you likened to having monstrous birds sink their "ghostly talons" into your head. "One each night, then two, three, four," you wrote. "I climbed walls. One hour of excruciating agony, then some fitful sleep, only to wake up screaming with pain."

You see, Mr. Capra: "Gene, my husband, has been suffering from this for over five years."

ONE WEEKEND NIGHT my family drove up to Poughkeepsie to visit McGonigle, the UFO enthusiast who had once set our lawn aflame with flares. We children itched with excitement, trying to imagine what he had in store for us this time. Would he, once again, affectionately call me an obscenity? Would he have flares on his own lawn? All we knew was that he made my parents laugh and laugh, which made us laugh as well, mostly in relief. And, as it later turned out, McGonigle did have a great prank in store. He had wired his house so that ghostly wails would emanate from the walls and almost certainly launch my father into asserting that the noises prove the existence of ghosts, prove that spirits never die, prove that—well, just imagine the implications!

That was the plan at least, but the joke never got to its punch line. On the ride up, my father began writhing in pain, like a lion shot in the neck. Between moans he explained to his stunned family that a headache had come upon him like a thunderclap—like no other headache he had ever had—and it would not ease. Hours passed before the pain did, and my father emerged as though he had been held underwater against his will: exhausted, and more than a little scared. A day planned for pranks and laughter had turned into one of anxiety, of Please kids, get out of here, don't disturb your father.

These incapacitating headaches returned repeatedly to exact whimpers and cries from my father. A succession of doctors diagnosed the attacks as chronic cluster migraines, for which no genetic or behavioral cause had been determined. All they knew was that these migraines usually occurred at night and struck with excruciating stabs of pain that could last for hours. Sometimes my father took the drugs they prescribed; sometimes he drank; sometimes he washed down the drugs with beer. Nothing brought comfort.

At first the headaches returned just often enough to bring horrible reiteration of an all too familiar lesson: be alert, all hell could break loose in an instant. One minute the six Barrys would be the model of 1970s suburban domesticity, watching television while the dinner plates dried in the dish rack and the dogs dozed in the hall; the next minute we would be five, with him upstairs, crying out for God's mercy, and we children looking to our mother, smoking her cigarette and exuding calm but all the while wondering whether he would be able to continue working.

Turn the sound down, she'd say. And say a prayer for Daddy.

Daddy tried. He was finally hitting his stride as a bond trader on Wall Street. Over were the days when Gene and Noreen wrapped the used toys of the nice family next door to present to their own kids on Christmas. He was making enough money now to take the family to Ireland—a quantum leap from those one-week-a-year vacations at a ramshackle dude ranch in the Poconos, with its swayback horses and dining room that smelled of mothballs. Not only would Noreen visit her homeland for the first time since she was seventeen, but the fresh air, the farmhouse cooking, and a few pints of Guinness might be just the tonic for these goddamned headaches.

The family flew over in the summer of '71. We children posed with goats and cows for the black-and-white photographs. We drank warm Coke while our elders drank stout and whiskey. Every day we ate potatoes and overcooked ham, then went outside to inhale the fresh, manure-tinged air. And when the Barrys left Shannon Airport in a flurry of tears and hugs, we had in our hold two plastic bottles shaped like the Virgin Mary, their caps her crown. Both bottles contained clear liquid: holy water in one, and poteen, the Irish moonshine, in the other. Maybe one or the other, or both, will help poor Gene's afflictions, God willing. They did not.

Still, my father continued to work. Two hours into the city, a full day hustling, two hours home, and then often up to bed to scream for the night. That was his routine, and thus ours, until he broke his ankle while clambering off that hell train of his. He spent half of 1973 drinking beer, scratching the inside of his thigh-high cast with an unraveled coat hanger, and serving as Counselor of Rage to the Senate during its televised hearings on Watergate. The bastard's lying, my father shouted, as a twitchy John Ehrlichman nervously testified before the hound-faced chairman, Sam Ervin. He's a goddam liar!

More than once I tried to sneak past my father to go play baseball on the corner. More than once he ordered me to fetch a beer for him from the fridge and join him in front of the television. This is history, Danny, he would say, before becoming absorbed in his civic duty.

The bastards! The goddam bastards!

Between his rants and headaches, my father calculated that if he went back to commuting on that goddamn train he'd be dead by fifty. But his skills were more cerebral than marketable—he only had a high school diploma—and when his cast was removed, he struggled to find a job on a Long Island reeling from a recession and skyrocketing gas prices. My mother typed his resume, but the o's punched holes like zeroes through the onion-skin paper.

He tried his hand as a manager-in-training at a Jack in the Box fast-food franchise in Bay Shore, but it was a disaster: a man who had dined at the Waldorf, who had sold bonds with the best of them, now wearing a paper hat and filling orders for Jumbo Jacks and onion rings, all the while wasted from the headaches and the lack of sleep. Each night, though, he brought home a few plastic figurines from Jack in the Box's knockoff of McDonaldland—family heirlooms now, hard-plastic relics from hard times. Finally, he took a job managing a check-cashing store on Commack Road, about two miles from our house and at about half his city salary. No more would we be visiting Galway.

By now the cluster migraines were coming nearly every night, staggering him like uppercuts to the head. A new routine, forged in pain and resentment, took hold. He came home from work beaten in body and spirit, the tingling sensation of another attack already creeping up the back of his skull. A quick beer or three—or maybe a couple of premixed vodka concoctions—and then up to his cool and dark bedroom to moan and curse and press his neck against the headboard in search of relief, so hard that it sounded like he was banging his head against the wall. And on days when the headaches briefly lifted, the rage came to fill the void. His childhood had been hard enough, but now, just when he was making some money and moving up in life, he was being waylaid by a condition that few can understand—no cast for it, no brace—a condition that directly attacks the vessel to his cherished brain. Jesus Christ. Jesus Christ.

His thundering, profanity-laced dialogue with God rang out from my parents' second-story window and onto the street, so loud at times that a neighbor occasionally came to the door to say that she prayed every night for Gene. On summer nights, Brian and I stood under a lamplight outside our house with other boys from the neighborhood and just tried to be kids. We beat rhythms on the hoods of cars, exchanged fake punches, admired the ability of one boy—nicknamed "the Beast"—to say an entire sentence in a protracted belch. We also tested in our mouths the foul words that seemed necessary to prove our Long Island mettle—

nicknames for body parts and sex acts—but which were dismissed by my father as low-class obscenities unworthy of us. If you want to curse, boys, he often told us, curse with relish, with class. Now his own epithets, sprinkled among the moans and prayerful pleadings, floated down upon us in the nighttime street like a teary summer mist, reminding us that we never could be just kids. We were doubly embarrassed; not only were we helpless to ease his public agony, we were also cursing in ways that were beneath us, and him.

Sometimes, when there were prolonged pauses in his moans, Brian and I looked up to the window of the room where Brenda and Elizabeth were probably conceived, a place of union that was now one of isolation. Maybe this headache had stopped; maybe he would be down soon to watch the *Ten O'Clock News* and enjoy a well-deserved bowl of ice cream. Almost always, though, a pause in the moaning only meant a howl in the offing.

Aaaaaagh. Aaaaaagh! Aaaaaagh!

Jesus Christ, Brian would say; Goddammit, I would say. As our father would say.

For us, being outside the house was better than being inside. Inside, there was no place to get distance from the anguish. The moaning and banging insinuated themselves into the daily household music, blending with the clatter of the washer and the rumble of the dryer. We ate dinner to it, watched television to it, did homework to it, all the while struggling to heed our mother's admonition to "keep things light"—the family code for not upsetting our father in any way. When a headache briefly lifted, he stepped heavily down the stairs, his every footstep a warning to make sure that everything was in place: lights dimmed, television sounds lowered, dinner reheated in case he was hungry. Often he trudged past the specially prepared dinner—of pork chops and mashed potatoes and cut green beans and huge dollops of applesauce, just the way he liked it—as though it weren't there, continuing on to the refrigerator for a half-time beer before the next headache took hold.

Nearly every night my mother sat alone on the couch, with no one to talk to about the malfunctioning appliances, the family's growing money concerns, the future. Nearly every night she asked one of us to check on our father and see if he needed anything. Reluctantly, we crept up the stairs and knocked on the door. No answer. Dad? No answer. Then we opened the door to his icebox of a bedroom. Dad, you need anything? No thank you, he might moan. Or he would demand, between gasps, another bottle. Sometimes this meant he wanted another beer. More often it referred to the Schmidt's beer bottles filled with frozen water that we kept stocked in our basement freezer; pressing these glass cylinders of ice against the back of his neck seemed to bring some limited relief. Late at night, after all the lights had been turned off, Brian and I would lie awake—as did my mother, as did my sisters—and listen to my father's moans, his begging God to ease his pain. We would silently join his pleas until fitful sleep came, and then start all over again in the morning.

One night I heard my father threatening to kill himself. He wasn't talking to my mother, or to any of the children; he was talking to God. I can't take it anymore, damn You! Why are You doing this to me? I'll kill myself! Is that what You want? I'll kill myself. Oh Mother of God!

He had made similar nighttime threats before, but this one struck me as naked and real. Maybe because the pain had intensified; maybe because he had been drinking heavily that night; maybe because I was feeling more vulnerable than usual. It did not matter. I was the oldest, I was the protector, I would not let my father kill himself. I got out of bed and went downstairs to hide the kitchen knives, the only weapons in the house other than our sharp tongues. Then I stationed myself at the top step of the stairs, between my parents' bedroom and the rest of the house. There was no way he would get past me, no way. I was the fourteen-year-old sentry, determined to save a teetering family from the abyss.

There I sat in the night's stillness, surrounded by the lingering aromas of dinner and the moans of a father in agony. As my eyes adjusted to the semidarkness, I could see the outlines of our living room and our world: my mother's worn couch, where she sometimes slept; my father's stuffed chair; the coffee table with the family's unread Bible; the Connemara marble ashtray from Ireland, with white cigarette stubs sprouting from gray ash. And on the wall beside the stairs, four diamond-shaped picture frames, each one containing a photograph of one of the Barry children. How young we had once looked.

Sometime around three, his snores replaced the cries. My shift was over.

WHAT ELSE COULD this Long Island woman do then, this worried working mother of four, but sit down and write that letter to the director of *It's a Wonderful Life*, a movie about misfortune and cruelty and, ultimately, perseverance.

Dear Mr. Capra.

Gene, my husband, has been suffering from this for over five years. He had to give up his job because of it. He commuted forty miles a day to New York City by train, but he was unable to continue because he didn't get more than two hours sleep at night because of the headaches. He was an executive salesman in Wall St. and he made very good money.

He went into a local hospital and had all sorts of tests done. His doctor called in experts in every field to examine him. Their final answer was "Cluster Migraine Headaches." They gave him pills for under his tongue, injections and antihistamines. These seemed to help for a little while and then the headaches came back full force.

He found a job locally and worked at this for three months. The headaches continued to get worse and he started to lose weight and get very on edge. He was out of work then for some time with no relief. We used up our savings and then he found a very easy job but the pay is poor.

He has had this job for almost two years now and there is no pressure there. I work to help make ends meet. He is still suffering and I don't know how long he'll be able to continue working with no sleep.

He is forty-three and we have four children and I'm afraid we will lose our home and Gene his sanity. If you found a cure would you let us know

*and we'll be forever grateful. I feel you'll understand because you have suf-
fered too.*

Thank you for your time.

Sincerely,

Noreen Barry

The refrigerator hummed, the washing machine kicked, the dogs
wheezed. Was that another cry from upstairs? Better go check.

Two months later, a typewritten letter was dropped in the metal mail-
box of the house of nighttime howls, postmarked Hollywood and dated
December 8, the Feast of the Immaculate Conception.

Dear Mrs. Berry:

*Cluster headaches! There is nothing worse. How I feel for you and your
husband. Mine started in 1961 and ended in 1971. I had to say good-bye to
my filmmaking career. . . .*

*In 1971 they stopped of their own accord. I have not had any headaches
since. So the only hope I can hold out for your husband is the rather forlorn
one that the headaches will stop someday. . . .*

Again, my deepest sympathies to you, and hang in there.

Warmly, Frank Capra

My father tossed the letter aside in despair. Hang in there; for Chrissake he'd been hanging in there for five years and where had it gotten
him. But my mother studied the short letter for a while, searching for
something, anything really, the way she studied clues to her beloved
crossword puzzles. Here. Here was something to hold on to: Capra said
that his headaches had suddenly and miraculously ended one day. Well,
at least there was that: the hope for one day.

Wasn't that nice of him, my mother said.

And she jotted off another note to tell her new Hollywood pen pal that
a mixture of vinegar and honey seemed to be giving my father "some
kind of balance back to his system," as well as some minor relief. "You
have given us hope that some day they will disappear, and hopefully it
will come soon," she wrote. "Thank you again for taking the time to write
and I hope you continue to enjoy good health."

In the years to come my mother would send an occasional Christmas card to Capra, each one indicating that my father was feeling better—which he wasn't. Her card from 1979 depicted Santa Claus smoking a clay pipe and carrying a bag of toys; in it she included a brief note to tell Capra about an inhalant called ergotamine, the latest "cure" that would prove to be just as ineffective as the honey-and-vinegar concoction of before and all the concoctions to come.

I wanted you to know and maybe you could help others. . . . Wishing you every happiness, Noreen & Gene & Family.

MY FATHER'S CLUSTER migraine headaches lasted for nearly twenty years, twice as long as Capra's. Because of the attacks, he missed four high school graduations, dozens of Little League and softball games, and hundreds if not thousands of family meals. His headaches, and the alcohol and pills he consumed to ease the pain, darkened our holidays, disrupted our nights, and left us always tiptoeing in his presence, for fear that the slightest misstep—the drop of a plate, the purchase of the wrong kind of cereal, the increase or decrease in the television's volume—might send him up to his bedroom to moan in pain. In our house of encroaching chaos, my mother's brief correspondence with Capra was quickly forgotten, as was the fact that she never received a reply to her Santa Claus card of 1979.

But Frank Capra had replied. A few months after the aged film director died in 1991, Leith Johnson, a friend of mine who works as the co-curator at the Wesleyan Cinema Archives, came across a curious batch of letters while cataloguing a trove of Capra's effects. He called one afternoon to ask an odd question.

Is your mother's name Noreen?

There, among the mounds of correspondence accumulated by the director of *Meet John Doe* and *Mr. Smith Goes to Washington*, *It Happened One Night* and, of course, *It's a Wonderful Life*, were my mother's letter and Christmas cards. There too was Capra's response to her 1979 Christmas note on a monogrammed card, along with instructions for his secretary: Flo, Send if you can find address. F.C.

Flo apparently never found that Deer Park address.

Dear Moreen Barry:

Forgive me in being so late in acknowledging your Christmas card. My desk is not a model of methodology; rather it looks like Fibber McGee's closet on its back.

On surfacing again your letter is a wonderful piece of news for people who suffer from cluster headaches—an inhaler "Ergotomine." I shall be happy to pass on this welcome information to all the sufferers who have written to me about cluster headaches.

Thank you for your kind thoughts for other sufferers.

Sincerely, Frank Capra

I hand-delivered a copy of the card to its intended address, 140 West 23rd Street, Deer Park. As my mother sat at the same kitchen table, reading Capra's words between Parliament puffs, I talked about the cynicism that often lurks in his movies—about the darkness inherent even in *It's a Wonderful Life*, despite the popular perception of it as a sappy Christmas movie. What's so sappy about George Bailey's suicide attempt? Maybe, I said, Capra was suggesting that life's wonders can only be realized through tribulation and hardship.

My mother looked at me as if I were not hers. And this is what she said: Wasn't that nice of him.

6

LISTEN, YOU LITTLE FUCK.

Not good morning, or welcome aboard, or that's a nice-looking blazer you're wearing today young man. No. It was, Listen, you little fuck.

The words remain anchored in memory, there beside the Prayer of St. Francis ("Lord, make me an instrument of Your peace"), the opening lines to a school song ("Onward to battle, on black and gold"), and simply, "Yes Brother." They conflict with one another and yet are inextricably woven together, echoing back in unsettling whispers: You little fuck listen yes brother make me an instrument of your peace fuck peace onward to battle listen Lord.

Hear each syllable to:

Listen

You

Little

Fuck

Hear the inner rhyme; note the perfect twinning of challenge and command. The subject's attention is unwavering now. He wants to know exactly what he should be listening for next. And this is what he heard.

Listen, you little fuck. Get off the bus and get down on your fucking knees.

Yes, of course, the knees. Get down on them. Submit, is what he's saying. But there must be some misunderstanding. I only wanted to start my first day at a Catholic high school, a Franciscan high school no less. I don't want to worship a school bus. I, I . . .

You fucking deaf? On your fu . . .

My knees hit the pavement before he finished.

Only an hour earlier, I had felt the first stirrings of purpose, of an end to juvenile aimlessness. I had put on the gray bell-bottom pants and the striped, maroon-and-white shirt that my mother had selected from the Mid-Island discount store on Deer Park Avenue, along with the brown vinyl shoes with inch-high heels and a round toe. I had chosen one of my father's newer ties, as wide as a dinner napkin and sporting a psychedelic design of violets and reds. Then I had shrugged into a brown corduroy blazer that would contour to my sloping shoulders for years to come.

I was no longer a child; I was a freshman. This was to be the first day of my first year at St. Anthony's High School, dedicated to preparing young Catholic men for the rigors of college "and for a life in some profitable occupation." So stated the *Friars Handbook*, the pocket-size student guide that went on to explain that the school I had chosen aimed to produce disciplined, cultured young men with "sound physical and mental health and a vocational purpose all directed towards his final goal—salvation."

For the first leg of that intended destination—salvation—I was to be ferried by the yellow school bus now idling before me, its churning engine adding to the heat of an already muggy September morning in 1972, a year when Richard Nixon would be elected president, again, and the Yankees would not win the pennant, again. The bus's doors had unfolded in welcome, but as soon as I took my first step up, the silver-haired man behind the wheel offered me the sweetest smile while saying, Get off.

I'm sorry?

Get off.

The driver's name was Steve. He had the vaguely sad look of someone already regretting what he would miss in his grandchildren's lives.

But, but . . .

It was then that the wild-eyed head of a teenage boy had sprung into view sideways, like the top to a malfunctioning jack-in-the-box, to utter the words that would stay with me all my life, to serve as my eternal greeting at the portals of young manhood. Listen, you little fuck. Get off the bus and get down on your fucking knees.

Now I was just that, a little fuck, inhaling bus fumes while Rice Krispies churned in my belly and gravel dug through my bell bottoms to pock my knees. Kneeling there, like a child prostrate before the Virgin Mary at Lourdes, only it was the corner of West 23rd Street, while neighbors drove past and wondered what one of those Barrys was up to now. Then came a voice.

Listen, asshole.

It was that jack-in-the-box again. I was an asshole now, not a little fuck, but I could not tell whether this was good or bad, a promotion or a demotion.

From now on, when this bus comes down your street, you better be on your fucking knees. And when you get dropped off in the afternoon, you stay on your knees until you can't see the bus anymore. We'll be watching. You understand?

I understood only enough to nod yes.

Then whattaya waiting for, he chirped. You're making us late. Asshole.

I climbed on board to see eighteen boys crammed into the first three rows, even though the rest of the bus was mostly empty. Spotting my friend and fellow freshman Donald Seibert, I offered the tentative smile that seeks a reassuring smile in return. No such smile came, although I sensed he was trying to tell me something. So were all the other boys I knew from Sts. Cyril and Methodius. Lips pursed, heads locked in forward position, they were all rolling their eyes, back, back, the way Abbott might signal to Costello that the Mummy was right behind him.

But. What. Were. They. Trying. To. Tell. Me?

Hey FUCKHEAD!

The jack-in-the-box was now vertical, and screaming like a drill sergeant into my ear. Even more unnerving was that a nearly identical jack-in-the-box was standing next to him, wearing the same maniacal grin. These, it turned out, were six-foot-six buddies, Leary and Geary: gawking rods of pent-up testosterone who never tired of plumbing the imperfections of others for humor. An overbite, a stutter, a tendency to cry, a habit of taking the hazing too seriously or not seriously enough—all these were giddily exploited by Leary and Geary and a few other sniggering upperclassmen. They considered themselves the great defenders of tradition on the Phelan Bus, the yellow rattletrap clattering toward St. Anthony's for yet another school year. They had been hazed three years earlier by seniors who had been similarly hazed when they themselves were freshmen. They felt duty bound: a failure to haze would have been to betray those who had gone before them, who, before heading for college or Vietnam, had dangled freshmen out bus windows, shredded their homework, looted their pockets, and greeted them every day with good-morning slaps to the head.

This was all a necessary introduction to life at St. Anthony's, they seemed to be saying: to be stripped of any sense of self-worth en route to school grounds, and then presented, *tabula rasa*, to Franciscan brothers who would tend to your formation as a Christian man bound for a "profitable occupation." Anyone who interpreted the hazing as sadistic and sophomoric simply did not understand the school spirit of this very special place called St. Anthony's.

Seeing no room in the first three boy-choked rows, I sat down in the empty fourth row, only to have Geary—or was it Leary?—shout at me to get the fuck out of that seat. Who do you think you are, a senior? Wrong, asshole, you're a fucking freshman. Find a seat in the first three rows where all fucking freshmen sit.

He shouted all this with a smile, a technique in the art of bullying that I knew well from humiliating experience. The victim is kept off guard because he doesn't quite know how to respond. If he begins to blubber in anticipation of a nosebleed, he is ridiculed as a pants-wetting baby. But if he relaxes and tries to join in on the joke, he exposes himself to the terrifying question: What the fuck are you laughing at?

The question is exquisitely suited to the purposes of bullies, not only because it has no correct answer, but because it lends itself so readily to broad and ever-shifting nuance.

For example, What the fuck are *you* laughing at? suggests that the victim was never invited to join in on the jokes being made at his expense, while What the fuck are you *laughing* at? indicates that the victim has woefully underestimated the gravity of his predicament. Then there is *What* the *fuck* are you *laughing* at?, which signals genuine outrage and therefore a sudden spike in the potential for violence. Not knowing what to do, the victim ventures a whimpering chuckle, all but ensuring that he will get his ass kicked because, you know what, there never was anything the fuck to laugh at.

I squeezed myself into a crack of space to become the fourth in a seat designed for three, and the bus lurched up Grand Boulevard, bound for St. Anthony's High School in Smithtown, fifteen miles to the northeast. In its hold were nineteen boys whose expectations for the first day of high school had been suddenly and considerably altered. Instead of talking among themselves about school supplies and classroom assignments, they sat in awkward silence, their bodies in half-clench, anticipating the next slap to the back of the head, the next summoning to the back of the bus, where only bad things happened.

The forty-five-minute bus ride provided more than enough time for daily riffs in the jazz of hazing. It emanated from the bandshell of an old bus, amid seats the color of congealing pea soup, windows streaked with phlegm, and the smell of corn chips and bologna belches and overheated teenage boys simmering in winter-jacket Crock-Pots. The music, a cacophony of shouts and laughs and pleas and slaps, rose and fell in relation to the distance from St. Anthony's. The farther from campus, the louder and more manic the music, whether we were bound for the school in the morning or pulling away in the afternoon (who knew what Brother might see?). Providing the beat to it all was the awareness of Phelan tradition, the standing dare to outdo the pranks and abuses of the past. Would anyone ever equal the psychotic reach of that student who answered his tormenters by wielding a knife? Would anyone ever dare to match the student who had taken the Phelan Bus for a joy ride while the driver was buying a six-pack in a deli? The very bus seemed to join in the taunting, its every gear shift sounding the grumble of top that, top that, top that.

Some of the hazing could be almost sweet in its traditional nature, as when upperclassmen used threats of physical harm to convince us of the value in learning the songs of St. Anthony's. Thanks to their forceful encouragement, I know the "Friar Fight Song" today as well as I do the Lord's Prayer:

Onward to battle, on black and gold,
Onward to victory, for young and old,
Fight for our alma mater's fame;
We'll cheer you on to win the game.
O Friars don't fail us; listen to our cheer,
On for St. Anthony's our alma mater dear.

But it was not all boola-boola. In the first few weeks of school, the seniors on the Phelan Bus expressed dissatisfaction with the names that had been given to us at baptism, and announced that it was time to rechristen all the freshmen. During the strangely formal christening ceremony, uninterrupted by the gasps and groans of the bus, each freshman was summoned to the back, given a new name, and ordered to return to his pea-green pew in silence, all while a junior solemnly recorded the names in a spiral-bound notebook. With the last freshman sent back to his seat, Leary—or was it Geary?—opened the notebook, cleared his throat with all the drama of someone trying to dislodge a grapefruit, and launched what would become a Phelan Bus practice for weeks to come. He took roll call.

Left Tit.

Billy Morrissey popped out of his seat and shouted, Here, sir!

Right Tit.

Here, sir, piped up Dennis Colbert.

On and on we traveled in this scatological tour of the human anatomy, through Scrotum and Douche Bag, Anus and Vagina, while passing through Deer Park and Commack, Northport and Kings Park, until there finally came the call of my own new name.

Penis.

I sprang from my seat. Here, sir.

I obsessed about my nickname; I could not decide whether to be honored or insulted. *Penis*, of course, is another term for *dick*, which is just about the most dismissive insult in the Long Island lexicon. Almost always used in reference to a male, it suggests that the person is clueless to the point of being annoying. By calling someone a dick, you are basically saying he is dickless. Then, in the throes of my agony, perspective would come like the snapped end of a gym towel. My home life alternated between *The Honeymooners* and *The Twilight Zone*, my acne-riddled face made others feel witty—Hey Barry, you look like the goalie for a dart team, *heh-heh*—and I had yet to speak to a girl my age, much less kiss one.

Get a hold of yourself, Penis, I told myself. Stop being a dick.

The bus became a rolling carnival, a fun house one day, a freak show the next, all for the entry fee of the twenty-five cents being extorted weekly by some Uriah Heep of a junior. One day we might be required to play "Pass the Orange," in which two-dozen freshmen used only their mouths to pass half an orange from one boy to the next; the first one to drop the slimy citrus was, of course, beaten. Another day we might be asked to "Make Out with Marsha," the name given to the emergency door at the back of the bus. The red light was her face, the bolts on the door her nipples. But before we were able to explore Marsha's plastic-and-steel delights—before we were allowed to thrust our hips in epileptic-like convulsions—we had to fight through the fists and kicks of upperclassmen guarding her honor. Then, as the bus jerked and snorted its way down Commack Road, the slobbering that we thought constituted heavy petting was bawdily critiqued by upperclassmen who feigned worldliness about the opposite sex.

One morning Leary and Geary caught the freshman sitting next to me, a blush of a boy named Schroeder, trying to hide a well-thumbed paperback called *The Choir Sings Sex* between his earth science and algebra textbooks. I felt sorry for Schroeder—whatever happened next would not be pleasant for him—but my cheap pity evaporated when Leary and Geary suggested that he stand up and, for the edification of his peers, read aloud a few excerpts from this unrecognized classic. Given the choice between freshman solidarity and prurient entertainment, we became the Phelan equivalent to the blood-lusting rabble clamoring before Pilate.

Make him read! Make him read!

Each morning on our way to instruction in the history of the western world and the teachings of Jesus, we were serenaded in erotica. Schroeder struggled to keep his dignity and balance as best as one could while standing in a moving bus, reciting smut to sex-starved boys on their way to an all-boys school. He read about rods of manhood and damp forests and luscious half-melons of delight, all in a quaking monotone that made the orgasmic rapture between a randy choirmaster and his voluptuous organist sound as exciting as the minutes to the last student council meeting.

Yes, yes, yes, she moaned. Harder, Trevor. Harder.

Jesus Christ, Schroeder, put some feeling into it, one of the seniors would shout. And read it like you're the one getting laid. Am I right, Left Tit?

Yes, sir.

Penis? Hey, Penis, you okay up there?

Yes, sir!

After a few weeks, the Phelan caste system became more defined to me. If you were an athlete, you were spared abuse; varsity players would be addressing your formation in the locker room. If you had an attractive older sister, you were also given reprieve, with the instruction to tell your sister how Leary or Geary had valiantly saved you from abuse. But if you were just a goofy kid, the oldest in your family, and the first to attend St. Anthony's—if you were, say, Danny Barry—you got slapped a little harder. And as bad as the goofy kids got it, others got it worse. If you were effeminate, hygienically challenged, or in any way a misfit, the Phelan Bus became your Bus of the Damned, no matter if you were a freshman or a senior.

Every morning a junior named Dominick Barone boarded the bus and bravely waded into this roiling sea of testosterone, clutching his books to his chest, now and then readjusting his thick, black-rimmed glasses. He and I soon formed a bond over old movies. My specialties, of course, were Abbott and Costello, the Marx Brothers, the horror films of Universal Pictures, and the gangster films of Warner Brothers. He preferred Bette Davis, Greer Garson, various musicals, and the choreography of Busby Berkeley. Still, there was enough cross-pollination, and enough interest in each other's disciplines, for us to talk at length about movies, often to the consternation of the seniors in the back of the bus. They took turns taunting Phelan's sole patron of the arts.

Dominick, that's a nice outfit you got on today. Real nice, ya fruitcake.

Hey Dominick, leave Penis alone, he's too young to be your boyfriend.

Dominick ignored the verbal bashing as long as he could, but he had his limits. Oh grow up, Geary, he would call over his shoulder and then, with an exaggerated eye-roll, tell me to just ignore the troglodytes in the back.

I strongly sensed that Dominick wanted to be away from all this. He wanted to be one of the tuxedoed extras in the backgrounds of *All About Eve*. He wanted to be a tap dancer clicking out rhythms on Busby's glistening marble floors, his arms locked around the waists of others, his face masked in ecstasy. He wanted to be gone. But every time he began to be transported—by talking about movies with this fidgeting freshman who knew more about Curly than about Bette—those troglodytes brutally returned him to the nauseating rock of his personal prison that was the Phelan Bus.

Hey Dominick, you got a dress picked out for the prom? Ya faggot.

That would do it. In a voice pitched high enough to impeach just about anything he said, Dominick would scream about the fucking animals in the back: how they were rude, unkempt, uneducated, and nothing more than a bunch of apes who clearly weren't sure of their own sexuality.

Thus challenged, one or two seniors would be obliged to lunge forward to throw a flurry of punches and kicks, until all that could be seen of Dominick was a single foot protruding from the edge of the seat, its gray Hush Puppy dangling from the toe. Then, after a few minutes, a hand would appear to grasp the back of the seat. A dramatic pause. And Dominick Barone would rise again, glasses askew, shirttail unfurled. A couple of freshmen would hand him the notebooks that had gone flying in the midst of the assault. Thank you, he would say dryly, and rest his head against a windowpane, yearning for that glorious moment when the bus would stop at his street corner, and he could escape to the set of a different movie, one in which the hero tap-dances to happiness.

For freshmen, though, there was no escaping the Phelan Bus. Like the pendulum on a clock, it swung back and forth, out to Smithtown and back to Deer Park, day after day, gradually hypnotizing us into accepting conditions and behavior that were unacceptable outside its yellow, tinlike borders. We were subjects in a social experiment on wheels and without supervision, re-creating the feral dynamics of *Lord of the Flies* as we rolled along in daylight, just another sunflowery blur in the endless Long Island flow.

But the day would come when the pendulum took pause, we were told; when we would find respite from our freshman fears and woes. On that day, the last day of school before the Christmas recess, the brutal and retarded sameness of our daily shuttles would end, and something wonderful would take place: the Annual Phelan Bus Christmas Party. Not only was this party the reason why that Heep of a junior had been extorting quarters from us for nearly four months, it also marked the day that our probation would end and formal Phelan acceptance would be ours. From that day on, all cuffs to the back of the head would be fraternal, not malevolent.

And what else, Penis? That's right, Penis; it is the day that we celebrate the birth of Our Lord. All you assholes bow your heads.

That December morning dawned as gray as the exhaust coughing out of the Phelan Bus's tailpipe. Still, it was the morning of the party and the last school day before Christmas, so we ignored the charms of Marsha and set aside *The Choir Sings Sex* to concentrate on holiday decorations. Up went the loops of silver garland to dangle from the metal ceiling; out sprayed the artificial snow to mask the windows in deceiving white. Holly-jolly music played from a tape recorder that bounced and jounced on a backseat as the bus rattled its way to Smithtown with some very happy boys aboard. It was a half-day of school, after all: Say "Here" in homeroom and "Amen" at Mass in the gym, and you're back on the bus without ever having opened a book.

When the final bell rang, we hustled to our Phelan Bus, idling there in the St. Anthony's parking lot with our grandfatherly driver, Steve, smiling at the wheel. Our guardian angel; our Clarence. Even now, though, we freshmen still did not know what we were rushing toward. What we knew of these Phelan Bus Christmas Parties came from the outlandish descriptions of upperclassmen more inclined to mess with our heads than tell us the truth. The rumors and the uncertainty made the party seem dangerous—even exciting. But the child in me, the one who wore pajamas, who lived for his mother's hugs, who still believed in the magic of days like Christmas, hoped that the celebration would be, well, un-Phelan-like. That it would have us all, freshmen and seniors, sophomores and juniors, singing good tidings to one another; that eggnog and tree-shaped sugar cookies would be handed out; that maybe even Steve would be our Kris Kringle, keeping gentle watch over a Christmas grab bag stuffed with the black-and-gold socks and shorts and T-shirts of our school, St. Anthony's. I tried hard to imagine being led in merry choruses of "We Three Kings" by those who had devised a left-tit-right-tit roll call.

The bus pulled into a small shopping strip about a mile from St. Anthony's, and several seniors hopped off. They returned a few minutes later with the supplies one might expect for a bachelor party in some paneled, musty basement: a dozen large pizzas, two cases of beer, a case of soda, pretzels, potato chips, Cheez Doodles, and about five napkins. The school bus chugged on, until Steve found a deserted corner in a Smithtown park, where foot and car traffic were sparse. He turned off the engine and accepted an offered can of beer.

Two hours later, all sorts of suggestions about what Santa could do to himself had been scrawled into the artificial snow. Smashed potato chips and Cheez Doodle orange dust carpeted the floor. At the front of the bus, our guardian angel Steve and a couple of freshmen were reminiscing over nursed beers like a group of regulars down at the VFW, while in the back, beer cans and empty pizza boxes were piled high enough to block metallic Marsha's view of the celebration. The air smelled of tomato sauce and beer and vomit, this last aroma the contribution of a senior from another bus who just wanted to experience Phelan, man.

The bus's resident scholar tried to ignore the festivities by immersing himself in some physics textbook, a strand of garland resting on his head, while boys just out of grammar school weaved down the aisle to collect another beer. Now and then someone would start singing a carol, only to trail off into forgetful nonsense.

And there, in the middle of this school bus bacchanal, sat Danny Barry. He was drinking a Coke, taking it all in, and not feeling so much like a little fuck any more.

7

WE KEPT HIM in sight, always in sight, this distraction, this teacher. Our minds shouted, Where is he now? Where is he now? Ah, there he is, at the front of the class, scratching out another x/y equation on the blackboard, the loopy sleeves of his black robe dusted with chalk. There he is now, leaning against the closed door, as if to block our escape. What was he thinking about—logarithms?—as he watched us squirm over another of his daily quizzes, every day a quiz, and woe to those who failed, a fate worse than failure awaited them. Him with his hands tucked within the slits of his robe, those hands at rest in the pockets of his pants, or was he even wearing pants as he watched us? Were those doughy hands at rest in pants, or were they rummaging freely about as he watched his roomful of fourteen-year-old boys? Pocket pool. That's what we wondered about during our cafeteria breaks, or in muffled conversations on the Phelan Bus ride home. He could be wearing shorts, which would explain the white socks and black shoes, so naked without the curtain of pants cuffs. Or he could be lining up his shots, eight ball in the corner pocket. And who's behind the eight ball this time?

Where is he now?

Of course. Right beside me, looming over my shoulder, reading the answers I have scrawled on my exam paper. I can smell him, a foul smell of whiskey and cheese, and Jesus, no wonder I suck at math.

Now he was kneeling before me, facing me, rubbing one of those fat-fingered hands on my cheek—caressing me, really—back and forth in a way that not even my mother had done when I was five, back and forth, making me flush with embarrassment and anger. My anger was mostly directed at myself, because had I been better at math, he would have had no opening to rub me.

Mr. Barry, he was saying, using words that had no relation to his actions. You might want to remember our discussions about coefficients and reconsider your answer to number three.

Yes, Brother Noel.

That was his name, like that of some demented sibling of Father Christmas: Brother Noel.

Another stroking swirl of the cheek, a slight slap to say good-bye or good luck or good boy. And then he was gone, off to give an encouraging rub to someone else's cheek, or maybe a reassuring massage to a pair of young, tensed-up shoulders.

Yes, Brother Noel.

He looked like an older, slightly disheveled Tyrone Power, with bushy black eyebrows made all the darker by a mane of white hair that he wore swept back. He spoke with a gravelly baritone that suited his great facility with the English language and his penchant for the dramatic; it was like having a Barrymore teach you algebra, each equation a Shakespearean riff. From day one, he addressed us as "Gentlemen," and in so many ways signaled that the time had come for us to put aside our childish ways.

He was by far the best-known teacher at St. Anthony's High School. Just a few months earlier, I was standing with some other boys in the parking lot at Sts. Cyril and Methodius, less than a week before our eighth-grade graduation, when a young teacher named Mr. Rafferty walked over and asked us where we would be attending high school.

Deer Park, one boy said. Holy Family, said another. Seton Hall, said another.

St. Anthony's, I said, already proud of it.

A Phelan Bus kind of smile creased Mr. Rafferty's baby face.

Oh-oh, he said, laughing. That's where I went. And let me tell you something. Whatever you do, watch out for Brother Noel.

Brother Who?

Brother Noel.

Why?

You'll find out, he said, laughing and shaking his head. You'll find out. Just watch out.

Now Brother Noel was standing in front of me, lurking behind me, genuflecting before me, keeping me off-balance with his shifting back and forth from furrow-browed scholar to baby-talking buddy, terrifying me with his daily quizzes, unnerving me. The daily quizzes, he explained, sharpened the mind and reinforced the lessons of the previous day. But if we failed a quiz, not to worry; we had a second chance to improve our grade by staying after school and taking a little quiz in his office, in an isolated corner of the old, red-brick building at the front of the campus.

The offer sounded more than fair, but I didn't trust it. I didn't trust him, this Franciscan skulking the aisles, angrily grunting—"Three minutes"—one day and cooing while kneading shoulders the next. He drove me to do something I never did before, and would never do again, which was to cheat. The students in his advanced math classes formed an unspoken pact to protect one another from whatever it was that he represented. A kick to the back of a chair, and the math whiz in front of me would slide his paper slightly to the left, just far enough for the rest of us to see. How a jumble of calculations came to the simple answer of 3, we did not know, we did not care. Three it was.

Other calculations were not adding up in my mind. After eight years at Sts. Cyril and Methodius, I was a parochial school veteran, and the concept of corporal punishment was as natural to me as breathing. You wise off, you get whacked; got it. But the grounds for physical contact between teacher and student at St. Anthony's were not always so clear-cut. For every Franciscan brother who swung his fists or whipped the ropes of his robe, there were several who never raised their hands, who chose reason or a withering comment to punish an offender. Interspersed among them, though, were a couple of brothers who freely invaded a boy's personal space, who incorporated back rubs into their lesson plans, who stroked cheeks that were years away from a razor's first touch.

In a classroom across the hall, for example, there was a brother with an individualized form of corporal punishment. He would grab an offender by the hair and rub his own red-bristled face against the boy's cheek, hard enough to scrape the skin. The practice had its own name—a "Barry Burner"—and if you saw a kid with a strawberry patch on his face, you'd say, What'd Brother Barry getcha for? A boy in my class got a Barry Burner the size of an egg yolk, and what could he say to his parents but that he had skidded on his face during a soccer game.

It was Brother Noel, though, who tormented us—the thought of him as much as the reality of him: a predator with puffy palms, slinking about my high school days, unnerving, unpredictable.

Here he was in a good mood one day, sauntering up and down the aisles as we puzzled and cheated over the questions of yet another quiz. Nothing out of the ordinary for Brother Noel's class: his eyes and hands upon us, his pat here, his rub there, his taunting observation that it looked like a few boys would soon be staying after school to take a makeup. Just another day, really—until he paused to read what had been carved with a Bic pen into the wooden top of an empty desk: "Noel is a Queer."

Our math teacher began to growl and then to wail, a guttural cry of pain you might hear from an animal caught in a metal trap. "Noel is a Queer" was the anti-cheer to the school's rallying cry of "Let's Go Friars." It was the phrase that might be shouted anonymously out of the Phelan Bus as it left the school grounds on a Friday afternoon, or muttered among the clutches of students in the cafeteria or out on the picnic bench near the St. Patrick's statue, where school rebels smoldered along with their cigarettes. "Noel is a Queer" may have been harsh, may, in fact, have been grossly inaccurate, but it had long since become part of the St.

Anthony's dialogue, and there was nothing that Brother Noel could do about it.

Cowering in my seat, I sensed that Brother's Noel's moans derived from something more than surprise. He knew that he could not control his compulsion. He knew what was being said of him in this environment. He knew, he knew we knew, and now, beyond the difficult concepts of mathematics, there lingered in this classroom of fourteen-year-olds the advanced themes of sexual confusion and rage.

Out! Out! Everybody out!

His screams chased us down the hall and into the cafeteria. Once safely out the door, I turned to see the Franciscan hurl the offending desk across the fast-emptying room.

That day had begun as a good day in the class of Brother Noel. Then there were the days that started off poorly and only got worse. If, for example, he came into class unshaven, then we knew that we would be paying for the night he had spent chasing demons.

There he stood one morning, the results from the previous day's difficult quiz clutched in his doughy hands, and you could practically smell the vapors of disgust coming off him. As he read the grades on each quiz, he released them into the air, one by one, as though they were unworthy of human touch. The tests descended in half-circles to the floor, gathering at his feet like white birds around St. Francis of Assisi.

Morrissey, 37, he said, as Morrissey's paper fluttered to the ground.

Pinkowski, 50; not half-bad. Another paper tossed.

Barry, 25; you ought to cheat off Pinkowski, Barry. Hebert, 17. Se-venteen, Hebert. Do you even have a pulse?

When he was a third of the way through the stack in his hand, Brother Noel barked: Barry, erase the board!

I rose from my seat, a boy flinching. I stutter-stepped toward the blackboard that stood several feet behind him, and tugged at the bottom of the map of the United States that had been used by an earlier class. The map obediently rolled up to reveal some anonymous prankster's masterpiece, a large-lettered message scrawled in chalk: NOEL IS A QUEER.

It was as though the combined thoughts of the thirty boys in the class-room had manifested themselves in chalk dust. Not that they necessarily thought the snarling, unshaven Franciscan before them was homosexual, although they might have, but that he was queer in the sense of odd, that he was a threat, a manipulator, the creator of discomfort and shame—that in this all-boy environment, the worst thing he could be called was "queer."

I froze, my mind sputtering, unable to decide what to do next. Did I have time to erase the message before he turned around? Should I pull the map back down? Should I run from the room? Panicking, I looked over Brother Noel's shoulders to see a roomful of students now upright in their chairs, their popping eyes telling me that whatever I decide to do, I better do it fast. If this man threw a desk because it was inscribed with "Noel is a Queer," just imagine what he would do if he saw the phrase in capital letters, appearing behind him like some Broadway marquee.

Erase! Erase all evidence! I scrambled for the eraser and furiously began wiping away the words. When the eraser popped out of my hand like a wet bar of soap, I improvised, using the sleeve of my shirt to smudge and blur the letters. Just as I was erasing the R in QUEER—the chalky indictment's last trace—Brother Noel wheeled around.

Barry! What the hell are you doing?

Nothing Brother, I said, a whisper to his snarl.

Then sit down. Maybe you can learn something for a change.

Inevitably, finally, I failed one of Brother Noel's quizzes; how could I not? The only consolation in my failure was that Brian McShane, a good friend of mine from St. Cyril's, had failed as well. We made a buddy pact to take the makeup quiz together. The school day ended, the Phelan Bus fled the parking lot, and two boys from Deer Park trudged up the narrow asphalt path that led to the red-brick administration building featured in all of the school's brochures.

I loved this building. A year earlier, when I was in the eighth grade, my mother and I had driven to St. Anthony's to see whether I would like it, and the atmosphere within its brick had sealed the deal. Gray-haired

Franciscans walked the carpeted halls, the rustle of their robes like whispered amens. Motherly secretaries brewed a coffee whose aroma mixed so enticingly with the hint of incense emanating from the dark-wooded chapel upstairs. Down one hall was the guidance office, where attentive counselors listened to the woes and aspirations of teenage boys. Down another was the library, where a very elderly Franciscan dozed at his desk between performances of his sole responsibility, which was to stamp the books being loaned out. Sometimes you had to nudge him—Brother? Brother? Wake up, Brother—to get your library book stamped; sometimes he blessed the book you had chosen with a drop of drool.

In this building too were the computer rooms, the domain of Brother Noel. In many ways he was ahead of his time in recognizing the value of teaching computer science in high school, and he enlisted a cadre of students—students who may have tucked their shirttails into their underwear but who would one day own the world—to feed stacks of IBM programming cards into a machine that looked as though it had been filched from the set of *Lost in Space*.

It was after school hours now, and the building was all but deserted. Brian and I shoved each other down the hall toward Brother Noel's office. We knew that this man had a way of getting physically close to us in an insinuating manner that we suspected was wrong but were not entirely sure. He was a Franciscan, after all, who always wore the black robe and matching cowl—garb that conjured thoughts of peace, of comfort, of ancient and mesmerizing chants of Latin prayer. After all, wasn't the chapel in this building named after St. Francis?

We made it finally to the threshold of his office, and peered in. There was Brother Noel sitting in a chair, with another freshman from the Phelan Bus straddled across his lap. He was spanking and dry-humping the boy at the same time, creating an awkward, flailing mish-mash of man and boy, of black robes and red faces. All the while, he cooed about the boy's failure to understand some algebraic formula.

Brian McShane and I ran. We tore down the stairs, away from the chapel and the library and the offices where the nice ladies made coffee.

We raced out the door and into the fresh autumn air, and then we were walking again, just walking, along a path on a campus of trees and grottoes and white statues of saints.

I shed my childhood that day; I set it aside like a heavy wool coat that was suddenly too small to ward against the winds of winter. This shove into young adulthood came with the instant realization that I would not tell my parents what I had seen. Before, I would tell them everything: what Sister had said in religion class, how many points I had scored in a pickup basketball game, why I preferred corn to peas, what the circumstances were when my brother had said the F word, on and on. The car could have a flat tire on the side of the narrow Southern State Parkway, and I'd be pulling my mother's sleeve to show her the scab on my arm that was shaped a little bit like Ireland. But this? Hey Mom, you'll never guess what me and Brian McShane saw at school today. No.

If I told my mother about Brother Noel, cheek burns, and the Phelan Bus, she would tell her husband, and then you could pretty much predict the rest: my agnostic father gunning the family station wagon toward Smithtown, muttering about black-robed sons-of-bitches and vowing to kick some good and holy Franciscan ass. I decided that the time had come for me to handle my own problems, even if I was not completely convinced that Brother Noel's actions constituted a problem. I was nearly fifteen: the age my mother was when she was sent packing to another world, the age my father was when he left school and started working. It was now time for me to tighten my necktie, shrug into a blazer, and commute to the job of growing up.

MY FATHER PULLED up to the house as he often did, with the slight skid of braking tires that announced he was home, so be alert. I was standing in our driveway, talking about nothing with a kid from across the street, as he slammed the car door shut. The door slam did not necessarily mean anything, because he always slammed doors, whether he was angry or content. He had a thing with doors, actually. If he held the door open for a woman at the entrance to a department store, it was as much a dare as an act of politeness. For if she did not say thank you, his stentorian send-off would chase her into the linens department: Have some manners, madam! Or, if he detected particular arrogance: Who do you think I am, your personal doorman? So the door slam might have been about nothing, just as the screeching brakes might have been about nothing, but you never knew.

My father stomped his way through our front lawn's obstacle course of Fire Island seashells and ceramic frogs, but even the stomp did not necessarily mean anything; although it looked as though he was forever snuffing out the cockroaches of his tenement childhood, the stomp was simply his preferred mode of movement. This time, though, he stopped in mid-stomp and turned to me. It was not to say hello; it was to make an announcement.

We're pulling you out of St. Anthony's. We can't afford it anymore. You're going to the public school next year.

He stomped on, into the house, completing the transaction with a slam of the door.

This news was as startling as if he had told me that I was in the navy now, not the army; a Methodist, not a Catholic; female, not male. I felt the stir of excitement that comes with the approach of the unknown, a kind of light-headed elation. Up to now, about the closest I got to the opposite sex was to breathe in the faint trails of Love's Baby Soft perfume left by the cliques of girls who roamed the Walt Whitman Mall in Huntington. The mere thought of sitting in the same classroom with girls excited me; they'd have to talk to me then, if only to ask for an extra pen (I would carry dozens).

I thought of all the guilt-riddled fears and duties that I would be relieved of with the filing of some simple paperwork: This is to inform you that Daniel F. Barry, Class of 1976, is withdrawing from St. Anthony's High School and will be attending Deer Park High School in the fall for his junior year. That was all that it would take and—instantly—I would no longer have to participate in, say, the yearly humiliation of St. Anthony's annual fund-raising drive.

ST. ANTHONY'S WAS a private school with a modest tuition, worlds removed from the likes of Andover and Exeter. There was no endowment to rely on, just its reputation as a training ground for the Catholic sons of Long Island's middle class—and its annual fund-raising event, the Franciscan Brothers Guild Drive. Since the Girl Scouts had cornered the cookie market and Little League controlled Tootsie Roll sales, the Franciscan brothers determined that they had no choice but to sell their core product, which was prayer. They did this by dispatching us students door-to-door to peddle ethereal wares. A three-dollar purchase bought a year's worth of prayers, said in someone's memory by Franciscans at an unspecified but assuredly holy location. Five dollars bought five-years' worth; ten bought ten. And for twenty dollars or more, people could ensure that the brothers would pray for them and theirs until the Second Coming.

During this protracted fund-raising push, the school administration worked the student body into an Amway-like frenzy, dangling sales incentives that pitted class against class, student against student. If your homeroom sold the most prayers, you, your classmates, and your teacher won a trip to Washington, D.C. And if you excelled individually—but were burdened by slouches in your homeroom—you could win days off from school. The more prayers you sold, the more days you could spend at home in your pajamas, eating bowls of Sugar Pops and watching *Hollywood Squares*.

Each day the loudspeakers broadcast sales updates. Homeroom teachers told their salesboys that second place—which might win a class trip to a Broadway play—wasn't good enough. One Franciscan brother, determined to beat a chemistry teacher who always seemed to win the contest, bussed his homeroom class of freshmen to a wealthy Smithtown neighborhood and ordered them to start ringing doorbells; they lost anyway. Troubled about trigonometry? Forget it. Confused over the concept of transubstantiation? Sell twenty bucks of prayers and we'll talk.

I had an easier time understanding the infallibility of the Pope than I did the fund-raising drive's mixed messages. Students with extended families living nearby usually sold the most prayers, thereby earning mini-vacations. Losers like me, with no relatives on Long Island and a family that was pretty much alienated from its neighbors, were essentially punished—by having to go to class. And participation was not optional; students were sent home with the news that if they did not sell forty-five dollars worth of prayers, their parents would be held responsible for that amount. My father, hobbled by the cluster migraines and working on Commack Road, not Wall Street, was at a stage of spiritual growth in which he would have likened the fund drive to a Mafia protection racket. He and my mother were concentrating on the hardships of this life, not the promises of the next. So, at dusk each night, I slipped quietly from the house and hit the pavement.

Connie Across the Street bought five dollars' worth, and I handed her a receipt for a purchase that she could neither see nor touch. She was my only street sale. As door after door closed to shoo me back to the curb, I tried to narrow my approach by searching for clues to Catholic domiciles: a Mary-on-the-half-shell on the lawn, a Marriage Encounter decal on the station wagon. But whenever I found a likely Catholic household, I lost the courage to ring the doorbell. I was a vacuum cleaner salesman with no demonstration model—only a vague outline of the machine's sucking power. For hours I wandered the west side of Deer Park, and instead of hawking prayers, I said them.

I wound up using my own money to meet my forty-five-dollar quota, drawing on birthday gifts and cash earned from odd jobs. I dedicated half of the bought prayers to my mother, half to my father. For this I received the solace of imagining aged Franciscans being roused from their sleep and forced to mumble prayers for my troubled loved ones.

A TRANSFER TO public school would mean an end to seeing Popeye-sized forearms jutting from the wide sleeves of dusky robes. Of neckties being grabbed and yanked as though they were strings attached to human yo-yos. Of head slaps and hair pulls and the thud that a skull makes when slammed against a hallway wall. It would mean an end to witnessing the daily St. Anthony's dramas, where typical high school confrontations between teachers and students often carried additional layers of tension: whether misbehavior was a sin; whether it warranted a demerit, a punch in the chest, or both; whether any of this was Christ-like—or Francis-like.

One afternoon a hapless student I knew from the Phelan Bus ran through the cafeteria and out the doors, then stopped, panting, to glare up at a second-floor classroom window. For a while his actions were only mildly amusing to those of us eating our lunches, until he earned our undivided attention by screaming, Fuck you, Brother! We ran to see what Herman was up to this time.

Herman was one of St. Anthony's walking wounded, the kind of kid who had no interest in preying on others, but whom other kids—and teachers—found too easy a target to resist. Freshmen were hazing him his senior year. Maybe it was his utter devotion to the anticommunist cause; he would try to inject the philosophy of the John Birch Society into bus conversations about the wonders of the female breast. Maybe it was his acne, or his poor basketball skills. Whatever the reason, Herman never seemed to know peace. And here he was, outside the cafeteria, screaming obscenities at a Franciscan and having the meltdown that God knows should have come years earlier.

Fuck you, Brother!

He kept screaming toward the second-floor window, like some psychotic Romeo, only to hear his Juliet answer in a voice too flat and calm to be in any way reassuring.

Herman, get back up here.

Fuck you, Brother!

Herman.

FUCK YOU!

Here was Herman, saying what so many students wanted to say at some point in their high school careers but never did. And yet we didn't cheer; we knew all too well the balance of power at St. Anthony's.

Her-

Fuck you!

Herm-

Fuck you.

Herman.

Fuck.

Herman's shoulders slumped. Seeing us, his peers, our faces pressed against the cafeteria windows, and then seeing the brother at the window above, he knew he had no choice. The incident was too public now, too egregious, no matter what cause he may have had for his rage. His body deflated with his sigh, and then, smaller somehow, he started back in. He walked past us in the cafeteria without saying a word and then disappeared around the stairwell.

We waited for the sound we knew would come, had to come. Whack! And another, and another, and—

Imagine! All this would be behind me once I left St. Anthony's and enrolled in public high school. No prayer peddling on secular streets. No fear that the making of the sign of the cross might conclude with a smack. No students walking the halls with beard scrapes on their faces, marking them for shame. No Brother Noel, no Brother Noel.

Imagine. Then why was I on the verge of tears?

I could not imagine not being a student at St. Anthony's. I could not imagine that yellow ship of perversity, the Phelan Bus, sailing up Grand Boulevard without me aboard. St. Anthony's was where my friends were, where my personality was taking shape. I shared a bond that had been forged by the Phelan Bus rides and the sidestepping of cloaked predators, and those First Friday Masses, when we sat straight-backed in the gymnasium stands while a hunched-over classmate whispered Happy Hooker advice from his father's latest *Penthouse*.

There was so much about the school that I loved—that, for better or worse, had become a part of who I was. I may have feared and even loathed Brother Noel, but I revered other Franciscans who had dedicated themselves so completely to the craft of teaching, and to our formation. We could almost smell the whiff of gunpowder when Brother Cletus recreated the Battle of Lexington; feel the power of word and rhythm when Brother Benilde read Eliot aloud; find the French language relevant, even vital, to life on Long Island when Brother Donan prohibited the use of English in his classroom. I knew that if I ever needed to, I could always call on Brother Pierre or Brother Peter—or Cletus, or Benilde, or Donan—to talk about any problems I might be having. I could, but of course I never would.

I loved how Brother Shane—"the Galloping Friar," they called him— raced across the field on horseback before every home football game, with the autumn leaves the color of butterscotch and tangerine, and the heat emanating from the small Styrofoam cups of bad hot chocolate, and the girls from other schools in the stands, their kissable noses like cherries from the cold, jumping up and down to stay warm as much as to cheer the Friars on, and the postgame sock hop in the gymnasium, where I leaned against a back wall, watching others dance and never, ever dancing myself because I could not summon the nerve. I was the bashful buzzard from the Bugs Bunny cartoons, stuttering duh-nope-nope-nope at the prospect of even talking to a girl.

I loved lunchtime, when I threw my tie and sandwich bag to the sidelines to play full-court basketball games in dress shoes, until the sweat darkened the front and back of my shirt and the friction of damp skin on corduroy pants irritated my thighs, and pools of perspiration settled in my socks. When the bell rang, I looped the tie around my neck, wolfed down my sandwich, and raced to take my seat in a cinderblock classroom beside other sopping students, not one of them a girl, for that would have changed our world. Sensing it more than knowing it, we were clinging to the remains of our boyhood, running and sweating without caring how we looked for fifth-period social studies, and why should we. We were boys, just boys, with our body heat steaming the windows and our sweat commingling to give scent to life's passage.

I loved the history of St. Anthony's the moment I stepped on its grounds as a freshman: how it had been founded in the 1930s as a boarding prep school for boys wanting to be Franciscan brothers; how its guiding principles were the work of a long-departed brother described in my *Friars Handbook* as "an exemplary and scholarly man." Even more than the history, I loved the myths that enveloped the school, the stories passed on from senior to freshman about eccentric brothers and long-ago pranks. We knew of the elderly Franciscan who was serenaded with quacking noises every time he turned to write on the chalkboard; the day he lost complete control was the day an actual duck was smuggled into class. We knew too of the courageous band of students who, a few years earlier, had prepared the proofs for two yearbooks—a polite, rah-rah one for the administration to approve, and a scatological one for the publisher to print. The cut lines below the photographs in this yearbook were obscene, mean-spirited—funny. No one was spared, not the oblivious principal, not even Brother Noel. The administration confiscated every copy of that yearbook within a day or two of its distribution, but how could the good brothers have known that one of their students worked part-time at the town dump and would be in position to salvage a few of the contraband yearbooks before they tumbled into history's waste bin. Thanks to that fast-thinking young man, I was able to sit on the Phelan Bus and listen to a senior lovingly recite memorized snatches from the notorious yearbook's glorious text, every word forbidden, and therefore brilliant.

This constant struggle between the holy and the profane confused me and drew me in, made me want to be a part, and apart. The school fostered a win-at-all-cost approach to life: it recruited students from as far as Puerto Rico to play on the state-ranked basketball team; it turned its

annual football games against Holy Family High School into holy cru-
sades; it packaged prayer as a commodity to be sold door-to-door. And
yet, nearly every week we recited the Prayer of St. Francis, asking the Lord
to make us instruments of peace; to help us to understand that it is in
pardoning that we are pardoned. Then does that mean, O Divine Master,
that we should pardon Brother Noel for rubbing us and making us feel
so threatened? Does it mean that we should pardon his Franciscan colleagues who did not slug him on our behalf?

O Divine Master. Oh Brother. God forgive me, but I wanted to stay.

FACED WITH LEAVING the place where I could feel my identity
emerging, I did what any tough, fifteen-year-old man-boy would do: I
cried to my mommy. One night, as my headache-stricken father moaned
upstairs, we sat at the kitchen table and reached a compromise. I could
continue at St. Anthony's if I helped to pay the modest tuition. I got a job
in a delicatessen on Deer Park Avenue, did some valet car parking, and
even worked at St. Anthony's itself, cutting grass, painting offices, working behind the counter at the bookstore.

I graduated from St. Anthony's High School in the June of our country's bicentennial, my various contributions recorded in a golden yearbook: member of the varsity baseball team; editor of the school
newspaper; member of the student council, the yearbook staff, the dance
committee, the National Honor Society, on and on—an official tally of
activities to prove my worth to the institution. In my senior portrait I am
wearing the wine-colored blazer that a salesman in the Sunset City shopping center helped my mother to select. It hung funny on me, but he convinced her to take into account those sloping shoulders. I am wearing
that wine-colored blazer, and I am smiling.

In the years to come, my dean of discipline would blow his brains out,
and my Franciscan principal would leave under a cloud of impropriety.
Brother Noel would be inducted posthumously into the school's Hall of

Fame. St. Anthony's would move to Huntington and become coeducational—a different school altogether. Other St. Anthony's graduates and I would drink our beer and analyze as much as reminisce. We have our friendships, after all, and our fond memories of brothers who shaped our lives for the better. But we also have Brother Noel, and the Phelan Bus, and the unshakeable sense of Jesus, what the hell was that all about?

In the years to come, I would stand before a deserted building on an abandoned campus, where nice ladies once brewed coffee, boys recited prayers in chapel, and a brother gave students the chance to atone for their mistakes in math. The "Friar Fight Song," I'd think. Onward to battle. Onward.

8

A FEBRUARY NIGHT. Inside the house, the tension before the father's headache takes hold: Eat, Gene, eat, you have to build up your strength. I'm not hungry, Noreen. I feel it coming on; just get me a beer. And the siblings tiptoe around, tripping into one another, sparking angry whispers and unspoken resentments about good times, normal times, not had. Outside, the susurrations of cold winds through leafless trees, and the distant sigh of a Long Island Rail Road train exhaling down the Ronkonkoma line. Then, added to the night sounds, almost in apology, the ping of a basketball on concrete, a ping that echoes off the shingled side of a neighbor's house just fifteen feet away, a ping specific in its time and place and like no other. I liked it out here, alone with my ball and my God.

I was just shy of eighteen, in every meaning of that phrase. In the tumult of our family life, my imminent adulthood had sort of snuck up on my parents and me. We had not visited any colleges together, nor held any serious conversation about what comes after high school; too much was going on at 140 West 23rd Street, always. It seemed that if I chose to attend college—and if I figured out how to pay for it—that would be fine. If I chose to become a circus roustabout, that would be fine too. Just remember: life is fragile; take nothing for granted; everything can change in the bat of an eye.

I needed solitude to sort out my future. And that was why I had stepped into my outdoor chapel, there on the side of the house.

A few years earlier, my brother and I sank a long steel pole into wet cement. It was a way of staking our claim, of declaring as our dominion a narrow strip of cracked patio that was always either wet or icy, thanks to the water forever dripping from a coil of twisted, disobedient garden hose. This would be our garden now, our Madison Square Garden, to hone our shooting and ball-handling skills so that athletic scholarships would solve the certain financial challenges of the future. We bolted a cheap wooden backboard to the top of the pole, attached a metal basketball hoop, and carefully pressed the loops of white nylon netting through the rim's orange eyelets. But our basketball hoop proved no less susceptible to failure than any of the other Barry brothers' projects, from the Sawyer-like raft that sank in Geiger Lake to the go-cart that just wouldn't go. The pole settled in the cement at a one o'clock angle.

After a while the right half of the backboard rotted and fell off, so we practiced layups from the left side. Soon after, the left half fell away, leaving a lonely basketball hoop to dangle in afterthought from a listing pole. Other families might have yanked this eyesore from the ground like some ugly metal weed; we did not. It was the Barry family's contribution to abstract sculpture, a symbol of our general distrust of rules, including the edict of organized sport that a basket be ten feet high and horizontal to the ground. Besides, this cockeyed basketball hoop had become my inanimate therapist, my mute confessor.

After nearly twelve years of Catholic schooling, I had neither the comforting conviction that God existed nor the certainty that He did not. I tried to pray in the dark of night, body entwined in bed sheets and face to the wall, but all I felt was the heat of my own breath rebounding off the painted sheetrock. What was there in this, I wondered, what comfort, as on the ripples of my subconscious bobbed the most frightening of nighttime childhood prayers: And if I die before I wake, I pray the Lord my soul to take.

But outside, in my concrete garden, it was different somehow. I found that I could talk to God, if not with Him, through a solitary form of basketball. Here was how my game of faith worked: hit ten foul shots and your wish, your desire—your prayer—will come true. It seemed no less theologically sound than other practices and beliefs of Roman Catholicism, from the healing powers of holy water to the purchase of indulgences to ensure one's place in heaven. Mine was a physical, almost interactive form of prayer, I reasoned, not unlike challenging Jesus to a game of one-on-one. Although Jesus appeared to be my height and weight—nearly six feet tall and 150 pounds—He had the distinct advantage of being the Son of God. On the other hand, it was my home court.

My rosary was the basketball. A basketball is best held with the fingertips resting lightly on the seams, so that when the ball is launched it will rotate as if in synchronicity with the natural order of things. For me, few sights were lovelier than that of my American Basketball Association basketball spinning like a red-white-and-blue pinwheel through a hoop's lacy blanket of net. I worked hard to re-create that soothing swirl, my fingers instinctively crawling across the ball's speckled surface in search of the seam, their home. On snowy nights, I shoveled a narrow path from the imaginary foul line to the basket and shot until the cold made my fingers too numb to feel the seam. And when my only basketball lacked the proper air to give it bounce, I shot it anyway, watching it plop lifelessly to the ground and then kneading away the dents left from the impact. I found an eerie peace in the repetition, in the skill, and in the bets at stake. My prayer game seemed to apply some ground rules, however artificially, to a life that grew more complicated by the day.

I took a few warm-up shots, seeking that mystical oneness of boy and ball. Nothing else mattered: the muffled arguments from inside the house, the weak light emanating from the closed kitchen door, the clouds of my breath hanging in the chilly night air. One bounce, then another, and then *fffft!*—the sound of ball falling cleanly through the net, a sound like a kiss blown. Now I was ready to present my silent challenge to the Almighty. If I made ten consecutive foul shots, then:

I will make the baseball team this year.

Or:

My father's blinding headaches will end, and with them his screams.

Or:

I will be tougher, stronger, braver—a man, somehow.

Through much of my adolescence there must have been some "tell" in my looks and body language: the acne-dotted face, the bow curve to the shoulders, the goofy, uncertain half-smile that was so often mistaken as one of mirth. The look, I suppose, of being apart. Whatever pheromones emanated from my trembling body, they attracted bullies like hyenas to a lame gazelle. Bullies boxed my ears at a Knights of Columbus carnival, pummeled me near the Abraham Lincoln School, slapped me along the shores of Geiger Lake. No corner of Deer Park provided safe haven. One day I was kicked to the ground in the lobby of Sts. Cyril and Methodius Church; another day I was slammed to the gravel in front of my own home, about thirty feet from where my parents were watching Merv Griffin. And every time I stumbled into the house with ripped pants and pummeled face, the same conversation took place.

What in God's name happened to you?

Nuffin', I'd answer, through swollen lips.

My father interpreted every beating as not just an attack on his firstborn son, but an attack on all Barrys: from Kevin Barry, the young Irish martyr, to John Barry, the father of the American Navy, to the ancient Barrys of Cork who lived by the family motto, *Boutez en Avant*, "Strike Forward." And here was this whimper of a Barry, creating a new motto: Stumble Backward.

Goddam sonsofbitches, he'd roar. Danny! Get in the car!

Yeth, Dad.

We would prowl the streets of Deer Park in the station wagon, searching for perps. He was the cop; I was the embarrassed crime victim, hunched low in the front seat. Is that the kid? he'd say, slowing down to glower at kids who were never "the kid," but who knew "the kid" and would report back to "the kid," ensuring that I would get another beating at some later date. Sometimes, after finding the ominous surname of the bully in the telephone book—Krudd, or McKill—my father would gun toward the suspect's address for a prosecutorial confrontation, itching to present me as his bloodied Exhibit A. These were never satisfying moments. The bully's beer-bloated father would stand behind a screen door, saying kids will be kids and smirking at the idea that casual violence was somehow bad.

Finally, in exasperation, my father enrolled me in a jujitsu school that promised to teach me self-defense. The teacher, a guy named Vic, had sideburns that hung from his face like stunned ferrets. Twice a week he stood before a dozen slump-shouldered students—walking bully bait, every one of us—and patiently explained how jujitsu uses the energy of one's opponent to defeat him. He emphasized his points by slicing the air with his callused hands, leaving us breathless.

Each session Vic selected a student to illustrate a certain defense technique, and each session he chose me as the would-be attacker. As Vic minded his own business, reading an imaginary newspaper, I reluctantly approached from behind, my every step summoning squeaks from the flat floor mat. Within a second and without a sound, Vic spun around and used my "energy" to lift me skyward, twirl me like a majorette's baton, and hurl me to the mat. My uncoordinated classmates managed to clap their hands together to applaud the rightful vanquishing of a bully, while I crawled back to my position, praying that Vic would someday be devoured by his own sideburns.

These classes no more protected me from beatings than had my father's intervention. One evening, two buddies and I were resting our ten-speed bicycles the way cowboys rest their horses. As we admired another sunset of that summer before our sophomore year, a Volkswagen Beetle pulled up alongside us. A disembodied voice grunted out a common Long Island greeting: Gimme a match.

I don't smoke, I answered, sounding a tad prissy.

That was all it took. The Beetle began belching bullies; they spilled out, one after another, like circus clowns erupting from a toy car. We had no time to saddle up. My friends got the worst of it because they were not accustomed to getting beaten up; they were shocked at being attacked for nothing, nothing at all. But I was already conditioned to understand that fairness and logic had no place in encounters like these. I fell to the ground, assumed the fetal position, and took my blows.

If matters of violence could be raised during my basketball dialogues with God, then so too could matters of the heart. A dribble of the ball, hardening now in the cold and not bouncing so lively. A Braille-like search for the seams. A shot lofted toward the darkened heavens, a schoolboy's challenge to his Maker.

Ten shots in a row and she will like me, I had once dared Him. You know: like like.

One.

Two.

Three.

In the months leading up to my junior prom, perhaps *the* social event on the St. Anthony's calendar, I paced the house like a penned-in colt, unable to find a place for proper and private brooding. Brian was always in the boys' room, playing his guitar or learning the words to "Johnny McEldoo" or some other tongue-twisting Clancy Brothers song. Brenda and Elizabeth were in the living room, doing their Sts. Cyril and Methodius homework assignments to the rhythms of Lucy-and-Ethel banter. My father was in the master bedroom, lights off, pain on, the groans seeping under the door and into the family bathroom.

I needed privacy to brood because of the nature of my brooding. I had never kissed a girl, never been on a date, and was naïve enough to misinterpret a girl's laughter for the coos of affection. Now here it was, the season of first courtships, and I could not summon the nerve to dial a certain telephone number. Where else to go but the kitchen, under fluorescent lights as bright as any interrogation room's, the domain of my mother, where another engaged cigarette was balanced on the lip of the Connemara marble ashtray, another crossword puzzle providing escape, another glass of fizzing beer. Flat beer was for washing hair; fizzing beer was for drinking. She looked up from her distractions to watch her eldest pace back and forth across her small linoleum floor. It must have reminded her of her youth on the farm, where the seasonal restlessness of animals was as natural as the growth of grass.

Everything all right? she asked finally, because she knew I wanted her to ask.

Yeah, yeah, I said, meaning no, no. It's just that . . .

What?

Nothing.

My mother reached for an unopened bill—they were strewn about the house like joyless confetti—and began to write on the back of the envelope. I looked out the small kitchen window and toward the street lamp; somewhere out there, just maybe, lay courage.

Here, she said, sliding the envelope past ashtray and puzzle, across the Formica surface. Use this.

Hello, Mary Ellen, she had written in her hurried, farm-girl script. *How are you? It was cold out today, wasn't it? How is school? I have a question. Would you like to go to the prom with me?*

I looked at the words, then at my mother's half-smiling face. How did she know I was worried about the? How did she know the name of? She was a witch of some kind, sitting there behind that Parliament-blue gauze, her hair dyed a forest-fire orange and styled in a kind of controlled wildness. But she was a witch from another time, another place. Although she was only thirty-seven, I thought her to be entirely out of touch with America—especially with the fears and longings of a teenage boy on Long Island in the mid-1970s. This wasn't Shanaglish; this was Deer Park.

Please! I wailed, pushing the envelope back across the table. Can I just have some privacy?

Do it yourself then, she said, though not with anger. She picked up her glass of fizzing potion, and then she was gone.

It could have been ten minutes later or it could have been an hour, but finally, and with my body shivering in the warm kitchen, I reached for the telephone. I dialed the number and pulled the yellow cord taut so that I could have even more privacy—outside, on the side of the house, my basketball sanctum. The father answered, and I stuttered, Is Mary Ellen home?

Who's calling please?

I hated that question; it took me a moment before I remembered. And when Mary Ellen challenged me by merely saying, Hello, I could not think of what to say. My mind turned to television snow. I was in the fifth grade again, about to break into nervous hysterics. My country 'tis of thee . . .

Hello? Danny?

I stumbled back inside and lunged for the envelope that my mother had left on the kitchen table.

Hello, Mary Ellen, I recited. How are you? It was cold out today, wasn't it?

Mary Ellen agreed to go to the dance—as friends. With all due respect, God, I had asked for like like, not like. But I like just like. To go as friends would be just fine, I decided, because I could use one.

THESE BASKETBALL PRAYER sessions of mine demanded a lot of God. I asked Him for help with girls and protection from bullies, and much, much more. I asked for it all; I shot for the moon.

Please take care of us, God, please. My father, my mother, take care of them. My brother, my sisters, take care of them too. And God, please God, take care of me. Ten in a row, God, and you'll take care of us, me.

One. Two. Three. A miss.

One. Two. Three. Four. A miss.

A miss.

One. Two. Three. Four. Five. Six. Seven. Eight. Nine.

My future and the future of those I loved now rested on this next foul shot, and no one knew it but me. The peek of light from the kitchen window formed my spotlight, my silhouette slanting across barren shrubs hard against a chain-link fence. I bounced the ball a few times to try to find a rhythm of composure. Imagine: If I hit this shot—happiness.

A miss.

A pause.

My basketball compacts with God were pure in their primitivism. There was no radio announcer's play-by-play coursing through my thoughts, no "Barry steps to the line, wipes his hands on his shorts. . . ." But there were no Gregorian chants, either. What I felt was a kind of peace, a sense of being in my proper place. I did not belong in a cloistered French monastery saying the rosary, or on a prairie communing with wolves. I belonged here: in the cold of a February night, beside some house in a Long Island subdivision. But time was running short here, wasn't it, God? I would be graduating soon; I would have to leave here, won't I, God?

Take care of them. Take care of me.

A dog yelped in the distance. A breeze rustled the trees. I waited for it to pass; once launched, a basketball belongs to the whims of the wind. When the chapel-like stillness had returned to my backyard, I searched for the seams, paused for breath, and lofted the ball again beyond the ambient light.

One.

PART TWO

Me eyes began to dazzle
And I'm going to see the races
With me wack fol-da-da fol-da-diddly-ida-day
— "The Galway Races"

9

A S I CARRIED two suitcases to the curb, my parents stayed planted like ornaments on the front lawn. He squinted into the sun that had become a stranger; she watched me with the one good eye and all the neighbors with that wandering other, so wonderfully witchy. Both suitcases still carried the Aer Lingus tags from the family's trip to Ireland in 1971; one of them even bore my immigrant mother's first stateside address from the early '50s. Two bulging suitcases, proclaiming that Danny was bound for a mysterious place that no one else in the family had ever been to, that no one had ever had the luxury of time or money to consider: college. And not just a college, but a university. St. Bonaventure University. Well!

I had briefly considered taking my baseball card collection with me, along with a few of the *Mad* magazines and Hardy Boys books that I jointly owned with my brother. I wanted them not for reading but to have as talismans of an evaporating time, and to protect them from one of my mother's whirlwind Folsom Prison cleaning jags. But there was no sense in taking them, really, and no room anyway, not anymore.

A high school friend and his parents were waiting for me in a car that was foreign to West 23rd Street. They would be driving me to St. Bonaventure, eight hours away near some place called Allegany, New York. The suddenness of my father's migraine attacks, on top of his usual volatility, made even the twenty-minute trip to the Walt Whitman Mall a risky venture, so the thought of my parents driving me to college had never been entertained. My father had to conserve his strength; the whole family did, in fact, for who knew what was next. It's better this way, my mother told me, as she slipped me a couple of twenties for school supplies and a meal for everybody on the ride up, and don't tell your father.

Our front-lawn farewell may not have been worthy of Norman Rockwell; I wasn't going to war, after all, and besides, what would Rockwell have done with the ceramic trolls and frogs scattered about the grass? Still, the moment warranted the catch in the throat, the hug tighter than usual, and the slow inhalation of my father's Old Spice, my mother's Chanel No. 5, and the cigarette smoke that clung to them both. It was an aromatic blend as unsettling as it was comforting: of parental love and parental defeat, a knowing submission to the dark promise foretold in smoke. I held them close.

I climbed into the strange car, and it slowly pulled away. From the back seat I saw the great metropolis of West 23rd Street begin to shrink, but my parents still loomed behind the hedge, giants on their third-of-an-acre lot.

THE RIDE TO St. Bonaventure University did not seem long enough, considering how different the campus was from my Long Island experience. It was tucked like a Franciscan hideaway into the foothill folds of the Allegheny Mountains, just outside the small city of Olean and three hundred miles from Deer Park. The campus sported some modern buildings—the athletic center, the friary, a few dorms—but its dominant features were the old red-brick buildings with dusky slate roofs that seemed to have sprouted naturally among the woods and meadows along the banks of the Allegheny River.

The campus essence was contained in one red-brick vessel in particular, the Friedsam Memorial Library, where the sweet smoke wafting from the pipe of the Franciscan bookbinder in the basement perfumed the air, creating a kind of scholastic incense. In many ways, Friedsam was like any other university library. It subscribed to the usual general-interest and academic periodicals and regularly rotated its displays of university artifacts. One month a collection of Hummel figurines, the next some mementoes of famous past students, including two members of baseball's Hall of Fame: Hughie Jennings and John McGraw, neither of whom graduated. But not far from a sign for the men's room was one for "incunabula," a treasure of manuscripts and books from the Middle Ages that were helping scholars to piece together the Franciscan influence in western theology. All the while, fussing about in the stacks with a heart that seemed to beat at twice the normal rate, was the Rev. Irenaeus Herscher, the wispy, white-haired curator of all things Bonaventure, and the university's living link to Thomas Merton.

While teaching English at St. Bonaventure some forty years earlier, Merton became so enthralled with the Franciscan way of life that he considered becoming a friar. He often returned from solitary walks through the surrounding woods to pose questions about God and faith to Father Irenaeus, who, despite the initial habit of addressing Merton as "Mr. Myrtle," provided encouraging and thoughtful answers. The Franciscans ultimately discouraged Merton from joining their order, which in retrospect was akin to telling a raw Mickey Mantle that he wasn't quite ready for the Yankees. Merton went on to become the most celebrated American theologian of the twentieth century—as a Trappist monk. Still, St. Bonaventure proudly celebrated its ties to Merton, who had written so fondly of the school in his autobiography, *The Seven Storey Mountain*. A weary student could gaze out the library's expansive window to see the mist-shrouded mountainside pasture called Merton's Heart, and moments later encounter the fluttering, generous Father Irenaeus, whom Merton immortalized in his autobiography as "this happy little Franciscan."

At first St. Bonaventure seemed so scholarly and serene, even sacred, that I felt like an intruder on its grounds. Not only did I come from a family in which the Holy Bible was more of a coaster for drinks than a guide for the spirit, but I had spent the summer after my high school graduation in a setting that would have melted Father Irenaeus's spectacles. Instead of keeping the Sabbath holy, I had spent the Sabbath consumed by a primal, pelvic-grinding beat, bump-ba-ba, bump-ba-ba, bump-ba-ba.

A spotlight pierced the smoky blue darkness of my summer Sunday nights to reveal Shera, Queen of the Jungle, a comely maiden forever in distress. Clad only in ivy, she stumbled through a forbidding, papier-mâché glade, trying to escape the clutches of a gorilla that lustfully pounded his plastic black chest to the beat of the drums, bump-ba-ba. Every time Shera broke from the gorilla's grasp, she paid the price with another piece of her costume; before long the beast had stripped the beauty of her every leaf. Aah, but Shera was wise in the ways of the wild and had the foresight to wear a g-string and pasties. She knew well the stripper's Morse code: two dots and a dash.

The two dots and the dash must have signaled, "Cut the lights," for every Sunday night Shera vanished from sight, unclothed but unharmed, leaving me to survey my own jungle: a dozen cocktail tables, around which prides of customers grazed on complimentary chips and lapped up the intoxicating waters of the house.

Another grasshopper, ma'am? I asked. More chips?

On my journey from one Franciscan institution to another—from St. Anthony's High School to St. Bonaventure University—I took a detour to the Catskills. I spent the summer working as a cocktail waiter at the Acra Manor, a working-class resort that catered mostly to Italian-American families from Queens, Brooklyn, and Long Island. The owners, the Fede family, also owned the check-cashing store where my father worked, and so a generous offer had been made to help me pay for my college tuition.

My mornings began precisely at 7:30, when the sweet motherly woman who ran the dining room flipped on the resort's public-address system to fill the country air with her subway rumble of a New York accent:

Testing, one two three.

"Oh what a byooteeful mawning, oh what a byooteeful day."

Good mawning, everybody.

Breakfast is now being served to the guests of the Acra Manna.

Although the Hamptons had all but usurped the Catskills as *the* place for downstate vacationers to go, the Acra Manor survived by creating the illusion for its hard-working regulars, the Bay Ridge cop and the Woolworth's clerk, that anything goes. A lunchtime beer, a poolside daiquiri—Hey kids, watch where yer splashin'—a dinner that began with melon and prosciutto and ended with anisette and coffee. Later in the evening, the guests gathered in the African Tiki Lounge, a pan-cultural wonderland where an African war mask glowered from the wall, a jukebox Jerry Vale crooned of the evil woman he loved, and Jimmy the bartender served the best Polynesian cocktails this side of the Rip Van Winkle Bridge.

Most nights the entertainment was one of a handful of comedians still working the Catskills circuit: there was Bobby, whose favored bit was to don a grass skirt and mouth the words to a Spike Jones record, and Joey, who did Boris Karloff and Bela Lugosi impersonations in Italian. But back then Sunday was burlesque night, featuring a troupe whose gags had resounded through burlesque halls before most of the guests were born. Even the strippers were of a certain age, from Shera, Queen of the Jungle, to a redhead who disrobed while singing "I'm Just a Little Girl from Little Rock."

I was there too, ducking beneath the spotlight's beam, serving drinks, sharing in the illusion. I wore a formal white shirt, black pants, and a black bow tie, an ensemble that went only so far in lending me an air of suavity. I was a gawky innocent, susceptible to the hypnotizing sway of that redhead's tassels, as she sang about punching the nose of that heartbreaker back in Little Rock. Like twin propellers they were—Hey kid, yer spillin' my drink—spinning clockwise and then counterclockwise, and clockwise again.

GOD WAS SHE TALENTED . . .

That was my summer: all strippers and maraschino cherries and Can I freshen your drink, sir? Now, in my fall, I was living in Devereux Hall, an old, vine-covered dormitory on the St. Bonaventure campus. Merton had once lived in a room two floors below. And just outside my window, cemented to the brick façade, were the terra-cotta likenesses and somber words of two great Americans: "Dare to do our duty," advised Lincoln; "Make our lives sublime," implored Longfellow.

Bump-ba-ba, thought Barry.

It took me a week or two, but gradually the Bonaventure dynamics came into sharper focus. Some students found the university's isolated setting just right for reflecting on life, God, and the future; they outlined their four-year college career as though it were a thesis paper, and strayed from its schedule only for the occasional batch of naughty, late-night popcorn. Other students saw the isolation not in terms of the potential it offered for self-discovery but in the distance it provided from parents. They cranked up the Pure Prairie League on the stereo, cracked open another beer, and mocked the professors they never saw and the co-eds they never approached. For all they knew, or cared, Merton had been a backup point guard on the great Bona basketball teams of the early 1960s. Merton feeds to Stith. Score!

I straddled these worlds. I drank with the serious drinkers: the guys who would polish off a quarter keg and then go down to Club 17 or some other Allegany roadhouse bar and drink some more. And when the bars closed, we would go to an after-hours party or just come back to the dorm to drink while we discussed how much we had just drunk. Weekends were lost to quarters, a moronic game in which the goal was to bounce a quarter cleanly on a table so that it tiddlywinked in the air and landed in a glass of beer. One time I drank so much that I almost tiddlywinked right into traffic, but fell into a snow pile instead.

If there was pride to be found in any of this, and that is a big *if*, it was that I never allowed my newfound fondness for alcohol to waste my days along with my nights. I had chosen to study journalism out of a vague

but persistent sense that I wanted to be a writer, and dutifully met its perfunctory demands: I attended classes, submitted assignments on time,
answered the questions posed to me by professors. This drunk-sober
duality of my life seemed to come easily. I had been conditioned to jug-
gle order and disorder and had witnessed firsthand how drinking and
functioning were not necessarily incompatible concepts. I drank my beer
and shot my pool. What kind of Barry would I have been if I didn't? But
I could not afford to take college for granted. Not when I was the first in
my family to attend college and not when my tuition was being paid
through a cobbled-together financial arrangement; "plan" would be too
grand a term for what it was. There were the sizable state subsidies avail-
able to me because of my parents' relatively low income; the money I
earned as a delicatessen clerk, Catskills waiter, and campus gofer; and the
modest support provided by my parents. We managed to scrape together
the amount needed, but only barely. One semester I cried poverty to the
Journalism Department, and its good-hearted chairman, Russell Jandoli,
somehow pulled a "scholarship" of a few hundred dollars out of his briefcase of tricks.

Tuition payments dogged me. One night, back in Deer Park for the
Christmas break of my junior year in college, I grabbed the slightly flat
basketball and returned to the patio on the side of the house. I lofted shot
after shot at the tilted hoop, trying to calm myself while waiting for my
mother to summon me. It was time again for that talk.

Inside, the Barry houseboat was still struggling to stay afloat. Every
now and then the call would go out that the sump pump had malfunc-
tioned again, sending a crew of us to the closet for galoshes and then
down to the basement to bail out water four inches deep and rising.
Using pots and old coffee cans, we'd fling the water out two small windows for an hour, restart the pump, and climb upstairs, wordless, because
this household chore seemed no different to us than making our beds.

The houseboat adjusted to the tides of time. Brian was no longer living at home; he was working as a unionized carpet layer and dating the
woman he would marry before he turned twenty-one. Brenda was in

high school and Elizabeth in junior high; both were out with friends old enough to drive cars. My father was testing yet another method to alleviate the pressurized pain of his headaches: a pulley-and-weights contraption that we kept clipped to the top of the bathroom door. He would come home from work—it would never occur to him *not* to work—slip his head into a cloth sling and slowly lower a bank bag of weights that was attached to the other end of the pulley. Then he'd sit in a chair, drinking his beer, reading *Newsday*, and flicking ashes into the bathroom sink. Although he vexed us, railed at us, darkened our days with his rage, we admired him. He never gave up.

You okay, Dad?

Yeah, he'd grunt from his head sling, which made him look as though the Three Stooges had just yanked his tooth. Get me another beer, willya?

This night, as usual, the Rube Goldberg contraption in the bathroom offered little relief, and my father was soon in bed, in agony again. My mother called me in from the side of the house, and we took our seats. On the kitchen table sat the latest tuition bill. We stared at it for a while, as though it had been postmarked in hell.

She said she didn't know what we were going to do this time. The washing machine was broken beyond repair, forcing her to lug the family laundry every few days to a laundromat near the Cream Puff bakery. Her husband was either hanging in the bathroom or howling in the bedroom, her pocketbook was weighed down with scrounged quarters and dimes, her free time was being dictated by the rinse-cycle settings of foreign machines, and here now was another one of those bills from Allegany, New York.

Years earlier my mother and I had had a similar sit-down to figure out a way to pay my high school tuition. But this tuition bill was several times larger; ten bucks here and twenty bucks there would not make up the shortfall. What are we going to do? I asked, a question that came out more like a plea.

Well, my mother said. Is there anyone you can borrow money from?

The way she said it, and the way that she looked at me, one eyebrow

raised above the rim of her beer glass, told me that this was my burden—
but that there might be a solution. I understood her meaning.

Carol?

My mother raised her other eyebrow but said nothing.

Oh Mom, no. Oh no, please.

Carol, a student at St. Bonaventure, was my girlfriend. Her family ran
a successful wholesale food business in Rochester, and she was pretty,
sharp-witted, and sweet enough to have spent the weekend at the House
of Barry—and to have returned several times. She had politely accepted
my father's moans as just another household noise and had helped my
mother fold the family clothes at the laundromat, making it all seem
almost normal for me, and not so profoundly mortifying.

Now my mother was suggesting, without uttering the words, that I ask
Carol's family for a bridge loan. I knew that if I made that call, the answer
would be an immediate yes, and that no one in Carol's family would
think less of me. Still.

My mother rose from the table. She picked up her glass but not the
tuition bill. She left no script on the envelope, as she had years earlier
when I could not bring myself to ask a girl to the junior prom. What
would such a note have said? *Hello, Carol. How are you? It was cold out
today, wasn't it? How is your family? I have a question . . .*

This wasn't high school; that was what my mother was telling me.
After a few minutes alone, I began to dial.

I DIALED FOR the usual reasons: the friendships I had formed, the
comfort I had found, the continuity I desired. Transcending all of these,
though, was the dawning sense that I was onto something at St. Bonaventure with journalism. If walking through the Allegany woods had helped
Merton to choose the religious life, then walking through the same
woods—and, God forgive me, stumbling out of bars at the fringes of
those woods—was helping me to choose the writing life. It was

grotesquely presumptuous but no less true. My friends wanted to be accountants and marketing specialists; I wanted to be a reporter, and I savored the distinction—even if I could not quite articulate an answer to the question, Why journalism? If forced to answer, I would have cited my mother's vivid storytelling, my father's distrust of the powerful—and, I suppose, my understanding of the underdog's life, of being the skinny kid with braces, the one who gets beat up so often that he might as well schedule appointments. I wanted to share the punching bag's point of view.

So far, though, my writing was not even good enough to be called sophomoric. I had worked for my high school newspaper, but everything I wrote was from the soda-belch school of journalism, full of sarcasm and sneers. I received the feedback that I craved from my classmates, the "Hey Barry, you're really fucked up" and other compliments. But when I wrote a farewell yearbook essay that was intended to sum up my class's four years at St. Anthony's, the only response I received was a two-page, typewritten letter from my English teacher, one of the Franciscans I most admired, Brother Benilde:

To say the least, I have been personally wounded by the cynical and sneering tone of your yearbook article. . . . I find the article sophomoric in outlook; cowardly in style; and singularly lacking in general clarity. I have been told in its defense that it is intended to be humorous—a foray into satire. If that is so, it is missing the double-edge that makes satire operate, for your essay is monotonously destructive and nowhere relieved by the kind of belief in the possibilities of human goodness that makes satire as grand as Swift's or as pointed as Philip Roth's. I have indeed failed you as your literature teacher. . . .

Years later I might have argued that the flashes of cynicism in my essay about St. Anthony's were warranted, even just; that I was subconsciously delivering a payback to an institution that had abetted the likes of Brother Noel. But I never could have made that point back then. Besides, Brother Benilde's critique of my writing was sound. He was teaching me still, and the Allegheny Mountains could not shield me from the echoing truth of his words.

Then came the jazz.

In my freshman year I was assigned to an English composition class being taught by a Dr. Richard Simpson. Masking shyness with a practiced look of indifference, I slumped into the last desk in the last row of a classroom in Plassmann Hall and waited to be challenged. Standing at the front of the room was this Simpson, a long-limbed, balding man with a goatee who began the class by saying there were a few things we ought to know about him. He was not from Upstate New York; he was from northern California—some place called Palo Alto. He was not Roman Catholic; he was actually raised a Mormon (A what?). He played tenor saxophone in a local jazz band, considered baseball to be the perfect game, and preferred the poems of the Romantics to just about anything else in the literary canon. All right, I thought. This is what college is about: learning to write from a baseball-loving, jazz-playing Mormon. Show me what you got.

He did. By the third class I had become attuned to his riffs of language, his ear for rhythm, his impeccable use of metaphor and allusion. Who else, I wondered, would read aloud the closing lines of "Ode on a Grecian Urn" (*"Beauty is truth, truth beauty,"—that is all / Ye know on earth, and all ye need to know*) and then compare its perfection to a Tom Seaver fastball, smoking down the strike zone at ninety-five miles an hour, unhittable, sublime. When Dr. Simpson implored his students to hear the music in language—to take risks in their writing—I paid attention.

The first assignment he gave us was to write a composition on a deceptively simple topic: "pressure to succeed." I instantly knew that I had a story to tell, a story so—so un-Bonaventure—that I could barely wait to write it down. Hustling back to my dormitory, across that emerald campus of old buildings and meandering Franciscans, all I could hear was the music of burlesque, bump-ba-ba, bump-ba-ba. I had to find a pen; I had to get *that night* down on paper—that summer night, a few weeks earlier, in the Catskills.

I HAD JUST FINISHED another shift as a cocktail waiter at the Acra Manor, and now I was the one in need of a drink. I made my way to the bar, unfastened my bow tie, and ordered a Coke, neat. On the stool to my right sat a sweat-drenched comic named Sammy, talking about how he had killed that night; if this were true, humor had been the victim. As I struggled with whether to mention that his toupee was a tug away from proper alignment, he opened his billfold to show me a snapshot of Sinatra straining to free himself of Sammy's clutch.

Me and Frank, he said, with house Scotch heavy on his breath.

Sitting to my left was my roommate for the summer, another cocktail waiter named Troy. He was twenty-four, had a nicely trimmed moustache, and considered himself the most dashing man ever produced by Halfmoon, a small town not too far from Acra. I had no right to challenge him, given that in the African Tiki Lounge of the Acra Manor, he was Cary Grant to my Jerry Lewis. Besides, on this night, there were two young women, friends from Halfmoon, who were laughing at Troy's every wisecrack.

Dan, he said. You want a drink?

Yeah, said one of the women, holding up her glass of viscous liqueur. Have one of these: an Angel's Tit.

As the trio from Halfmoon collapsed in giggles, I stammered a good night to the African Tiki Lounge and walked across the lawn to the ramshackle, clapboard building where the waiters and waitresses lived for the season. The room I shared with Troy had two old beds side by side, a single light bulb dangling from the ceiling, and some phosphorescent-orange graffiti from the 1960s: loopy flowers, peace signs, and odes to love and dope. I put on my Deer Park High School sweatshirt, a pair of gym shorts and some white socks, and reached up to turn out the light.

It was well after three in the morning when I heard the slam of a screen door, the approach of uncertain footsteps, and a boozy shooshing for quiet. I watched through squinted eyes as Troy opened our bedroom door and peered in.

He's asleep! he practically shouted, eliciting peals of laughter from two women.

Two women, I deduced in my drowsiness. Two.

The three drunks stumbled into the room and fumbled about for a minute or two in the semidarkness. Clothes flew in the air, shoes—many shoes—clomped to the floor, and then the three of them were in Troy's bed, fumbling about some more. I didn't want to move, but I was on my side, facing them; I didn't want to watch, but I couldn't help myself. Who could? I was terrified, not aroused, and itching now in my casing of white socks and sweatshirt.

The inevitable calculus of their situation soon took hold. The Half-moon hunk rolled to his left to concentrate his who-loves-ya-baby affections on one woman, and in doing so yanked the covers to unveil the second woman: a pretty, naked brunette whose breasts were the first—and therefore the largest—that I had ever seen. With a huff she turned away—only to notice me, scared as a rabbit, my two Thumper-like eyes staring at her.

After a few minutes of being jostled about by activity that excluded her, the woman slipped out of the bed and got into mine, with the casualness of someone changing seats on a bus.

Throughout my adolescence I had dreamed of such a moment: of a naked, attractive woman—she was the one who had been sipping the Angel's Tit—climbing into my bed, just like that. Oh how I would prove my manhood. Oh how I would ravish her. And me still a virgin. Oh. It would be like living out a chapter from *The Choir Sings Sex*, the book that poor Schroeder used to read aloud on the Phelan Bus. No, better than that: one of those *Penthouse Forum* letters we used to read during First Friday Mass in the gymnasium (*One summer I was working as a cocktail waiter in an exclusive summer resort . . .*). Now it was happening, and, and,

and. And I was mortified. Paralyzed. Traumatized. All I wanted to do was to jump out of bed and flee.

She nuzzled me, then slid her hand down my side and onto my manhood, which fear had shrunken to the size of one of those salted pretzel nuggets in the African Tiki Lounge. I gently lifted her hand and placed it by her thigh, and sort of patted it, as if to say, There, there, let's just get some sleep, shall we? She did it again and so did I, pat pat. She did it a third time, a little insistently, and so did I. Pat. Pat.

My bed guest became so annoyed that she turned over and passed out.

I stared at the ceiling for a long while, itching in my white socks and Deer Park sweatshirt, not exactly the kind of apparel appropriate for a *Penthouse Forum* moment. About an hour before dawn, I extricated myself from the sheets, tucked my bedmate in for the sake of modesty—mine, if not hers—and tiptoed from the room, a pair of pants in my arms.

Sunrise found me in an Adirondack chair on the porch of the servants' lodgings, trying to reconcile what I had just done and what I had not. I could have been the gorilla, pounding my plastic black chest. But I was just Danny Barry, nothing more.

I SKETCHED OUT several drafts of this story before it said what I wanted it to say. Then I wrote it down one more time on clean sheets of loose-leaf paper and handed it in to fulfill that freshman writing assignment on the subject of "pressure to succeed." The moment I walked out of the classroom, though, I felt the familiar dampness of embarrassment at the back of my neck. Dr. Simpson and I barely knew each other. And yet in my very first writing assignment for him, I had chosen to describe naked women and bed romps and unresponsive private parts. What is he going to think? What would Merton think? What have I done?

A few days later, Dr. Simpson returned our compositions. I studied his face for any sign that he now considered one of his students to be a sexual deviant. If he felt this way, he didn't let on. He just handed me my paper, which he had marked with a grade of A and three glorious words: "What a yarn."

Those three words provided the validation I sought for pursuing the life of a journalist. I could do this, I thought. I could tell stories for a living. In the back of my mind echoed the baseball chatter of my childhood, those chants of encouragement that seemed almost to rise from the dirt and grass of the diamond.

Now you're set. Now you're set.

10

M Y COIN ON the pool table's edge gave the silvery wink, announcing to all that the next game of eight ball was mine. What more could a young man want than what was before me: a field of green felt, a bunch of balls and a stick to bang them around with, and a bottle of beer to leave me thirsting for more. There is a song like that, ancient and Irish and known to me since the age of ten:

> What more diversion can a man desire
> Than to sit him down by a snug turf fire
> Upon his knee a pretty wench
> Aye and on the table a jug of punch

Outside, on the vacant village stage of deep-night Allegany, November thundered like a truck convoy down Main Street, carrying with it the shivers felt just moments before in Jamestown, Salamanca, Riverside Junction. Even the street signs shook. But inside the Club 17 bar, I tucked myself under the window-steaming exhalations of others, my beer full and my coin winking. What more could a young man want.

Yes, of course, that too: female companionship. But Carol had graduated and moved to Boston, and besides, there would be time enough for courting. I was in the bullpen warming up for life's game, pacing like a rookie pitcher beside my good friends and fellow seniors, Seibert and

Conlon, Farrell and Fay, Ying Yang and Bear. Freshman year had nudged into sophomore year, which had blended into junior year—all, it seemed, in about the time it took to play a game of quarters. Now, suddenly, we had six months to go before our college graduation, after which society would require us to declare something more than the next game of barroom pool; we would have to declare ourselves. Until then, all we had to do was get passing grades and avoid expulsion. We were not ones to attend career-counseling days or to pester professors for contacts in that daunting place, the working world. That world would come to us in time, as measured by the plastic-arrow quivers in the bar clocks of Allegany. Tick, tick, tick, we did not watch those arrows so much as sense their movement, while we waited at Club 17 or the Burton bar for graduation, and after that the next thing: a job, a wife, a house, a baby, and then, one day, something—a death, or maybe just a song—would fill us with aching wonder at what had happened to us, how had we gotten here, and why couldn't we be back in the warm human crush of Club 17, when the answer to what more could we want seemed so obvious, because it was nothing.

On this, another blur of a night, she came crisply into focus, a young woman with long blond hair that broke like sunlight through the blue-gray barroom cloud. She maintained an air of grace at the scrumlike counter, sipping just so while those around her lapped like livestock at a water trough. I knew her vaguely, but I did not know her. A junior, I thought. Mary Something.

Although in our fourth year of college, my friends and I still clung to deeply flawed preparations for mixing with the opposite sex. We played quarters and other drinking games to find the nerve to speak to women, a nerve that always seemed to lurk somewhere beyond the next glass. When finally we marched into the social fray, we often discovered that the nerve we had strived to summon was numb, that the poetry with which we hoped to beguile the Mary Somethings of the world was always just a tongue's twitch beyond articulation. It was all so frustrating and embarrassing—so childish, really, in the self-infliction—that we often remained in the poolroom sanctum at the back of the bar, broadcasting the limits of our evening's expectations with the quarters we placed on the pool table's lip.

I looked down to see the eight ball drop into the pocket. Game over, and my quarter was next. But Ying Yang, my pool partner, had vanished, swept away in the feverish jostling to place wet dollar bills in a bartender's hand. It all made for wondrous timing: quarter up, Ying Yang gone, and Mary Something at the bar, surrounded yet alone, sipping, oh my God, she was sipping a seven-and-seven—in this beer hall an act of defiant sophistication that I found dangerously alluring. Beguiling verse suddenly came to me. I had to make my move.

Hey, I said, fumbling with my pool stick. I got a quarter up. Wanna play?

And she said—I'll never forget what she said—she said, Sure.

So it began, while balls clicked and clacked on beer-stained felt and Bobby Darin sang "Beyond the Sea" on the jukebox. We won a couple of games somehow, and I bought her another seven-and-seven that she did not finish, and my friends along the cue-pocked wall looked at one another and then jerked their heads toward me, the gesture that says, Are you seeing what I'm seeing? Something to bust Barry on later, but God don't I envy him. I escorted her the blustery mile back to her dormitory on campus, where we sat in the lounge and talked and talked in the filibuster of attraction, for neither of us wanted to say a simple goodnight. She told me her full name, Mary Katherine Anne Trinity. I asked her whether a nun really ought to be drinking highballs and shooting pool so late at night.

Trinity was her surname, she assured me, an Irish name, with no clear roots in any of Ireland's thirty-two counties, although there were strong rumors about Kilkenny. Her paternal grandfather, John Trinity, was off the boat and had worked the counter in a Philadelphia tavern owned by another Irish immigrant, the wealthy and trusting Reardon. This barman named Trinity had the audacity to court the owner's precious daughter, Mary, who had gained some regional attention at the time for her elabo-

rate and patriotic "Flag Dance," which lifted the home-front spirits during World War I. One evening Mary Reardon stuffed her best dress into
her violin case, told her parents she was off to music practice, and eloped
with that spalpeen Trinity, and what kind of an Irish name is that
anyway.

Soon the light of dawn crested over the Southern Tier hills to kiss the
top of Merton's Heart. But the exhausted granddaughter of a dissident
debutante and an immigrant barman was still being subjected to aimless
interrogation by a young man who could think of no other way to court.

Where do you live?

In New Jersey, in a town called Maplewood.

Sounds made up. What do your parents do?

They're schoolteachers.

What are their names?

Mary and Joseph.

No, really. What are their names?

Mary and Joseph. Mary and Joseph Trinity.

Jesus. Got any precocious brothers I should know about?

I have three younger brothers and one younger sister; they're nice, but
no need to worship them. I also have an uncle who is a Franciscan missionary in Bolivia—he went to St. Bonaventure—and an aunt who's a
Sister of Mercy.

Wow. Sounds like the Barry family.

Really?

Uuh, no. So let me get this right, Mary Trinity, daughter of Mary and
Joseph Trinity, niece of Franciscans and Sisters of Mercy. Do I have to
make the sign of the cross before I kiss you?

And what about you, Dan Barry?

You're changing the subject.

That's right. Tell me about you.

Just a kid from Long Island.

WHAT WAS I going to tell her? About my own family? She might have a Franciscan missionary for an uncle, but I have an uncle who used to wear a gorilla's mask while driving around Long Island in a convertible. Yeah. That would go over big with the Holy Order of Mary Trinity Relatives.

What was I going to tell her? About the UFO searches? And the cluster migraines, and the decorated artificial Christmas tree in the garage, and the alcohol, and all the rest? So I told it flat: just a kid from Long Island, the oldest of four. Father grew up in the city and runs a check-cashing store; mother grew up in Ireland and works as a clerk somewhere.

At the same time, I was slightly miffed that this Mary Trinity did not already know who Dan Barry was. Where had she been, living among the incunabula in the library basement? I bragged that sitting before her was a founding member and co-editor of a campus magazine that came out not once a year, but twice, with a circulation of a few hundred, easy. Hadn't she read the magazine's devastating critique of student government, or the hard-nosed examination of the university's arbitration system? Didn't she know that I was the one working diligently to challenge the Franciscans' well-publicized commitment to poverty, based on a hazy tip that cases of Chivas Regal were being delivered to the back of the friary every month?

But she was easy to forgive, this Mary Trinity. So instead of telling her stories about my family, I told her the story of Tony Oni the janitor.

In the old Devereux dormitory where I lived for three years, night often spilled into morning like an upended pitcher. Along with the radiator rattles and shower hisses, the sounds of a new day in academia included the jangling of cans and bottles being dragged in a black garbage bag along the beer-soured carpet by Tony Oni. He was short and wiry, with a gaping overbite and slick brown hair that was parted with an engineer's precision. Every morning I greeted him with "Hiya," and he returned the greeting, "Hiya," which was basically all that he ever said.

If students ever saw janitors at all, it was as fixtures to the university infrastructure, like shower nozzles or bed frames. But Tony Oni was more than just another janitor; he was a cult figure, the subject of legend. In the first week of my freshman year, some of the newcomers to Devereux Hall were escorted down to the Allegheny River and made to chug beer while balancing themselves on the tops of kegs. Only then were we considered worthy of learning the secrets of Devereux, which loomed like a Gothic mental ward over the rest of the campus. Check this out: two students once held a black Mass in the Devereux attic—true story—so never go up there alone. And here's something else that'll blow your mind: Tony Oni, that goofy janitor? He's Sophia Loren's cousin.

There was nothing in Tony Oni's face—in the overbite, or in the eyes set a little too deep—that remotely reminded me of Sophia Loren, but what did I know.

Hey Tony, I said one morning. You really Sophia Loren's cousin?

His eyes widened. Yeah, yeah, he said. Sophia Loren my cousin.

How many times had this poor man been asked that question by wise-ass Bonaventure students as he cleaned up the morning wreckage of their nighttime revelry? Hey Tony, hey Tony, hey Tony. You Sophia Loren's cousin? She pretty? Yeah? Yeah? Big breasts, yeah? Yeah?

And how often had he basked in his moments of distinction, no matter how meanspirited? How many times had he responded exactly the way he had to me? Yeah, yeah. Sophia Loren my cousin.

But was he? I had to find out; there was a story there, somewhere.

Another janitor told me that Tony Oni had a photograph of Sophia Loren hanging in his bedroom. Tony seemed to confirm this and agreed to let me borrow the photograph to reproduce in the campus magazine I was editing. One afternoon I went to the rooming house where he lived, along a dog-breath stretch of downtown Olean called "the Strip." The rooming house was a decrepit shelter for housing-code violations, all pocked sheetrock and rat droppings and overloaded electrical outlets. And there was my host to greet me, looking formal somehow in his flannel shirt and dungarees, out of his Bonaventure uniform of work-clothes blue. He was glad to see me—Hiya, hiya—and led me to his fetid room, where he proudly pointed to a crinkled movie poster of Sophia Loren taped to his otherwise bare wall.

Oh, Tony, that's so beautiful we should leave it where it is, I said, and he agreed. I left as quickly as I could because I was ashamed. All those years of cleaning up the mess of the privileged at a Franciscan university, of shaking out the last dregs from tossed bottles, of big breasts, yeah, yeah, and then coming home to this.

If there was truth to this Sophia Loren story, it would be found in the basement of the university library, where Father Irenaeus, that old friend of Merton's, still puttered. His mind was a repository for all things Franciscan—Alexander of Hales, William of Ockham, Duns Scotus—and yet there was more than enough room for campus tidbits and trivia. He was nearly eighty by now, hard of hearing and with a chalky whisper of a voice, but as eager as ever to fulfill his mission as researcher. He said that the story of Tony Oni and a famous relation sounded vaguely familiar, and he invited me to flip through the bound copies of yellowed campus newspapers. Maybe something had been written once.

Every day for a week, I finished my classes and headed to the library basement, where the air was redolent of the Franciscan bookbinder's pipe, and the rest of the campus—the beery howls in Devereux, the clatter of utensils in the dining hall, the cheers in the gymnasium—seemed a continent, a century, away. Back I went in Bonaventure time, through stories about unforgettable basketball games already forgotten, and photographs of young men yet to be aged by Vietnam. Finally, I came upon it: a short news article and a photograph of a much-younger Tony Oni, his arm around an icon.

Sophia Loren my cousin.

I TOLD MARY Trinity my Tony Oni tale, which was meant to demonstrate my love for stories and my big heart and my derring-do. After all, hadn't I ventured down to Olean's Strip—nearly two miles off-campus!—in search of the tale? And hadn't I broken the story of Tony Oni and Sophia Loren? Not technically, no; some other student journalist had written about it years earlier. But I *had* resurrected the truth behind the Tony Oni legend. Hadn't I? Wasn't I something?

She smiled, and nodded, and said that she would like to see the article about my adventure. She knew exactly where Tony Oni lived, by the way, because every weekend she helped to run a soup kitchen just a few doors down on the Strip. Tony was a regular, in fact.

She told me this with no hint of pride or one-upsmanship—only as a polite way to signal that she had been listening and that she understood. Still, I felt embarrassed. I knew nothing, nothing at all.

For reasons that were probably rooted in sleep deprivation, Mary agreed to see me again that night. On our first formal date, we went to the most romantic movie playing in Allegany, which was also the only movie playing in Allegany: *Apocalypse Now*. I had already seen the movie, and so I blathered on and on about the movie's literary allusions—this reference to Conrad, that reference to Eliot. She listened and nodded, but now and then she would gently correct me or offer another interpretation. She was better read, more analytical, and gave as good as she got, but somehow did so without the sarcasm that I presented as wit.

At some point between Robert Duvall's tribute to the smell of napalm in the morning and that first glimpse of a bloated Brando in the shadows, my date nodded off. Studying her lovely face, I wondered, What's to become of us, Mary Trinity, what's to become of us? I slid my arm around her and drew rare comfort, as all around me a virtual war raged on.

11

Y OU RETURN HOME, Mr. Big-Shot College Graduate, and they present you with a new portable typewriter: a Brother and baby blue, it's our gift to you, you've made us so proud. Feel the power in that instrument, son, the power to make people think and laugh and cry with the stories you write. The power to take down those sons of bitches, those motherless bastards: the two-faced politicians, the permanent government, Henry Kissinger, the Trilateral Commission, Archer Daniels Midland, the oil companies that Ida Tarbell wrote about so long ago and it's still the same, nothing's changed, the bastards, the motherless bastards, they suck the very marrow from the bones of people like us.

Gene, keep it light. Keep it light, Gene.

Noreen, do you have any idea? Do you have any idea what these sons of bitches have done to this country? Oh don't get me started. They shove their goddamned commercials down our—

Gene. Please. Light.

Anyway, son. Congratulations.

Now, college graduate, you are living in the basement, your bachelor pad beside the sump pump. Every now and then your wincing father thumps heavily down the stairs, a pirate in pain, to grab another Schmidt's beer bottle from the freezer. It is a beer bottle, yes, but no beer in it. That beer is history, uncorked long ago with a thumb-and-forefinger flick to release a sound as common to the household as the tea kettle's whistle, a sound somewhere between a hiss and a sigh, and aren't both appropriate, Mr. Big-Shot Writer. Relieved quickly of its contents and then filled with water, the beer bottle was resealed—Save those caps, kids!—and tucked into a freezer-hair bed, between frozen string beans, ShopRite frozen orange juice cylinders, and other frozen-water bottles. Now my father was using that beer bottle to alleviate pain, again, only he will work the back of his neck with its hard coolness in a bedroom's black, hoping to massage away another cluster migraine, his hundredth, his thousandth.

Clump. Clump. Clump. Down the stairs and into the basement, your bedroom.

Dad, you say into the dark. You need help?

No, he gasps. G'night.

Good night, Dad.

Clump. Clump. Clump.

Sometimes she falls asleep on the living room couch, her office. Wrapped like a sarcophagus in a swirl of worn blankets and floral-patterned sheets, hair in flamingo-colored curlers, a glass of water within a hand's reach on the coffee table, where the glass of Schmidt's had been, next to the ashtray. Most of the time, though, she joins him in their bedroom, usually after the top of the *Ten O'Clock News* on Channel 5. Him aarghing and beseeching so violently that the bedposts have dented the walls. And her beside him, sleeping or trying to, willing things to be normal by acting as though they were.

Then morning, and your mother is calling down the basement, Danny, it's 6:30. But you know that already, the smell of their coffee has already slapped you in the face. They like their coffee strong—make that muscular: twelve heaping scoops of Maxwell House percolated into just eight cups of water to create a caffeine concoction the color and consistency of spent motor oil.

She sips her coffee while arranging her hair in the upstairs bathroom, studying herself in the mirror, blowing gently on the coffee's mocha surface between drags from her second cigarette. She is immaculate in her appearance when she leaves for work, always. No matter that her office is a hole in a gigantic cinderblock on Route 110, where women like her toil at gray-metal desks over purchase orders for cheap cosmetics, the kind you see at a discount drugstore's checkout counter. No matter that she and the other girls long for their ten-minute breaks, when they can grab a smoke and rest their eyes from squinting. No matter that lunch is thirty minutes, barely enough time to wolf down the Tupperware lump of last night's leftovers and take a smoke walk around the factory with a girlfriend. They mutter and joke during their industrial-plant constitutional, about the supervisor with the permanent fisheye, about who's kissing up to whom, about how this multi-million-dollar business rewards people for twenty years of service with a gold pin the size of a baby lima bean and bearing the company logo, as if you'd go out to dinner one night with your husband, dressed up and wearing a company endorsement on your lapel. I don't want to be here for twenty years, say my mother and the factory girls. I don't want that stupid pin.

Noreen Barry never wears sneakers or dungarees to work, as some do. Noreen Barry always wears a skirt, a blouse, and heels, always keeps her back straight and her eyes ready to return any gaze, so that when she walks into the place, she might very well be heading for the door that says Executive Vice President. They may have her, but they don't, this foreigner who stopped registering with the I.N.S. long ago. She was not the most Irish of the Irish. She was not one to sit there with the *Irish Echo* and a cup of tea, studying the familiar surnames under the posed photographs from the latest dinner dances, the Rose of Tralee this and the Ancient Order of Hibernians that. But she refused to become an American citizen, an act that would have formalized her assimilation somehow. This factory, this country, they don't have her, no; she belongs to Gene, to the four kids, to Ireland.

She calls into the bedroom she shares, a battlefield of twisted linens and damp towels and beer bottles filled with defrosted water, where her husband has a beaten pillow wrapped across his eyes to block out that damned morning light.

Woochin, she says, using the made-up term of endearment they shared before they were married, before any of us were born. Woochin, it's seven o'clock.

His footsteps fall like dead weight down the stairs. He slumps at the kitchen table and turns the radio on and wouldn't you goddam know it, someone's changed the station. He works the dial like a safecracker, listening to every tic and cough, until he finds the music of his life, News Radio 88, traffic and weather on the eights. He reaches for the *Daily News* that is laid out for him like a table setting. And when, finally, he takes that first sip of coffee lava, he moans like Gleason: Aaaah.

Aaaah, the Barry greeting to the day. I made it through another night, you bastards, so now what.

The days of competing in Manhattan are long gone: of dining at private clubs and fine restaurants, Delmonico's and the rest; of being that baritone in a downtown glee club who always hit just the right note; of double Windsor tie knots and silver cuff links that wink with promise. Gone, so gone they might as well have been lived by another man.

He will dress in the pants and shirt that his wife has ironed, but no goddam tie, Lord knows he's worn enough of those in his day. He will throw the *News* into his briefcase, alongside the collection of stories by Mark Twain, or the complete set of Sherlock Holmes, or some other doorstop of a book that has caught his eye—anything from a history of reincarnation to a study of the Vietnam debacle—and click the briefcase shut. The only way to unlock it is to know the Gene Barry code, the numbers that he lives by, 6-8-5-7, a date more important than his draft date, than even his own birth date: the date of his wedding to Nora—Noreen—Minogue. (You wonder whether you will ever feel that way about a woman; and if you do, will she be the lovely Mary Trinity?) He will drive the two miles to the check-cashing store on Commack Road and wait in his car for the arrival of an armed security guard, usually some cologne-sopping ex-cop who by all rights should not be carrying a gun. One of these Barney Fifes was demonstrating his prowess with a .38, twirling it like a toy right there in the office, when the damned thing went off, sending a bullet too close for comfort into the back wall.

See what I have to put up with? Gene moans to the gods and to his family. See what I have to put up with?

As odd as it sounds, though, he needs the armed escort; there had been holdups and shootings at check-cashing stores throughout the island and the city. One time a man walked up to his counter and, without a word, blew a hole through the Plexiglas window with a shotgun, covering his book-cluttered domain with glassy snow. Another time, late one night, a couple of knuckleheads cut a hole in the ceiling to find nothing more than a safe as tight as a nun's lips and a paperback copy of the Warren Commission report.

He will sit at the counter from 9:30 in the morning until 6:00 at night, cashing checks for the landscapers, the factory workers, the welfare recipients, the orderlies from the Pilgrim State psychiatric facility, the people getting soaked under the trickle-down policies of the current president. Most days, he sees it as his private mission to make them think or at least laugh, using a style that is equal parts Noah Webster, I. F. Stone, and Jonathan Winters. He issues challenges on the etymology of certain words, commiserates on the conspiracies of big-business bastards, provides counseling on vexing personal matters—and then slips into a convincing Yiddish accent to tell a joke (the Orthodox Jews on the Street used to call him Boris, for the great Thomashefsky of the Yiddish theater). If you prune the shrubs of the rich, or inhale chemicals in a factory, or take punches while restraining patients, sometimes a bright spot in your week's drudgery is coming to see the man behind the scratched Plexiglas, the man called Gene. He gets it; he gets how hard it can be sometimes; how sometimes all you want to do is laugh. So you take in the stuffed duck, wearing glasses and a tie, that he has dangling from the ceiling; you read the latest "Far Side" cartoon that he's taped to the window; and you chuckle at how his voice imitations segue from W. C. Fields to Topo Gigo to John Cleese.

On some days, though, Gene will feel another headache coming on, or think of the what-ifs of his life, or brood about how he is trapped like a caged animal in this office because you can never leave the money, and he looks past the Plexiglas fog to see no peace and quiet on the horizon, which was all he ever wanted. On these days, if you the customer do not meet what he considers to be the minimum standard of civil discourse— if you do not acknowledge his thanks and good wishes that you have a nice day—he will bellow, for all to hear: I SAID: THANK YOU AND HAVE A NICE DAY! Gene Barry deserves at least that—as we all do. A sign on the window gives fair warning: Courtesy Is Free; Have Some.

WITH EVERY MORNING comes that ritualized rousing: the radio chatter, the coffee smell, the cigarette-blue smoke, the hacking coughs that sing out from upstairs and downstairs like mating calls, back and forth, up and down, reassuring two life partners that each other is awake, alive. Now too there is you, returned to your nest but a visitor somehow.

At this very moment, in Mechanicville and Binghamton, in Norwalk and North Babylon, your fellow Bonaventure graduates are also dressing for the day. They are putting on dry-cleaned suits and pressed shirts and power-red ties, and they are earning a salary. You, though, are putting on your clay-smeared dungarees and work boots and a T-shirt, and you are earning four dollars an hour by digging ditches on the lawns and construction sites of Long Island.

No question: you have a career problem. You spent four years and a lot of money, not all of it yours, toward earning a bachelor's degree in journalism, and now that you have that admission ticket to your Adulthood, you realize that daily journalism is not for you. All those requirements to be objective, to answer the who, what, when, where, why, and how of a story, to follow the "inverted pyramid" theory of presenting the most important facts first—well, you think, invert this. You want to be Jimmy Breslin, Hunter S. Thompson, and Nellie Bly all rolled into one—not the prettiest sight to imagine, but still. You want to travel the country in search of civilization's fault lines, to chronicle those failures for *Rolling Stone* and *Esquire* with all the wisdom of your twenty-two years. You want to pay back all the predatory bullies and clerics, all the taxmen and traitors, all those responsible for everything from the Great Hunger to the Great Depression—anyone who has brought suffering to the people at 140 West 23rd Street, and those like them. That would include every single tobacco company, the bastards. Not the beer companies and distillers, though; leave them be for now.

But the classified sections of *Newsday* and *The New York Times* reflect scant demand for the likes of you. There are no calls for "Righteous Young Writer" in the help-wanted ads, no solicitations for journalists at all, in fact, except with trade publications dedicated to solid-waste management. Public relations and advertising firms are offering entry-level positions "with potential to grow," but you cannot imagine telling your mother and father that you had landed a job, say, as a flack for Archer Daniels Midland. You might as well leave your surname at the door on your way out.

So, every morning, you muster alongside other men in a dirt lot outside the cinderblock office of the Ace Lawn Sprinkling company, on a desolate, scraggly-pine stretch of Long Island Avenue that straddles the Ronkonkoma line railroad tracks. These men beside you spit out the taste of last night's beer, draw aimless lines in the dust with the toes of their boots, and wait for Mike, the crew boss, to emerge with the day's assignments. When he appears, the men come to him like iron filings to a magnet.

Hector, Willie, Manuel, you guys go with Bob. Eddie, Perfecto, Sammy, Danny, get in my truck.

You climb into the back of his gray Ford van and push aside picks and shovels to make room for your ass on the metal bed. First comes the necessary stop at a delicatessen, where the men get their obligatory ham-and-eggs on rolls, their white Styrofoam cups of coffee, their Ring Dings, Devil Dogs, Yankee Doodles, and Susie Q's. Sammy always gets two bot-

tles of Schmidt's for breakfast and Eddie always gets one can of Bud, sixteen ounces all. Then back into the van to root for fuck-ups: traffic, rain,
bad directions, anything that eats into the time you'll spend swinging a
pick. Before long you are being rocked into dreaminess by the equidis-
tant ruts in the Long Island Expressway asphalt, while the rakes and
shovels beside you clank together like tuning forks in search of a proper
note.

An hour later, maybe less, maybe more, you grumble out of the truck
and into the midmorning light that graces a corner of Sands Point, Mut-
tontown, or some other place where landscapers become suspect after
sundown. Your job: to dig trenches, lay water lines, plant hidden spouts,
cover up the trenches, and leave no trace that you had ever set foot on the
client's property. By evening, though, your work will have almost mysti-
cally granted to some cardiologist or sewing-thread heir the power to
control nature. With the flip of a switch, he will be able to create a soft
mist to dapple the pachysandra around his doorstep, or tommy-gun
sprays of water that shoot thirty feet across his blue-green sod.

You and your scraggly coworkers are the rainmakers of summer,
really. You pause from work only for true rain, as if in deference.

Mike, an ex-Marine with a cigarette-smoke squint and tattooed arms
like bridge cables, almost never speaks to the customers, so bald is his
contempt for them. The only time he seems to truly enjoy his job is when
some client starts to whine that a certain part of the lawn is not being
watered by the newly installed sprinkler system. Tell you what, Mike will
growl, eyes on the ground because he cannot bear to look at these people. You stand on the spot, I'll turn on the system, and we'll see what's
what.

It always takes Mike a minute or two longer than anyone else to hear
the cries of the drenched doubters.

You and Mike are as tight as two men in this world will allow them-
selves to get: you shoot pool, swap baseball trivia, discuss the genius of
Hank Williams and how he really was crying at the end of "Cold, Cold
Heart." About the closest Mike ever comes to revealing himself is to recall

that when he was growing up in some coal-dust dump in Scranton, the upstairs neighbor came home one day with a recording of Tennessee Ernie Ford singing "Sixteen Tons"—and played it nonstop for three weeks.

I hate that fucking song, he confides.

There are other men you have come to know and like. You sweat together, curse together, and arc your piss streams together against the shadowed sides of Long Island mansions that you will never see from the inside. Sometimes, while burping up soda and beer gas during a late-afternoon break, these men pause from discussing the amenities at the county jail in Riverhead to razz you because you are different. This is a way station for you but life for them, and everyone knows it. But that's okay. You dig your trenches, you get your balls busted, you bust back; most of all, you laugh.

Yo, Danny. What's the name of that fucking school again?

Uuh, St. Bonaventure.

Bananaventure? That where all the fruits go?

Bonaventure.

Wherezat?

Upstate. Near Olean.

Never heard of it. You got a degree and shit?

Yeah.

And you're still this fucking stupid? Man don't even know how to swing a pick. Maybe I should go to Oh-lean, be the dean or some shit.

There is Sammy, who naps in the trenches he digs after those two Schmidt's, then breaks into his lunch bag well before noon. Usually his lunch consists of two pieces of bread separated by five inches of mashed potatoes, but there was that time his afternoon sandwich was made from the disoriented squirrel that the crew had seen him waylay with a shovel the day before.

There is Perfecto Santiago. He always wears the Perfecto uniform of sweat-stained Panama hat, green work pants, and loose-fitting shirt, and he always keeps the plastic end of a spent Tiparillo clenched in his teeth.

With all this he is still naked without a pick in his hand. He is a virtuoso on that instrument, able to swing it with great force and unerring accuracy. For four bucks an hour, he would pick and dig through a minefield. And he has his principles, conveyed to Mike through a translator: Perfecto never, ever works on Good Friday; if man pierces the soil on that day, blood comes out.

The only time Perfecto talks to you is when you take the lunch order. Meatball hero, he mutters, in broken English. Orange soda.

The delicatessen often has neither, forcing you to imagine what this strange man might eat and drink. When you return, Perfecto glowers at you, snatches the bag from your hand, and walks twenty yards to eat alone, consuming his ham-and-cheese and Pepsi in bites and slurps of anger. In the awkward afternoons that follow, after the food has been consumed and the garbage buried in the trenches, you stay well behind him and his Excalibur of a pick.

Finally, there is Eddie, by far the company's best laborer, who instinctively knows the electronics and strategy needed to install sprinklers. But the owners will not make him a foreman, a Mike. They tell him he needs more experience. Eddie is thirty years old and has worked for the company for five years. He thinks it has to do with other matters: his modest criminal record, his prodigious drinking, his anger-management issues, or maybe, just maybe, his being Puerto Rican.

Come on, Danny, he says. You think the owner wants the bitches in Old Westbury to open their doors and see me as Mr. Ace Lawn Sprinkling? Riiiight.

That is how people on Long Island talk; they say "right" for "wrong."

Eddie deals with these realities by working and drinking, working and drinking—and seething. His fury competes with the angry sun that has baked the steel of our tools, teaching us always to pick them up by their wooden handles. He raises his pick and holds it high above his shoulders, pauses, a thrusted middle finger of a man, then sends his instrument crashing down to strike the earth, for he is as furious with the ground as he is with the sky. Again and again, as sweat flees from his taut arms and

scraggly black hair. He keeps his rhythm by cursing the clay. Motherfucker, he says. Motherfucker. And when dusk comes, a deli beer stop is
made, and soon Eddie's eyes are shining like wet brown marbles.

With the day done, the gray van stops at the corner of your street and
you climb out, slathered in dirt and dried sweat. You pause to watch the
van pull away, its shovels and picks rattling in song and Perfecto Santiago
glaring out the dusty back window. All he wants in life is a meatball hero
and an orange soda, and you bring him what—a ham-and-cheese? A
Pepsi? He will not forget; he will never forget.

Another day is done for the college kid, another thirty-two dollars
before taxes.

Magna cum what?

You walk wearily down West 23rd Street, noticing again how things
change and never change. A nostalgia that you know is premature and
artificial begins to take hold; you are twenty-two, but you are only
twenty-two. Still, these squat little houses contained the Micawbers and
Fezziwigs of your childhood, and now some of those people, characters
really, have gone. Mrs. Spitz and her family have moved from this house;
she has gone to who knows where to drink her grasshoppers and shuffle
her mah-jongg tiles. Big Tom from that house died a couple of years
back, and no one could believe it, he was so strapping and strong. And
here is the Bernardi house, where your parents shared so many bottles of
Chianti over platters of antipasto, and the kids who had been sent to play
in the basement furtively listened to every word, hoping to crack the
coded, double-entendre language that had all those adults crying with
laughter. Maybe there was something there, something you could say, to
defuse future situations.

The Bernardis, though, moved to Arizona, which might as well have
been Malaysia. You've heard that their daughter Sharon, who spent her
father's cherished silver on Bungalow Bar ice cream, has kids of her own
now, kids who no doubt will avenge their grandfather someday, maybe
by taking scissors to her prized collection of *Tiger Beat* magazines.

The Bernardis; they once loomed so large in your family's life. Now someone else is living in that house, and the Bernardi name is mentioned only when your dogs sneak out of the yard.

Where did you find Gypsy this time?

Down by the Bernardis'.

THERE, AT THE crenelated hedges that surround the Barry compound, stands your mother, cigarette in lips and garden hose in hand. On summer nights she races home from work so that she can slip into some beat-up clothes and escape into puttering. She mows and clips, rakes and waters, moves and moves again the frogs and ducks of her ceramic menagerie. Her Galway manner of greeting you is to hose you down like some workhorse just in from the fields.

Your father comes home and it is a good night, considering; a headache has not yet taken hold, but the imminence of one dampens his mood. How can it not. Racing against time, they grab a couple of bottles of their life's champagne, beer, and head for the backyard, which over the years has grown into a kind of leafy fortress, where too tall hedges and tangles of forsythia discourage over-the-fence chats and thwart prying eyes. That free-flowing neighborliness of the early years on West 23rd Street is over; the only ones to visit now are the birds that feed on the rye-toast crusts from breakfast. The Barrys have put out the not-so-subtle signal: they want to be left alone. Gene wants peace and quiet, and when he does not have peace and quiet, his kind of peace and quiet, then no one in the family has peace and quiet, so that is what Noreen wants: Gene's kind of peace and quiet. This means the backyard. Sitting in the summer-evening shade on old metal lawn furniture, a few feet from the crooked, backboardless basketball hoop. Sipping beer. Crushing smoked cigarettes on the patio. Her telling stories about this one from work, and him complaining about the sons of bitches who—

Gene, look. A bluejay.

Where?

There on the grass. Next to Danny's Tree.

That is what the family calls the backyard's looming maple. Gene and Noreen had planted it more than twenty years ago as a way of staking their claim in Deer Park, of saying that here was where they would raise their children.

You retire to the basement to write for an hour or two on the baby-blue Brother, next to the sump pump. Here is where you write a bad short story about grammar school, a slew of cover letters to magazines in search of employment, and scenes from your day—from Sammy's mashed-potato sandwiches to Perfecto's oneness with a pick, to the way that the sky looks like a fish's belly just before a thunderstorm. You have no idea what you will do with these bits and pieces. All you know is that you want to capture what you see with words, you want to preserve moments and then turn them upside down to see what truth lies beneath. You want to entertain, inform, engage, enrage. You want epiphany—through words.

It is late now. Your Galway mother is sleeping on the living room couch, your tortured father is coming heavily down the stairs for a shot of that ice in a beer bottle. And you, you are looking for the words.

12

I BORROWED THE RED TIE. The black belt. The blue socks that were long enough to reach my knees. The black shoes with the small silver buckles. The blue blazer that still had half a roll of his favorite snack, Rolaids, in the pocket. My father weighed a good thirty pounds more than me, and so everything, even the tie, seemed too big. I was awash in a Gene Barry sea.

But I had to look my best. I had an appointment with a Miss Cummings at *The New York Times*, after all, to inquire about a job as a news clerk at that august newspaper. My mother asked me to say it again, and so I did. The Noo Yawk Times, doncha know, said the duke of Deer Park, earning that sh-sh laugh of hers, a kind of whispered, whistled exhalation of mirth. Sh-sh-sh.

How do I look? I asked, as I treaded water in another man's clothes.

Very handsome, said my mother. Like a million bucks, said my father. But don't forget to mention the Mark Hellinger Award from St. Bonaventure.

I didn't win that award, Dad. I came in second.

It's still prestigious. And that reminds me. Maybe you ought to bring up that award from *Newsday*. You might even wear that nice lapel pin they gave you.

Dad, a bunch of students got those pins. Besides, *The New York Times* doesn't care about high school newspapers.

Every little bit helps, son. Don't forget: I know something about selling yourself in the city.

On her way to her job of poring over orders for nail polish, my mother dropped me off at the train station in Wyandanch. Working behind the Long Island Rail Road ticket counter was a neighbor of ours, a man known as "Groucho" because of his explosive rage if a Spalding happily bounced upon a blade of his grass. I had spent many nights as a child speculating with other neighborhood kids about how many balls he had confiscated and what he had done with them all. We had decided that he practiced juggling while chortling about so many hours of childhood fun denied. Now here he was before me, bent in the back and still with that same, pickle-weaned expression, and I knew that he had missed the train for Scrooge-like redemption. His legacy was sealed. One day sooner than later, the solemn word would be shared over an open box of Entenmann's or a couple of Buds, or both:

Hey. Didya hear Groucho died?

Really? Huh. Want another beer?

I shoved my money toward him and said, Penn Station, round trip. He answered by shoving back a ticket that would get me out of his sight.

I stepped out onto the Wyandanch train platform. Down to my left was the yard where all the Bungalow Bar ice cream trucks were parked for the winter, row after row of little trucks shaped like cottages, forming what looked like an off-season village for old ice-cream men like Baciagaloop. Directly across from me was Otto's delicatessen, where long ago my confident father used to flip coins with Otto, double or nothing, for a six-pack of beer, a pound of potato salad, a pack of smokes. And behind me, the long, long row of parking slots. God, I thought. How much time had I spent there, squirming in the backseat against my siblings, sensing my mother's worries, praying for the next Ronkonkoma train to return that sixth piece of us, our father.

A train arrived, bound for the other direction: New York, Penn Station. I found a window seat and stared through a fine veil of soot as a Long Island panorama—Pinelawn, Farmingdale, Bethpage, Hicksville—

moved past. The repetitive blur of small houses, delicatessens, and train-stop bars can be mesmerizing, and before I knew it the train was pulling into the Jamaica station in Queens. Oh my God, I thought. I'm about to have the most important job interview of my life and here I am, nose pressed against the window like a kid on a school trip.

I was not one of those eager young journalists who scrutinized every issue of *The New York Times*, analyzing the placement of front-page stories, deciphering the cryptic meanings behind the typeface, tracking bylines. I followed the tabloid names of Breslin and Hamill more than I did those of Reston and Apple. Still, I knew that when my father lugged home the *Times* on Sundays, he was carrying the official record of the previous week's events. I also knew that to land a clerk's job at the *Times* was akin to being admitted into an elite private club. Beyond collecting a salary that paid more than a starting reporter's job at most newspapers—and more than what my father was earning a year—a clerk at the *Times* could learn the newspaper craft from its masters and perhaps be hired as a *Times* reporter someday. It was the journalistic equivalent to being a stable boy for the Knights of the Round Table.

But the woman who oversaw the clerk program at the *Times*, this Miss Cummings, was a famously proper woman. As I understood it, her main mission was to cull from the hordes of applicants anyone—anyone!—who might someday bring the rosy hue of embarrassment to the Gray Lady's pallid cheeks. My mission, then, was to mask my rabble essence: to turn the facts that I had not gone to Dartmouth, that I was not the scion of some corporate lawyer, to my advantage. My only chance, I thought, was to win her over with my working-class charm and easy command of the language. I had to present myself as someone who might be a little rough around the edges but could still toss out the word *hyperborean* in describing the bitter upstate winters at St. Bonaventure.

I fantasized for a while about using the word *hyperborean* in the interview before coming to my senses. Using *hyperborean* was not enough; I need to sift through my modest experiences since college, and figure out what—and what not—to mention.

The train doors closed at Jamaica station in Queens. New York, Penn Station, the conductor called out. Penn Station. Next and final stop.

My deadline, a ten o'clock appointment, was approaching. Think, Dan, think. What have you been doing these last three years?

FIVE MONTHS AFTER leaving St. Bonaventure with a degree, I was back again, ensconced in Allegany because a weekend visit with Mary had turned into an eight-week sabbatical. In exchange for occasionally proofreading her class assignments, I ate her food, slept in her bed, and borrowed her money.

One snowy night, while Mary studied for final exams, I sat down at the bar counter of an all-but-deserted Club 17 to have a couple of beers with one of the many people in my world named Sullivan. This Sully was graduating in a couple of weeks. Midway through the second Genesee, he asked me a rather forward question.

So, he said. What are you going to do?

Sully was not asking whether I wanted another beer; he was asking what I planned to do with my life. Give me a break, I thought. I'm only twenty-two. Then, slowly, I felt the weight of my years. By the time he was twenty-two, my father had served two years of a three-year army hitch, and was living in Japan. By twenty-two, my orphaned, immigrant mother had married, bought a house, and given birth twice. And here I was, nearly twenty-three and with no answer to the obvious question: What do you do? Staring into the bar mirror, I saw a faintly familiar young man—Noreen and Gene's son—with an unkempt beard, a beer bottle that came too easily to his lips, and no answer for even that softball of a follow-up question: What do you want to do?

I don't know, I said to the mirror.

I know what I'm doing, he said. The day after Christmas I'm driving to Denver to work at the big livestock show they have there every year. Gonna gas up my Vega and hit the road.

Good for you, I said, and I meant it.

We sat for a while in the bar's churchlike quiet, two supplicants deep in prayer. Through the large storefront window we could see the snow falling, floating, really, in that light and aimless way that entices you to think about fate, and choices, and how good and warm the beer makes you feel, so much so that you want another.

Wanna go with me? Sully said finally.

I knew instantly that I would say yes. It was both frightening and enthralling to realize that I had no better offer than to drive two thousand miles to sling beans for a bunch of cattlemen. Yes, of course. Why not Denver! We sealed the deal by lightly clinking together our brown Genesee bottles, a kiss between men.

I didn't see much of Denver, really. For twelve hours a day, I stood guard over a steam table, making sure that no rancher or cattle hand ever wanted for beans and scrambled eggs. Then, exhausted, I retreated to a foldout bed in the basement of a house owned by a friend-of-a-friend's parents, where in the late-night darkness I tried to divine a future that did not include shovels or buffet tables. I knew that with the stock show almost over and the job market poor, Sully had decided to apply to graduate school. So had Mary. What the hell, I finally decided. I dashed off a request for an application to New York University's master's program in journalism, and reached for my bean-spattered apron.

The Journalism Department at NYU gave me a kind of poor boy's graduate-assistant position that paid for my tuition and provided me with a small stipend. I moved in with four Providence College graduates, including two of my classmates from St. Anthony's, in a railroad-style apartment on Henry Street in south Brooklyn, where the tight quarters and the infantry of cockroaches gave me a faux sense of my father's Depression-era experiences. We upended a ping-pong table and hung a blanket to transform half the living room into my unventilated bedroom. At night the boisterous conversations from the Italian social club directly below my room wafted through a large hole in the floor, along with clouds of cigarette smoke that satisfied any homesickness I had for Deer Park.

At NYU, I took a second shot at trying to write coherently on deadline, only this time my attempts sparked a love for daily journalism that I did not have at St. Bonaventure. I found myself craving the rush of adrenaline that came with trying to write a clear yet surprising lead, and then following it with a narrative that would hold the reader's interest through to the kicker of a conclusion—all while dutifully ringing those six bells: who, what, when, where, why, and how. Not only could I still go after bullies in this medium, I realized, I might actually be able to earn a living by telling stories. Imagine: getting paid to tell stories.

In newspapers, though, the crush of failed expectations is as much a part of one's apprenticeship as learning to type. It gives you a sense of the heartbreak that awaits you in the days ahead, when you will forever interpret the placement of your story—on the front page or buried near the classified ads—as a reflection of your worth in the eyes of God and humankind. In that sense, my apprenticeship prepared me for a future in newspapers.

It began well enough when I landed an internship at the *Daily News*, the newspaper that had dictated the order of my childhood mornings. On Sundays, my mother would turn to the crossword puzzle in the newspaper's magazine and then gradually fade from our presence, clouded in smoke and deep in concentration. My father would assert his privilege as family patriarch by being the first to read the comics, because life was hard enough without diving immediately into the reports of daily misery. Best to see what Moon Mullins was up to, or better yet, Smokey Stover, whose nonsense phrases like "Notary Sojac" had become part of the Barry family lexicon. Brian and I would grapple for the main section, which was read from back to front, from the sports section to last night's murder, for what else mattered if Bobby Murcer had failed again to be our generation's Mickey Mantle, if he had not been able to will the Yankees beyond mediocrity?

Now I was parading twice a week into the *Daily News*'s Art Deco building on East 42nd Street with an outsized sense of purpose: ignoring the huge globe in the lobby (that was for tourists), saluting the security guard, holding the requisite cup of jo in my hand. Jo: Isn't that what newspaper people call their coffee? It didn't matter that I actually had tea in that cup; I was working, sort of, at the *Daily News*. When the Son of Sam wanted to taunt a city, he didn't write to the *Times*; he wrote to Breslin, care of the *News*.

My hustling stride slowed to a gawking amble once I reached the newsroom, where reporters and editors, copy clerks and photographers, hurried about in a caffeine-fueled frenzy, as though the borough of Queens had just been reported missing—again. But no one ever shouted, Hey kid! Get yer ass over to the East River. We got a floater! No one even looked up. So I kept on walking, dawdling really, until I reached a hushed sanctuary in the corner of the newsroom: the food-and-living section, my internship assignment. Me, who grew up on Pasta Barry—macaroni-and-cheese-with-chopped-up-hot-dogs—now working in the food-and-living section.

My first assignment was to write a story about getting in shape for the approaching ski season. My knowledge of skiing was limited to one day in Denver, when I had upended my instructor and then slid on my ass down the bunny hill, never to return. And all I knew about the person I had been assigned to interview, the professional skier Suzy Chafee, was that her endless endorsement of a lip balm had earned her the nickname "Suzy Chapstick." Still, I was determined to write the definitive story on this important subject by interviewing Suzy Chapstick as though she were imparting wisdom for the ages.

What you're saying, Ms. Chafee, is that if I repeatedly hop over an ordinary kitchen chair, I can build up the leg muscles that will power me on the slopes come winter? Fascinating.

My debut in a major New York newspaper embarrassed me. There was nothing about a "limbering up for the slopes" story that was hard-boiled, or edgy, or, quite frankly, particularly relevant to anybody I knew. The housewives back on West 23rd Street, for example, were not suddenly hopping over kitchen chairs between drags from their cigarettes.

But there was more at play than just my inflated sense of self-worth.

My mother distributed Xerox copies of the article at work, out of pride and in defiance; it was her way of thrusting a fist at any boss who might dismiss her as just another mousy clerk. My father went one step further. He had the Suzy Chafee article mounted on a plaque that would hang in a place of honor, just above the clothes dryer, for years to come.

Over the next few months, I wrote feature stories for the *Daily News* about the wonders of champagne, the dangers of overeating at Thanksgiving, and the proper way to behave in Irish bars on St. Patrick's Day, as if I had a clue about any of these subjects. The publication of these stories convinced me that I had proved my mettle—that I was ready to tackle some down-and-dirty deadline reporting—so I applied to take a writing test for the Associated Press, the world's dominant wire-service news agency, at its majestic headquarters at 50 Rockefeller Center.

Some world-weary editor, impatient with my exuberance the moment he shook my hand, led me through the newsroom to a typewriter whose battered keys suggested that AP reporters banged out their stories with ball peen hammers. He handed me a printed test containing some garbled notes that he said represented the hastily gathered facts of several news events, including a fire at a schoolhouse, a college football game, and the dramatic rescue of a boy stuck in quicksand. My challenge, he explained, was to use the information to write clear and concise news stories on deadline. He informed me that I should complete the test as quickly as possible, and then he returned to the AP hubbub.

I fed a piece of paper into the typewriter and studied the notes for the fictional fire. In the town of Mount Vernon; some injuries, but not clear how many or how serious; occurred at 11:45 A.M., just as the students were preparing to go home for lunch; at the Pennington School on Central Parkway; the alarm sounded and children and teachers filed out. There were also snippets of quotes from school and fire officials.

I tried typing a lead to the story, but my paper looked like a journalistic crime scene. Infinitives lay split and dead on the page, alongside panting, tortured adverbs. Beneath this carnage I had also managed to bury the critical fact that some people had been injured in the fire. What's more, some of the keys of my tired typewriter kept sticking. Feeling the pressure of time, I set aside the fire story and reached for the notes about the imaginary football game between Oklahoma and the heavily favored Kansas.

My father had always taught me to hate football—a blood sport for idiots, he called it—and now I was paying for it. I didn't know a tight end from a loose end. I yanked my half-hearted Dick Young impersonation out of the typewriter and reached for another piece of virgin paper to defile. Now where were those notes about the rescue?

Two boys named Mark and Jeremy, accompanied by a dog named Ginny, were hiking along the Tallapoosa River in Wetumpka, Alabama. Mark fell into quicksand and could not get out. Ginny then led Jeremy—who, by the way, was Mark's uncle as well as his playmate—along the river to his grandfather's house. The grandfather followed Jeremy and Ginger back to the scene of the accident and dug Mark out just in time. Ginny had saved the day!

And Mark, the notes added, "was not harmed by the ordeal."

But I was. Just like that, I was Danny Barry again, failing in the "pressure to succeed" category of life. An hour into my deadline assignment and all I had to show for it was a wastebasket full of crumpled-up paper carnations—a floral arrangement commemorating the demise of my career. Everywhere I looked, men and women were reporting the events of the day against a succession of deadlines, and here I was, choking on make-believe. I was a professional fraud.

I reached for one last piece of paper, having decided to sum up the day's news in one story rather than three. What I wrote might have been a bit too concise for the editors of the AP, but it got to the truth quickly and was finished well within my imaginary deadline. I shrugged into my jacket and headed for the exit, leaving my story to dangle like a white flag of surrender from the typewriter's hold. All it said was:

I don't feel well. I'm sorry. Thank you.

———

THE TRAIN DOORS opened with a hush at Penn Station, and the people of Long Island began trudging up metal stairs to join the rush of Gotham. Marching in step with all the rest, I felt a rare spike of self-confidence in my ability to wow this Miss Cummings of *The New York Times*. My meltdown at the Associated Press would go unmentioned, of course, as would the ditch-digging, the drinking, the lounging about in Allegany, and the bean-slinging in Denver. There were plenty of other accomplishments to cite: the body of work at the *Daily News*, including my interview with that world-famous celebrity, Suzy Chapstick; the hard-nosed investigations of student government at a university in "hyperborean" Upstate New York; the honor of placing second in the prestigious Mark Hellinger Award for outstanding student journalist at that same university. Oh, and don't forget that humor piece—an extended letter, really, about commuting—that was published in the Long Island section of the *Times*.

As I strolled up Eighth Avenue toward the *Times* building on West 43rd Street, I tried to come up with a few ice-breaking comments to store in my arsenal. Maybe I would compliment her on the lovely _____ she was wearing—brooch, necklace, whatever. Maybe I would make admiring reference to "that smart piece by Apple in today's editions." Maintain eye contact, I told myself. And relax. What's the worst that could happen?

I saw him coming, but there was nothing I could do. He had emerged from one of the darkened storefronts between 40th and 41st streets, about three blocks from my destination, and now this glass-eyed stranger was weaving toward me, a paper bag strangled in his meaty fist. All I wanted to do was get past him, but he mirrored my every step, as though the two of us were on the deck of the same heaving ship. I went left, he went right; I went right, he went left. Then, just when I thought I had successfully dodged him, my dance partner executed a pirouette that concluded with the smack of his paper bag against my chest. The resulting cascade of malt liquor brought a wet sheen to my father's blue blazer.

The revolving doors at the front of the building at 229 West 43rd Street spun like hamster wheels turned on their sides, hurrying people in and out in reinforcement of the message that *The New York Times* is an important place with no tolerance for nonsense. Glancing up, a bystander on this day would have seen a clock that gave the official time as determined by the *Times*, as well as a row of orb-shaped light fixtures, each one inscribed with a single word: *Times*. Glancing down and just a bit to the left of the revolving doors, a bystander would have also seen this: a young man in shirtsleeves, snapping his blue blazer like a matador's cape.

And then there I was, reeking of Colt .45 cologne while sitting across from this crisp woman of no-nonsense propriety, this Miss Cummings, whose every word and gesture—from saying good morning to reaching for a pen—signaled that she had my number, mister. Clearly, I was the kind of wastrel who would violate the sanctity of the *Times* chapel by beginning the morning with a pick-me-up at the Blarney Stone.

I did not mention Suzy Chapstick; I did not utter the word *hyperborean*. I just sat there in my father's beer-soaked blazer, watching her lips move and hearing only a stray phrase or two—including one particular question: How many languages do you speak? I took this to mean that dozens of multilingual Dartmouth graduates were interested in the position that I had dared to inquire about. Dozens who, by the way, could keep sober until at least déjeuner.

Soon we were saying good-bye. I slinked out of the *Times* newsroom, leaving an impression that surely lasted no longer than my vaporous trail.

Au revoir, Gray Lady. *Au revoir*.

13

I NK. THE BUILDING smelled of ink, spilled and bled. It was a tart and chemical smell, the kind that weaves into the fabric of your clothes and then under your skin, the kind that comes home with you, sits with you at the dinner table, tells you constantly what it is you do. Car mechanics know their smell, as do fishermen and hair stylists, nurses and short-order cooks. You may consider yourself to be first a parent, a lover, or a child of God, but your scent says otherwise. You are a man who chases halibut, a woman who perms hair. You smell of it.

I waded into that invisible veil of ink, inhaled it deeply, allowed it to wash over me. It smelled of words and phrases, rants and ideas, sports scores and felony arrests, announcements of marriage and notices of death. Maybe the chemical-like aroma was inducing hallucination, but I doubted it. In a squat concrete building, no different from all the others in a drab Connecticut industrial park, I was experiencing a moment of revelation—an epiphany, really, at the age of twenty-five.

This is what I do. Baptize me in ink. Praise the Lord.

Pinned like a manifesto to a bulletin board in the center of this ink-perfumed building was a typewritten note from my new employer, announcing that on this day, October 17, 1983, I would begin working as a reporter for a daily newspaper. The note formalized my calling in life with a splash of perspective that would stay with me forever:

Dan is a former intern at the Daily News *in New York and a graduate assistant for the journalism department at New York University. His writing has appeared in the* Daily News, *the* New York Times *and the* Rocky Mountain News. *Soon it will appear in trashcans throughout north-central Connecticut. Please make him feel relevant.*

Reading the note, I thought, I'm home.

FINDING MY WAY had not been easy. The internship at the *Daily News* had ended, the graduate degree from NYU had been shoved in a drawer, and I had returned to living beside the sump pump in my parents' basement. I spent my days splitting sod for Ace Lawn Sprinkling alongside Eddie, who had taken to calling me "Professor," and my nights typing out professional love letters to the *New London Day*, the *Asbury Park Press*, the *Poughkeepsie Journal*, the *Stamford Advocate*, the *Anywhere Clarion-Bugle-Star-Record-Sentinel*, and every other Northeast newspaper that I had never read. Round and round I spun in a journalistic Catch-22: the newspapers wanted reporters with experience, but young reporters cannot get experience if newspapers hire only reporters with experience.

Late in the summer of 1983, I came home from digging ditches to find a rare positive response to my mass mailing. Chris Powell, the managing editor of the *Journal Inquirer* in Manchester, Connecticut—where?—did not have any openings at present, but if I was ever in the area, please stop by. I called Powell the next day.

What a coincidence! It just so happened that I was planning to be in the Manchester area in the next week or so. Uuh, where is Manchester again? About ten miles from Hartford?

Powell met me at the receptionist's desk. He was a short, boyish man in his mid-thirties, with several pens in his shirt pocket and a kind of amused frown on his face that suggested a worldview of what will they think of next. He led me past a small newsroom where mounds of old newspapers and overstuffed folders sprouted from every desk. Now and then a reporter would pop up from behind the hills of paper, like a gopher sniffing at the wind, but most of them stayed burrowed, coaxing information from the phones pressed to their ears. The smell of ink wet the air, and distant presses hummed with news.

As I followed my host, I heard a faint, persistent jingling noise, as if I were being tailed by an elf. I didn't find its source until I almost stepped on it: a black dust mop of a Scottish terrier that had joined Powell in escorting me to his office.

Powell sat down behind a desk in a cramped office, and the dog hopped onto his lap. This is Terry, he said, as the dog and I sized each other up. Now. Tell me about yourself.

The decorations in his office, particularly the framed photograph of the Three Stooges, told me that this Chris Powell was—different. A newspaper portrait of Adolf Hitler from 1940. The last front page of the old *Hartford Times*. Several awards for editorial writing, and a couple for softball. A framed quote from *Henry VI* ("The first thing we do, let's kill all the lawyers"). I would come to learn of Powell's editorial gifts, his sharpness at puncturing the pompous, his gift for inappropriate comments, his biases and peeves (He maintained, for example, that accusers in rape trials should be identified, to preserve due process and to dispel the false shame that rape victims often feel). The *Journal Inquirer* was pretty much all he had ever known. He had joined the newspaper as a punk newsboy when it first started publishing in the late '60s, and, instead of graduating from college, had worked his way up to become the gadfly of Connecticut. He was keenly intelligent, thoroughly antisocial, and chronically skeptical; he was the quintessential newspaper editor.

But on this day, all that I knew about Chris Powell was that he had a photograph of Moe, Larry, and Curly on the wall, a dog named Terry in his lap, and a work environment that reeked of ink. I told him everything I could summon that was even remotely flattering about myself, and begged him to call me the moment a job opened up. He promised that he would, but left me with the clear impression that he would first have to talk it over with Terry.

A few weeks later, in the fall of 1983, the *Journal Inquirer* of Manchester, Connecticut, offered me a job as a reporter, at a beginner's salary of $262 a week—or $13,624 a year, which was about $5,000 more than I was making as a ditch digger. I accepted.

I said good-bye to my colleagues at Ace Lawn Sprinkling. In a few weeks the ground would freeze, and picks and shovels striking the fist-tight earth would send sparks shooting like miniature flares to announce the futility of it all. Eddie would soon be warming himself with flasks of peppermint schnapps in the back of an unheated van, waiting for that fast-approaching day, sometime around Thanksgiving, when the boss would tell him and the other laborers to have a nice winter, see you sometime in March.

We went to a Deer Park bar called the Kozy Kabin, shot some pool, drank some beer.

Take care, I said. I'll see you around.

Yeah, said Eddie, with those shining eyes that would never see me again.

I borrowed Mary's 1971 green Dart. I made arrangements to sleep on a college friend's couch in Enfield, about twenty miles from Manchester, until I found a place of my own. And, once again, I prepared to move out of the house at 140 West 23rd Street, from which north-central Connecticut might as well have been the Wicklow Mountains. Even though I had spent most of the last several years living away from home—in Upstate New York, Denver, and Brooklyn—we all knew that this was it. Danny has a purpose now; it's taking him a good three hours' drive from here. Far, far away.

My mother fixed my favorite, Swedish meatballs on a bed of egg noodles, for my last meal, but my father did not join us. The headaches had him up in bedroom darkness again, begging the Mother of God to intervene. I went up to say good-bye. He held up one hand to shield the invasion of light slanting past the door, and stuck the other one in the direction of my shadow.

Good luck, son.

I reached for his hand. In bed and in pain, he still responded with a firm Barry handshake, because there is nothing worse, son, than a dead fish of a handshake. A firm handshake is a measure of men; shake their hand and look them squarely in the eye. And that is what we did.

Take care of yourself, Dad.

I teased my mother once more about her brogue: say "Port Authority" once more; say "butter." She called me a brat, demanded that I call when I got to wherever I was going—What's the name of this place again?— and gave me a final hug. Pulling away from my childhood home, I could see her standing at the gate. Noreen Barry in the Long Island gloaming. She would stay there, too, watching until my taillights disappeared like cardinals in flight.

FROM MY DESK along the far wall, I could see it all. The huge presses at the back of the building began their hum and rattle by late morning, providing a lullaby for the sportswriter who dozed off the night's late scores and late beers in the men's room. Then, just about 11:30, an ink smudge of a man emerged from the pressroom with copies of that day's first edition, warm as bread just out of the oven.

His first stop, of course, was the glass-encased office of the publisher, Elizabeth Ellis, tall, immaculately appointed, and with hair the color of flint. She had lost one of her three children, a son, to leukemia years earlier, and now this newspaper was her baby. On her wall hung a sign: "A good editor has no friends."

After the publisher's office, then Powell's office, and then the ink smudge trudged on to the library: the morgue. Here, a row of filing cabinets contained thousands of clipped newspaper articles, all of them kept in neat manila folders, ready to be yanked on deadline for instant context—and instant errors. If, years earlier, a reporter mistakenly gave the dog warden of the town of East Windsor the middle initial of *A*, the error might be repeated in every future story that mentioned the man, including his obituary. For the most part, though, these cabinets offered an accurate recent history of north-central Connecticut, as recorded by *Journal Inquirer* reporters come and gone. Reading the old clips, fragile to the touch, you could almost hear the words that had been said, see what had been seen: the shouts at public hearings, the flames consuming wood-frame tenements, the crackle of police radios at a domestic turned fatal. The contents of these filing cabinets sang of life's inevitabilities, the distressing and the reassuring. Children will drown in backyard pools and children will be rescued from lakes, again and again.

Then the ink smudge headed toward the epicenter of it all: the newsroom, a place of finger taps and beeps and whispers and occasional hilarity, as when a sheriff waving a subpoena chased a reporter around the desks and out the door. In the corner, the sports reporters, bleary-eyed from taking dictation over the phone about every high school basketball game in the region, every cross-country match, every swim meet. Along the wall, the maps: from the deserts and oceans of the world to the hills and ponds of Enfield and Vernon. Close by, the Associated Press's Wirephoto machine, serving as the newsroom's television, slowly grinding out images of the day, moment by moment, sometimes while reporters and editors gathered around it, mesmerized, unable to turn away. As when the state treasurer of Pennsylvania held his last press conference, and the photographs stuttered into view, one after another: he reaches into an envelope; he places a gun into his mouth; his eyes egg, his hair flies up; he crumples.

Then the gaggle of editors, their legs nervously bouncing and jouncing as they raced against a twenty-minute deadline to read five stories of 500 words, 800 words, 1000. They had to make sure that the stories made sense, were newsworthy, and avoided libel. An inaccurate characterization of a certain town councilman slips by, and the newspaper could wind up being called *Harold Bissonette's Journal Inquirer*.

Finally, the reporters, twenty or so of them, sipping cold coffee from cups that said "Whole Donut," jazzed that they were informing forty-five thousand readers but fretting that they had failed, yet again, to summon the muse of Dylan Thomas in their stories about zoning boards and school budgets. When the ink smudge walked past with his armful of warm and fresh newspapers, they could smell that smell, of words and photographs, news and opinion. They had written their stories only an hour earlier, and knew how and where it would appear in that day's edition, but they still needed to see it for the rush of having captured a moment, however imperfectly, in print.

Hey, can I get one of those? they'd ask. And the ink smudge would oblige, like some trainer in a locker room, knowing exactly how to ease his players' pain. Here you go.

And there it would be, in that day's *Journal Inquirer*.

"Planners Approve Smaller Mobile Home Park." Bam.

"School Officials Resistant to Manager's Budget Cut." Bam.

"Seven Arrested in Drug Raids." Bam.

So it was written. So it was.

THIS WAS THE other Connecticut, a world's remove from Darien and Greenwich. This was East Windsor. South Windsor. Stafford Springs. The Talcottville section of Vernon. The Scitico section of Enfield. Bolton. Meandering along secondary roads in Mary's old Dodge, I could see the awkward juxtaposition of past and present. Fields of strawberries beside subdivisions straining to consume any open space in view. Two-family houses deflating along a riverbank, rows of them, their foundations warped and green with moss. Ghostly mansions gaping from a hillside, with ionic columns and front porches in desperate need of repair. And then the sorrowful explanation for why these mansions and row houses had come to be: a brick dinosaur of a mill, two, three, four stories high, its broken-glass windows jagged in the fleeting sweep of headlights.

None of this was anything like the post-war landscape of my childhood, where the Kozy Kabin bar was considered a Deer Park landmark, and people reminisced about the 7-Eleven that used to be on Grand

Boulevard. I was so enchanted by my new surroundings that I began to see a potential news story at every turn in the road, in every old man's face. Powell eased my hyperactive mind by finally assigning me to a specific beat: the town of Vernon, including the strange nucleus at the center of this bedroom community, the tiny former city of Rockville.

Rockville was once an industrial and cultural anchor for the region, with massive woolen mills energized by the Hockanum River, which cascaded through the city center. It was a city that supported two opera houses, a city deemed worthy of visits by the likes of the real Tom Thumb. But the demand for wool gradually declined. By the mid-twentieth century, most of Rockville's mills had shut down, leaving the tiny city to gasp along the Hockanum shores. Every year the town council sounded the call to revitalize Rockville, and every year Rockville seemed to lose a breath's more vitality, as if any public confirmation of the city's dire condition would only hasten its demise.

Still, I found Rockville magical.

Liquid bouquets of pink and white suds sometimes gushed from the sewer grates, a kind of accidental performance art provided by a dyeing manufacturer whose cleaning agents had found their way into the river. Now and then one of the local businesses, an edible-panty manufacturer, sent a strawberry-coconut aroma wafting across the tired town green. Thinking that the business might make for an interesting feature, I knocked on its door and posed a question that I would ask only once in my lifetime: Do you make edible panties here? While the owner considered the question, I considered the erotic potential of the sacks of flour and sugar behind him. These considerations were brief, though, and the slam of his door enveloped me in a whoosh of fruity fragrance that stayed with me longer than it should have.

Edible panties and cotton-candy effluence were the least of it. Rockville had character, and characters: From the lady who caused traffic snarls every afternoon by leading a parade of ducks and geese across a busy roadway to the firefighters from different volunteer departments who brawled in the glow of houses ablaze.

But it was in Town Hall—built in the late 1800s as a Civil War memorial—that I found the latent insanity of everyday life, the wisps and strands of chaos that, when knotted together, form what is known as local government. I sensed this nearly every afternoon as I walked through the dark-wood portal to see the rotund receptionist, squeezed into a booth and surrounded by certain essentials: a large bottle of soda, a bag of chips, a smutty paperback, a telephone. Every few minutes she answered a buzz on the switchboard with a protracted exhale of a greeting that suggested the gradual crushing of a heart: Town-n-n Hal-l-l-l.

Upstairs reigned Marie Antoinette Herbst. Years earlier, she had had the temerity to challenge a good-old-boy incumbent who girded to teach this pushy grade-school teacher the electoral lesson of her life. And he would have—oh he would have—had he not driven away after hitting a parked car, inside of which was a civic-minded teenage girl who recognized Hizzoner's sedan. Word of a police report eventually leaked out, as it often does in the land of the *Journal Inquirer*, and one day the newspaper received a copy of the girl's statement in the mail. No name on the envelope, no return address.

Now Mrs. Herbst was Mayor Herbst, an elected official whom Powell once described as "conscientious to the point of being annoying." And now a welcome part of my day was receiving a morning call from Her Honor—a verbal tip sheet that always began: Dan? Marie. Did you hear that so-and-so has a conflict of interest on that matter before the zoning board? That what's-his-face, you know who I mean, missed another subcommittee meeting last night? That . . . That . . . That . . .

Yes, Rockville had it all. The fussy town clerk, with leather visor and musty ledgers, who did not see how any computer could improve upon his meticulous way of doing things. The town secretary who in middle age had bought her first house but who was too busy working three jobs to spend much time in it. The town official who aspired to manage the affairs of larger, more prestigious municipalities—New Britain, perhaps, or even Danbury—but saw no chance, and so drank.

And the earnest young reporter, with a beard that made him look unkempt, not older, and a desire to write about the town of Vernon as though it were the city of New York. That is why, every day, he dialed the same telephone number, disrupting a large woman's paperback reverie. And that is why he gladdened to hear that groaning voice of democracy.

Town-n-n Ha-a-a-lll.

FOUR HUNDRED MILES separated Mary Trinity and me; four hundred miles that might as well have been four thousand. She was living in a small apartment beside the railroad tracks that skirted St. Bonaventure, where she was earning about a dollar an hour as the social action coordinator for the campus ministry. Her charge was to encourage students to put into practice the Franciscan ideals they were being taught, to reach out to the rural poor of the Southern Tier who lived just beyond the comfortable confines of the campus. Every day she drove a station wagon jammed with students to open the Warming House, a soup kitchen and gathering place in downtown Olean. There, especially in winter, she would find the regulars—Young Darrell and Old Grace, Kenny Who Liked Pancakes and Mary Who Smoked a Pipe, Big Joe and Little Joe and Harmonica Joe—already gathered at the door, hunched in old coats against the eye-tearing cold, creating a Reagan-era portrait of poverty worthy of Dorothea Lange. Some were just flat poor, captives in a remote little city whose flush days had passed; others were slightly retarded, or alcoholic, or emotionally scarred from childhoods spent in the surrounding hollows. Some were children. They came for the tomato soup, of course, and for the weak coffee. But they also came to be comforted by the friendly Bona's student with long blond hair who had graduated and then come back to listen to their stories, give them rides to clinics, help them with their City Hall battles, hug their children.

Mary and I ran up our telephone bills by talking nearly every night, and tried to visit each other every month or so. But we struggled to close another gap that went beyond geography, the gap between reporting on life and living it. I was immersed in the land of the *Journal Inquirer*, and Mary was not. She lived beyond my circulation area.

I once enticed Mary to drive eight hours and spend the weekend in Manchester, in part by promising to treat her to a lavish dinner of fresh New England seafood. She arrived at the *Journal Inquirer* on a Friday evening, weary from the journey but excited to see me. Some of the reporters were going for a quick beer, though, at a bar that just happened to be almost directly below my apartment. Mary gamely agreed to go for one. Several hours later, she gently interrupted one of my stories about Rockville arcana—And then the secretary of the Democratic Town Committee says . . .—to remind me about our dinner plans. Seafood, remember? I reached across the bar counter and presented her with a snack bowl of Pepperidge Farm Goldfish. The boys and girls of the *Journal Inquirer* laughed and laughed.

It was not quite a matter of loving my job more than I loved Mary; it was that I had become my job. It gave me purpose, allowed me to buy food and pay taxes and split the rent with my college friend Bear for that apartment next to the bar. More important than any of these, I finally had a socially acceptable answer to that inevitable question.

What do I do? Well, I'm a reporter—for the *Journal Inquirer*.

The mere mention of the *Journal Inquirer* offended some people, particularly those who thought that a newspaper's purpose was to publish photographs of self-important boosters handing plaques of appreciation to one another. They called it the "Urinal Inquirer" because it was a tabloid, because it occasionally ran graphic photographs of car accidents, because Powell's editorial positions—that the names of women alleging rape should be published, for example—brought them to apoplexy. They blustered about the state's journalistic Goliath, the *Hartford Courant*; now *that* is a newspaper, they'd say. Of course, at the *Journal Inquirer*, the David of Connecticut, the *Courant* was both envied for its resources and disparaged for its pomposity. If a *Journal Inquirer* reporter or editor accepted a job at the *Courant*, as many did, Powell considered the act to be treasonous. Clean out your desk and get out, but don't you dare take any files; they're the property of the *Journal Inquirer*. You may have once played third base for the *Journal Inquirer* softball team; you may have given seven years of your young adulthood to this newspaper; you may have even met your spouse here. But as far as Chris Powell was concerned, if you left for the *Courant*, you never existed.

As absurd as this attitude was, I ate it up. I loved the *Journal Inquirer's* bulldog reputation, its outsider status, the oddball ways in which it promoted itself. It even paid for radio promotions to be recorded by Orson Welles (who was renting out his vocal talents to the highest bidder), then continued to run those ads after he died, supposedly in tribute of the late, great actor. I would be driving down some back road to yet another meeting of the Vernon Zoning Board of Appeal when suddenly the sonorous, God-like voice of a dead man would sound through my car radio to plug a newspaper, my newspaper: "*The Journal Inquirer* tells it like it is. Somebody has to."

But my all-consuming crusade—to tell it like it is—seemed to lessen in importance with every one of the four hundred miles that separated Mary and me. The antics of the town council, the pitched battle over a proposal to build a Super Stop & Shop on Route 30, the ups and downs in the hothouse environment of the *Journal Inquirer* newsroom—none of this translated very well over a telephone line, particularly to someone who was quietly immersed in trying to address this poor kid's case of lice or that old man's need of a winter coat. After a while, the prospect of spending sixteen hours in a car in three days—Manchester to Olean, Olean to Manchester—lost its romantic appeal. There were better ways, it seemed, to spend my time, including with a wonderful young woman named Nancy, who worked at the *Journal Inquirer* and whose parents had come from Ireland.

Mary and I broke up finally, by phone. I was scared. For the last five years of my life, she had been my one source of strength, understanding my anxieties, my family—me. I mewled about remaining friends, even— you never know—being lovers again sometime. But Mary said she didn't think that was such a good idea.

Why not? I demanded, in late-night telephone calls of word staccatos and dead air. I sat on the edge of my bed, eyes closed and cheeks wet, and the phone line stretched taut as a high wire.

How can you rule it out? How do you know what might happen in the future? Isn't anything possible?

Mary?

Mary?

Mary? You still there?

Yes, Dan. I'm still here.

14

A S A NEWSPAPER reporter, I could fill my gaps with the written word. I could filibuster in ink; I could shed myself. All I had to do was dial the telephone, mutter an incantation or two—Good morning, chief. Anything going on?— and bam I became someone else: historian of the day, avenger of the wronged, political analyst, sleuth. Complete transformation, though, did not occur until I was staring into the winter sea of my computer screen, dropping letters like stones into its vastness. Hours vanished like deleted words.

I wrote news stories by the hundreds, as many as four a day. I wrote about budget shortfalls, per-pupil costs, and bond referenda; child abuse, drug dealers, and the murders of several gay men; public corruption, old-boy networks, and prison breaks. About the Catholic cult created by a delicatessen clerk who convinced people that he was the twin of Christ. About what it was like in the American Legion bingo hall in Manchester, when a man named Pinky called out "O-66" and all the women smiled wicked smiles and rang tiny bells. Stories, stories, stories, just tell me a story, and my little net of hasty words just might snare a butterfly moment before it darts away forever. Late one afternoon, a salesman came to the quiet newsroom with a contraption that made absurdly large soap bubbles. I called for a photographer and wrote a story.

There I was, at the bar of the old and gasping Polish National Home in Enfield, talking to the regulars about what it was like back then, when you'd finish your shift at the Bigelow-Sanford carpet mill and stop for a Cremo beer and a pickled egg, and maybe later head upstairs to bowl a string, or join the polka dancers whirling like pinwheels about the auditorium. All that was gone now, the mill nothing but a block-long brick shell, the auditorium dark, the duckpins and balls kept in a wooden box. Except there was still this old Polish social club, with old men swallowed up in windbreakers and drinking from short glasses, and a back room with stacks of unused stationery dated "192-," just waiting for someone to fill in that last digit.

There I was, at a convention of the Invisible Empire of the Ku Klux Klan, who had been invited to East Windsor by a large landholder eager to make a point about property rights. I tucked my notebook inside the back of my shirt and wandered about the "sacred ground"—no cops or reporters allowed—to absorb the flea-market atmosphere: the "Klan Youth Corps" T-shirts, the fifteen-dollar Klan earrings, the one-dollar raffle for a handmade throw pillow embroidered with the empire's red-and-black insignia. I loitered long enough to see the Klan leader, cigar in mouth and torch in hand, light a kerosene-soaked wooden cross to honor Jesus Christ as the "light of the world."

There I was, being waved past the steel gates of the maximum-security prison in Somers to attend a meeting of the Pardon Us chapter of the Sons of the Desert, a Laurel and Hardy fan club. Perhaps to discourage frivolous media requests, prison officials chose a murderer to be my host. Steven Wood, a bearlike man with bags under his eyes that were the color of mortar, was known throughout Connecticut for his lurid homicidal acts. One day a couple of years earlier, he had gunned down his ex-wife and her boyfriend, drove to another location to kill his former mother-in-law and his young stepdaughter, then held the police at bay for several hours before surrendering.

Now he was my movie date.

As we were escorted to the projection room, Wood confided that there were few opportunities in prison to "let out a belly laugh," but that sometimes—while watching these old comedies—"I'll laugh until tears come down." We sat together and watched in silence, as other inmates in prison-issue brown filtered in. The lights dimmed, the guard at the door blended into the darkness, and a few couples cuddled together. Steven Wood kept his hands in his lap, though—a gentleman throughout.

The short feature for the evening was a 1931 Laurel and Hardy film called *Helpmates*. Hardy enlists Laurel to help clean up the aftermath of a wild party before his wife returns home. Soon the house is in worse condition than when they started, as pots and pans, dishes and bodies, go flying through the air.

Sitting there in the dark, beside the killer of four, I lost myself for a while in the ancient comic travails of Stan and Ollie. "Turn it up!" one of the inmates shouted, and I agreed: Turn it up.

I FOUND SANCTUARY in the newsroom. Often unable to think of anywhere else to go, I fled to its embrace, where the aroma of ink had displaced the smell of my mother's cooking as the scent of home. I became as much a newsroom fixture as the vending machine that excreted bad coffee into paper cups, and justified my omnipresence by reasoning that someone might call at any moment with a story. A murder, perhaps. That would be nice, a murder; it would mean that I could continue to set a few things aside for a while. Mary was weary of my never-say-never pleas, Nancy was weary of my surreptitious contact with Mary, and I was weary of being so wearisome.

Another Saturday afternoon and I was sitting again in the deserted newsroom, staring at the telephone. The *Journal Inquirer* did not have a Sunday edition so there was no need for anyone to be there, but I was, waiting for someone—anyone—to call. A friend, a crackpot, a politician; yes, I would even have talked to a politician, and gladly too. Without the diversion of a story, I was naked in my loneliness. I dialed Deer Park.

He was upstairs again, my mother said, using that family code for the wall bangs and cries loud enough to set the neighbors praying. Gene, with those migraines that would not submit to old reliable, the drink. And Noreen, with the music of her life a serenade of screams that followed her about the house—on the couch, by the stove, in the bed. This was no Irish love song she was hearing, more like the ceaseless groans of a broken bagpipe. Who could blame her for seeking the salve of the house?

Noreen was in a storytelling mood this day, I could tell.

Oh Danny, she began. Celeste Down the Street died last week.

Oh Mom, I said. I'm sorry.

Celeste Down the Street was one of the first neighborhood pioneers to go. Like so many others, on West 22nd and West 24th, in Lindenhurst, Amityville, and beyond, she had moved from the city with an eager young husband, raised some children, and fully expected to be a very old suburban matron one day, sitting in the kerosene-scented shade of her open garage, watching a sprinkler's water fall upon her eucalyptus, her maple, her property. You could see it in that we've-finally-made-it expression she flashes in the home movies my father stored deep on his closet's top shelf, next to the stack of old *Playboys*. There she is, pretty in youth, mugging and laughing in images that flickered across the living room wall we used for private screenings of the past. Celeste the mocking Rockette, rolling her shoulders and kicking her legs high above our baby hedges.

She had been among them, that city crowd new to the island and new to property, drinking Manhattans and running barefoot on grass. But in her last days, our Long Island Rockette could only sit in a wheelchair kept locked in place at her front door, where she gazed at paradise through a screen window's mesh.

The right thing, of course, would have been for the Barrys Up the Street to attend the wake. Although the families had not talked in years, there was still that bond among pioneers. But my father's headaches had prevented the Barrys from getting to the funeral home on either of the two nights, my mother explained. I could tell that she felt uneasy about this; the Irish go to wakes, period. I could tell too that she wanted absolution from her eldest.

We sent flowers that cost forty dollars, she said. Your father said they were six feet high. Don't you think we did right?

Plus, my mother said, she did leave work for a couple of hours to attend the funeral Mass at Sts. Cyril and Methodius, where she had not been since Elizabeth's Confirmation, nearly a decade earlier. She sat in the last pew and saw her widowed neighbor, a man she had never seen in a suit before, coming down the aisle behind the hearse and crying. Oh Danny, he was crying so hard.

But we did right, didn't we, Danny? With the flowers, I mean. And I did go to the Mass. Don't you think we did right?

Yes, Mom, you did right by them, I said. Don't worry. But promise me one thing.

What's that? she said, though she knew.

Take care of yourselves, please, I said in another family code. Please take care.

IT WAS ADVICE that I freely dispensed but routinely ignored. Sometimes I filled my gaps more with beer than with words, as I did at yet another wedding reception of yet another friend who had figured things out. I had stayed too long and drunk too much, and now I was wandering the late-night streets of Hartford's West End, trying to sober up so that I could devote full attention to self-pity. Bear, my roommate, had moved away. Nancy, my girlfriend, had broken up with me. Mary, my ex-girlfriend, was beginning to date other people. And every time I visited Deer Park in search of comfort—the phone calls were too painful—I left carrying the smoke of a hundred cigarettes in my clothes and hair, the breath of my parents, coughed out, moaned out, laughed out, sighed. So I had reason to be walking alone through my urban valley, appearing and vanishing in accordance with the streetlamps along Capitol Avenue. I was a ghostly young man, joining my father's quest for some peace. That's all I wanted, goddammit. Some peace.

Behind me, the hurried slap of shoes against pavement broke the midnight quiet and became louder and louder. No peace. I started to run but stopped when I realized that I would never reach my apartment door, just a few yards down Beacon Street. I turned toward two men whose faces were veiled by the night—true ghosts.

Give it up, one of them said, panting.

Fuck you, I said, and was knocked to the ground for my pluck.

Give it up, fuck you, give it up, fuck you, that was how our breathless dialogue went, like some operatic refrain, as they punched me and kicked me and rooted about for a wallet that contained about ten dollars. I fought back and even connected with one of my punches, feeling my knuckles go deep into someone's cheek. Never having hit anyone in the face before, I felt a brief rush of manly pride, until a fist from nowhere crunched against my eye to remind me that there were two attackers, not one. I was too angry and too drunk to consider that they might be armed. My attitude was, I'm lonely, I'm disconnected, I've got enough problems. So fuck you, fuck you, and fuck you. I could not give it up.

My screams may have scared them, or maybe they were just bored; my two assailants soon ran off without my money but with a good chunk of my dignity. My pants were torn, my face was bloodied, my eyes were swelling shut—another fine mess, as Oliver Hardy would say—and for what. Because I resented the interruption of my drunken self-pity?

When I returned to the *Journal Inquirer* two days later, my editor took one wincing look at my battered face and ordered me home. I was disrupting the newsroom, he said.

It was time to go, oh God was it time to go. Through half-closed eyes I looked about the newsroom and realized that many of my closest friends were gone, having moved on to other, larger newspapers. I was surrounded by recent college graduates who saw me as a throwback, an elder statesman—at twenty-nine. Here was Peter, the new reporter covering Enfield, and no way was he shaving yet. Here was Eileen, just assigned to cover the Manchester school board; I remembered when she was an intern. Here was Kara, the new Tolland reporter, and the way I tried to relate to her was to plumb our shared interest in Bugs Bunny cartoons. Monsters meet the most in-n-n-teresting people, I would say, and she would smile, as you might to placate a clueless older brother.

It was time to go. There were whispers of job openings at a newspaper in Providence, a place that a good friend of mine, another reporter named John Hill, called a "reporter's theme park." I sent my resume and a few clips. That was where I needed to be, I thought, in a place called Providence.

WITH MY APPLICATION to the *Providence Journal* pending and my face several weeks clear of fist marks, I walked into the *Journal Inquirer* newsroom one afternoon with the casual assuredness of a man returning to his living room. But Bob Boone, the tall and professorial news editor, was blocking the path to my desk, and he looked about ready to cry. He led me into Chris Powell's small office, the same office where— almost four years earlier to the day—Powell and his dog had convinced me that I was destined to work for a small newspaper in north-central Connecticut. Powell's head was bowed; he no longer looked so boyish. He did not look up when he finally began to speak.

Kara Laczynski, who loved Bugs Bunny and the New York Mets, had been murdered. Kara, who would rush to her desk in the morning, black hair still shimmering from a hurried shower, had been found that morning on the floor of her apartment. Kara, who would slam the telephone down whenever a town official refused to tell her what the hell was going on, had been strangled. Kara, who lived just a few blocks from me in Hartford's West End, who sat just ten feet from me in the newsroom, gone at twenty-four.

The three of us sat in the silence of shock for a while, with words that

we routinely, even cavalierly, tossed around in the course of a day—
murder, body, dead—now left unspoken. All those afternoons and nights
spent in the newsroom, waiting for the telephone to ring with a good
story—a good murder, as reporters like to say—so that I could find
diversion from my petty woes. After all, what is a stranger's death to a
reporter but material for a solemn yarn that explores, yet again, the
fragility of our existence? That allows us to cluck and memorialize and
find cheap context? Now the gods of journalism had granted my request.
Here you go, they had said—asshole. I could barely breathe.

Powell lifted his head and said with uncharacteristic softness that we
had to cover this family tragedy as a news story. Of course, I said. I'll go
now. I opened the door to find a newsroom in suspended animation. No
one answered the ringing telephones. Some reporters and editors sat at
their desks, not moving; a few others were frozen in shared hugs. I heard
someone weeping as I left the building, but I could already feel that professional numbness of emotion taking hold, steadying my quivering legs.

I edged my way through the crowd in front of Kara's apartment
building, using my notebook to protect me from the television crews
jockeying for position. When I identified myself as a reporter from the
Journal Inquirer, two detectives waved me under the cordon. Instead of
me questioning them, they questioned me. What kind of woman was
Kara? Did she have any boyfriends? Was she dating anyone at the *Journal Inquirer*? What kind of sex was she into? You can tell us. I could only
stammer that I really didn't know much about Kara's personal life; she
had been at the paper just seven months. I didn't think she was dating
anyone at the newspaper, but I could be wrong. She was just . . . a nice
person.

Then the detectives talked. Kara had been found naked and face down
in her tiny ransacked apartment. She apparently had been interrupted
while taking a bath. Her hands had been bound with leather straps cut
from two of her purses. The belt from her terrycloth bathrobe had been
wrapped tightly around her neck. A pair of scissors—with her name
written on a piece of paper and taped to one of the blades—had been

found about a foot from her head. That's pretty much all we know. I understand, I said, though I did not.

I rejoined the crowd on the cordon's other side, where I asked question after question of anyone who caught my eye. Finally, sometime near midnight, I realized that the only two people left were the police officer guarding the lobby and me. And all I was doing was staring at Kara's small gray car. It looked so out of place not parked in the *Journal Inquirer* lot.

I got to the newsroom at seven the next morning, flipped on my computer terminal, and began to type. A few reporters stopped by to offer encouragement; one of them brought me coffee. Then Boone was suddenly at my side, gently telling me that my time was up.

HARTFORD—Kara Laczynski, a Journal Inquirer reporter described by her editor as a "beautiful young woman with a beautiful future," apparently was strangled in her West End apartment between Sunday night and Monday morning, according to police.

With that, I became the lead reporter in the *Journal Inquirer's* investigation into the murder of one of its own. I was the keeper of the Kara file, which each day overflowed with more notes from interviews with detectives and neighbors, more crude maps of the West End, more tips to check out—many of them from other *Journal Inquirer* reporters and editors. An editor remembered talking to Kara about hairstyles and suggested that I ask Kara's beautician about shared confidences. A reporter recalled that Kara had begun to pursue a tip about trash-hauling corruption. Another reporter filed a "profile of Kara's killer," developed by a local psychic. It was all a part of a newspaper's grieving.

In that file I also kept Kara's original job application to the *Journal Inquirer* (*Dear Mr. Powell: Do you have any openings in the news department for reporters? If the answer is yes, please consider my application*), as well as her recent request for a fall vacation that she never lived to take (*I hope that these days are convenient. Thank you for your consideration*). I wanted her to remain vivid in memory while I pursued the story—and the son-of-a-bitch who killed her. His unmasking became my great obsession, my unhealthy diversion—despite knowing in my marrow that I lacked the ability. I returned to her neighborhood at night to knock on doors. I stopped people on the street. I checked in with shopkeepers a second and third time. Time and again I interrupted the drinking sessions in the neighborhood bars. All to say, Hi. I work for the *Journal Inquirer*. On October fifth a friend of mine was killed . . .

Here I was again, a child, believing that if I just set the table, if I just peeled the potatoes and made the beds, then everything would be all right; my parents would be happy, we would be happy, Mary would return to me, the killer would be found. And here I was again, an adult, realizing that no matter how many potatoes I peel, no matter how many doors I knock on in Hartford, no matter how many calls I make to an ex-girlfriend, some things cannot be fixed.

As the days grew colder, so did the trail to Kara's killer. The police began to describe the death as "baffling" and "mysterious." In mid-November, the *Journal Inquirer* printed leaflets offering a $10,000 reward, and its employees—from the newsroom, from circulation, from advertising—began distributing them throughout the West End. We were paired off, assigned city blocks, and instructed to strike up conversations and take notes. The exercise turned up little new information, but in our own way, we had honored Kara. We had plastered a corner of a city with her image, as if to say that we had not forgotten and would not forget.

A few days later, I got a call from the *Providence Journal*, offering me a job. I asked to speak with Bob Boone in private, and when I told him the news, I nearly broke down in tears. How could I leave now? I asked him. Wouldn't I be letting the paper down? Wouldn't I be letting Kara down? Maybe I should stay.

Boone was the father of the newsroom, and he looked the part, all furrowed brows and cardigans, always brushing his hand back and forth across his gray hair, as if trying to summon the wisdom culled from decades in journalism. I respected him more than anyone else in the newsroom; he seemed to inject just the right measure of maturity into the *Journal Inquirer*'s raw style. And now he was smiling at me, ever so slightly. He already understood some things about journalism, and life, that would take me years to realize.

This, for example: The story is always, always larger than the reporter.

And this: Some stories have no end.

No one has ever been convicted of Kara's murder.

Take the job, Boone said. If you don't, I'll fire you.

With that, I was released into Providence.

15

Come won't you please to Providence. Let me guide you through Providence. We can live together in Providence. Please, in Providence.

Up and down and all around the streets of Fox Point, this longshoreman's neighborhood where George M. Cohan once clicked his heels and where now I shamble. Into the Portuguese bakery just around the corner, with bread that dissolves sweet on the tongue. Maybe stop for a drink at Babe's on the Sunny Side, where a collie circles the pool table as if to corral the balls into a perfect rack, and Rocky Marciano and Willie Pep stare down from the black-and-white past, fists cocked to pop you just for looking. Then up to the top of the Fox Point hill, just outside my door, where car fumes from the interstate below charge the Narragansett Bay air, filling you with a light-headed wanderlust that compels you to explore New England, Rhode Island—Providence. Breathe with me, and we'll explore together.

That Louis Armstrong tape is still stuck in my car's cassette player by the way, a good thing. He blows happy-sad honky-tonk while I drive, thinking how glad I am to be here, how sad I am to be here, alone. Join Satchmo and me, won't you? Up to the city of Pawtucket, just three miles away in this Rhode Island urban clot, all factories and row houses and bars. I know a hole-in-the-wall Irish club there, run by an elfin man in a white shirt and narrow tie, name of Pat. And an ancient minor league baseball stadium, where has-beens and never-weres frolic on grass set aglow at night, and the locals receive psychotherapy at grandstand prices, heaping life's frustrations upon head-bowed strangers in cleats: Hey Number 8, you suck, give it up. Pawtucket oh Pawtucket, where the mayor will soon be indicted, I just know it. I know it like I know the seasons.

And farther up the mighty Blackstone River to the province of Woonsocket, with its French-Canadian social clubs and its fierce hockey and its Most Precious Blood cemetery, where a girl named Little Rose is buried. They tell me she would bleed from her hands and eyes while talking to Jesus. They tell me thousands came to her funeral in 1936 for one last look at the "Stigmatized Ecstatic of Rhode Island." They tell me they disinterred her body years later to prove how clay could never corrupt their teenage saint-to-be. They were wrong, of course, and now her aged sister runs a tiny museum to Little Rose out of a cold back room, visited by busloads of shrunken men and pursed women, all searching for the elusive proof of faith to make their final journey's destination more certain. There's a story in Little Rose, don't you think?

Or we could head down to Washington County, past the farms and fruit stands and antique stores, on to the beach roads that chuckle in wonder along the shores of the Atlantic. That is the thing about Rhode Island—only twelve hundred square miles, and no place is more than an hour's drive away. I can show you where rusted fishing boats bob and clang, where piping plovers glide on sands that glitter at evening tide, where daylight dissolves into night, like that sweet bread on your tongue, as you sit in your car, sipping take-out coffee and listening to music that seeps through radio static. Somewhere along these shores I once found an Irish pub, where a musician teetering on a stool played all the songs of my childhood while the owner fed him pints for balance. I joined him in a pint from a distance and listened to him sing "Whiskey in the Jar," a song about a man on the run, looking for connection. Then I was looking up, afraid that someone might have seen the hint of wet in my eyes, and wouldn't that have been a cliche: Danny Boy at bar's end, weeping so sad into his cup. A bar napkin quick! Dab dab, and now I'm a stone-faced rebel.

And if anyone can aid me, 'tis my brother in the army
If I could learn his station in Cork or in Killarney
And if he'd come and join me we'd go roving in Kilkenny
I'll engage he'd treat me fairer than my darling sporting Jenny.

The Atlantic sighed just outside the door, and I thought of my own brother, Brian, where was he, and my sisters, Brenda and Elizabeth, grown up and gone from the house now, and my parents. Maybe at this very moment they too were at the ocean's shores, drinking beer and spooning cups of clam chowder at Jones Beach; they liked doing that when he felt well enough. Or maybe they were searching the sands for loose change again, or pocketing a few beach rocks to display on the front lawn back on West 23rd Street. The two of them, light as piping plovers, leaving the barest of footprints in the sea-packed sand before they fly away—and they will fly away someday, won't they—and what can Danny Boy do about that?

And you, my darling sporting girl, you would never betray me like Jenny in that song. You would never steal away my rapier or fill my pistol's charges with water. Come, please. Come to Providence, and let me show you. Oh the stories here; I stick my pen in the waters and the fish spear themselves.

I know, I know. I know that I told you how hard it was at first. How no one here knew anything about me. About my give-it-up mugging, or my obsession with Kara's murder, or the way I see Irish ghosts all about me, the way I half expect UFOs to crisscross the night sky. All they knew was that a *Providence Journal* editor had scolded me for being so enamored of pretty words that I was burying the news, missing my deadlines. This isn't working out, he had said. Maybe you ought to consider another career.

Well Jesus Mary and Joseph, I thought. I'm nearly thirty. What other career? Molecular scientist? Manager of a Jack in the Box?

I know how I called to tell you all this, struggling not to cry, dab, dab. I told you how his counsel was like a cleaver, cutting me from my sense of who I was: a reporter. How he told me things weren't working out and then assigned me to baby-sit the city of Providence on New Year's Eve:

Another reporter will write the feature about First Night festivities in downtown, Dave—I mean Dan. The only way you'll be writing is if the governor is caught with a goat. Just walk around with this walkie-talkie, then come back and do your cop checks. Got it?

Got it.

So on that last night of 1987, a night so cold it hurt just to breathe, I wandered the ice-glazed city streets in search of goats. I shouldered my way against the flow of First Night revelers, past the closed storefronts and deserted alleys, then lingered before the reflections of a city on the brink of abandonment or renaissance—no one knew which. The small park in Kennedy Plaza, where vagrants doze in sleeping-bag cocoons amid the scruff of shrubs. The deserted Shepard's department store, once the Bloomingdale's of Providence and now a block-long pigeon coop. The seedy Fountain Street strip club that long ago, in another life, was where the wayward got fed in exchange for being lectured about God's abiding love.

Whenever the pitch of this New England winter's night seemed about to swallow me, I used my walkie-talkie as a lifeline to a place of light, the newsroom. Just checking in, I'd say. These conversations, though, were brief and impersonal. I stayed out in the cold. Three hours to the new year; two hours; now just one.

I returned just before midnight to the newsroom, where I was not so sure I belonged. The editor's comments earlier in the night had suggested that many are called but few are chosen, as though journalism was a kind of priesthood. Maybe I should take the hint, I thought. Maybe by this time next year I'll be gone from Providence, gone from journalism. And then what? Those were my thoughts that night, the thoughts of a man with no one to call on New Year's Eve.

Where were you that night?

But I *did* have calls to make, more than sixty in fact. I still had to make my cop checks, which meant contacting every police department in Rhode Island and southeastern Massachusetts to make sure that, God forbid, news had not broken out somewhere. I dialed and heard a voice.

Attleboro Police.

Hi, this is the *Journal*. Anything going on?

All quiet.

Okay, thanks, I said, and started to hang up.

Hey wait a second.

What?

Happy New Year.

Oh, I said. Oh yeah. Happy New Year.

The cop check ritual of anonymous reporters calling anonymous desk sergeants and dispatchers was perfunctory, even adversarial. Neither party trusted the other, and why should they; there was no eye contact, no sizing each other up. But that "Happy New Year" from some stranger of a dispatcher in Attleboro was like a child's wave fluttering from the back seat of a passing station wagon, a goodwill gesture with no ulterior motive—a blessing, the first of many. From Barrington to Cranston, from Lincoln to North Providence, from Smithfield to Westerly, dozens of strangers wished me the best, their words sustaining me as I sat alone in a deserted newsroom.

Happy New Year, the people of my new home said.

Right, I answered. Happy New Year.

I TELL YOU, that night changed me. With a new year and a new start, I tempered my pretty words, made my deadlines, became accepted in a city-state of a million people where everyone knows everyone. If your name is Urso, it means you probably come from Westerly; if it's Potvin, West Warwick; if it's McBurney, Pawtucket. The state motto is "Hope," but it might as well be "I know a guy." By now I know a guy or two myself, and they are begging to tell their stories, just as I am yearning to write those stories down. Come to Providence, if only for the story of it.

Let me escort you past the Colonial-era homes and mansions of College Hill, where the Providence bluebloods would exist above the city's grit and grime were it not for that profane and plotting ex-mayor living in their midst, in a carriage house off Benefit Street. Italian, Catholic, and sharp as broken glass, he believes his presence only raises the neighborhood's level of class, and I'm with him. Buddy Cianci isn't the one descended from Brahmin slave traders.

And let me tell you about Buddy. He's worth the pause.

A blackjack of a man, he became mayor back in the 1970s, when Providence was slipping out of control, when zoo animals were wandering onto the interstate. He fixed things up a little, soared like an eagle within the Republican Party, then fell like a shot duck. First, a bunch of hacks in his administration, guys with nicknames like Buckles and Cha-Cha, were convicted of the low-brow corruption you'd expect from guys called Buckles and Cha-Cha. Buddy dodged a close one that time. But then he goes and assaults some contractor because the man is supposedly having an affair with his estranged wife. It's not the assault but the manner of assault that is so—Buddy. While a city police officer guards the door, he beats the guy up with items now so notorious in Providence—an ashtray, a fireplace log, and a cigarette—they might as well be embossed on the city seal. He pleads guilty to assault, gets a suspended prison sentence, and is forced to resign.

Maybe another city would abandon its disgraced former mayor. Not Providence. He's still everybody's Buddy, even mine. Some afternoons I grab a coffee at Dunkin' Donuts and crawl my car through this strange new city, watching the winter sun slip behind creaking triple-deckers, listening to my radio.

AND NOW YOUR HOST—BUDDY CIANCI!

Pete from Wanskuck. You're on the air.

Buddy?

Yeah, Pete. What's on your mind?

I just wanna say that you were the best mayuh this city ever had.

We can listen to Buddy on the car radio when you come to Providence. Off goes Satchmo, on comes Buddy, and away we go. Up to Federal Hill, the old Italian neighborhood, where the salami and provolone hang like fishing trophies in the storefront windows, where the cannolis are cornucopias overflowing with ricotta cream, where the red wine at Angelo's restaurant comes in short water glasses so snug in the hand. We can take a walk along Atwells Avenue, past the Coin-O-Matic store that used to be the headquarters of the New England mafia. The Old Man, Raymond L. S. Patriarca, used to lounge in a chair in front of this store, clenching a cigar in his livery lips and waving to the detectives rolling by in unmarked cars. No one will ever know how many millions he made as mob boss or how many people he had killed; he wasn't the type to brag. After years of claiming that he was too ill to stand trial on the latest round of racketeering charges, Patriarca died with a fuck-you flourish—in the apartment of a woman who was not his wife. He died of a heart attack. Or, in the parlance of the city he dominated for so long, the Old Man "took a hot."

The Old Man's dead but Baby Shacks isn't. We can stop for gelato at the café where he sits in the back, sipping espresso, watching without looking, waiting his turn as the next mob boss. When he was on the lam a few years ago, he supposedly spent some time dressed like a woman, but please do not mention this in his presence when I take you there, when you are living here, with me, in Providence. For heaven's sake.

Let me show you the streets I roam late at night in the newsroom's radio car—Car One, they call it. It is fully equipped: coffee-stained dashboard, police scanner bolted beneath the overflowing ashtray, matching set of used sixteen-ounce Dunkin' Donut cups on the floor, heaping collection of yellowing newspapers in the back seat, ever-present whiff of another reporter's buried, half-eaten sandwich. I drink my coffee, I eat my cruller, and I palm the wheel, steering my boat in whatever direction my police-scanner muse takes me, skimming along the Providence seas toward islands of misery. There, to the hot edge of a mill engulfed in flames. There, to a scene so quiet after murder, with bloody handprints fresh upon a wall to mark a young man's last stand. There, to the river-bank, where a small bicycle on the ground, looking so awkward and empty and out of place, might be the defining detail to call into Marty the rewrite man, the detail that says it. The boy who's missing, he's been murdered. You just know it.

And when night, according to the *Providence Journal*, has yielded, when the paper is put to bed at one and there is nothing I can do even if I found the governor with a goat, I join others from the newsroom's late shift at a bar around the corner called Hope's. Owned by a *Journal* reporter, it is named not to echo the state motto, but rather to honor O'Neill's iceman, which adds to the despairing feel of the place. When closing hour comes like a plague to Providence, the slumming Brown kids are hustled out the door: Good night, safe home, get the fuck out of here. The locks are thrown, the front lights dimmed, the shades drawn. And we chosen few, we accomplished reporters and editors of what we believe is the finest newspaper in America, cower behind the bar counter, sipping long-neck Buds, waiting for quiet to come to Washington Street. After a while the bartender gives the all-clear, and we rise from the worn wooden floor like thirsty crocuses, reaching into our pockets to cover the next round and saying, Now where were we. We might have been discussing the sworn challenge of some reporters to slip past the editors and into print a certain meaningless phrase: "As if by the wave of an occult hand." The trick, we agreed, was to bury the phrase deep into a story filed well past deadline, so that the harried editor might glaze over a sentence like, "As if by the wave of an occult hand, the zoning board voted to postpone discussion of the matter until its next meeting." Or we might have been discussing the ubiquitous Charlie Zabluski, who had the uncanny knack of providing the perfect, pithy quote to a reporter desperate to fill space. There was no Zabluski, of course; a mischievous *Journal* reporter had created him decades earlier. And yet he existed, in a way, earning his own file in the *Journal* morgue (ZABLUSKI, CHARLIE, Allover, Rhode

Island), his fabricated observations preserved in newspaper clippings fragile to the touch.

But we would not have discussed what it was like to feel that fire's heat, to see those bloody handprints, to sense a boy's murder by the riverside. Why go into that? Hey Len, one more?

Two o'clock comes, then three, then time to go. I weave through the predawn hush of my adopted city. Maybe I stop for a fried-egg sandwich at Haven Bros., the nocturnal diner on wheels that disappears at dawn, as if only imagined. Then over the river I go, up Wickenden Street to Fox Point, where Yankee Doodle Cohan once lived. He was from Rhode Island and went to New York; I'm from New York and now I am here in Rhode Island, but you know what? I belong here.

And so do you. Please won't you join me in Providence? For the hundredth time, for the thousandth time, for the love of God, won't you join me here? Reassemble me here? Here in Providence?

AND SHE DID, did Mary. Yes, Mary did.

16

MARY HAD HER stories too, better stories in fact, reported back from the front lines rather than from the scribbling shadows. After years of managing the Warming House, that drop-in center near St. Bonaventure, she became the director of a soup kitchen in a rough patch of Stamford, Connecticut, learning only later that it was the slash of a patron's knife across the face of her predecessor—a nun—that had created the job opportunity. Mary thrived there, though, finding purpose in the whiff of homelessness off a man's coat, in the wind-whipped face of an aging debutante gone to drink. Then she returned to New York's Southern Tier to work in Wellsville with the mentally ill. There was Alice, who thrilled to hear the trucks barreling past her home so close to the highway, rattling the cheap china on the pressboard shelf. And Willie, a black man who had spent decades in a psychiatric institution; all he had done was flirt with a white woman in 1940s Syracuse, and, well, one thing led to another. And, of course, legless Ralph. Mary trundled him up in her Dodge Colt one Christmas Eve and drove him to New York City to see his sister. A couple of days later, her matchbox of a car was fishtailing through a snowstorm to get back to Wellsville, with old Ralph swaying beside her, urging her onward because he didn't like being away. The Colt slid off the highway and became lodged like a red hockey puck in the snowbank boards of Hornell. And there Mary stayed, at Christmas week, in a paneled motel room where the guest down the hall called every hour asking, When are we leaving? When are we leaving.

Mary left Wellsville for me. She left the Texas Hot restaurant, with its enormous homemade pies, and the bar just down the street called Better Days, and the Friday night fish fries. She left the azure evening skies of the Southern Tier: the hot-air balloons that float by like Technicolor clouds, the cool breezes wafting from the hillsides, the cleansing snow, the Allegheny River. She left her small apartment just above the flower shop. She left her many friends, including legless Ralph, so that she could come and live with me, a reporter with prospects, in Providence.

ON THE LAST morning in June, in the New Jersey town of Maplewood, in the house of Mary's childhood, where no dinner conversation ever centered on alien abductions and no pots of pasta ever sailed out the door, we prepared for our big day. The air was summer sticky, the sky oh so clear. Mary drove into the village to have her long blond hair braided and pinned. I laced up my sneakers and jogged into her parents' backyard, where a basketball hoop was hanging in open invitation over the garage door, and where my brother, my friends, and my three future brothers-in-law were waiting to fulfill my wish: some premarital basketball.

Mary did not mind, but her mother thought it was an unwise exercise to engage in so close to the wedding hour. Many times before she had looked through the kitchen window to see her sons and me playing body-slamming basketball—and it worried her. What if I sprained my ankle on the uneven asphalt? How would that look, coming down the aisle with my new bride on one arm and a crutch under the other? What if I got poked in the eye or had a tooth knocked out? Forever and ever, the wedding pictures would suggest that Mary had married a barroom brawler whose mouth was faster than his fists. Evidence of violence, no matter how innocent, would become all the more pronounced at a wedding ceremony, given that Mary managed a battered women's shelter in Providence.

The men gathered beneath the basket to discuss ground rules; some of them still wore the "Mary and Dan 4-Eva" T-shirts that had been custom-made for the previous night's rehearsal dinner. The ball was out of bounds if it hit the car, the garage, or the grass. But no one is allowed to foul the groom, they said; just this one time—this one time only—Dan gets to do what he wants on the basketball court. The next hour was like a gym rat's wet dream. Every one of my layups was uncontested, it seemed. Every one of my jump shots went in. And the day only got better.

Mary Katherine Anne Trinity, agleam in her mother's wedding dress, and I, in a rented tuxedo, were married on June 30, 1990, in a cavernous church whose name, Our Lady of Sorrows, must have tested the motivational skills of its school's cheerleaders (Let's go Sorrows, Sorrows let's go!). We permitted no sorrow in the church that day, though, as we exchanged vows before witnesses from nearly every period in our lives: people who had changed our diapers when we were infants; who had heard me sing "My Country 'Tis of Thee" at St. Cyril's; who had worked beside Mary at the Warming House; who had endured us as a new couple, an ex-couple, and a reunited couple.

Later, when Mary and I were finally alone in a hotel room strewn with unopened envelopes and tuxedo parts, we reminisced about moments just hours old, while I removed all those pins from her long, braided hair: How Mary's mother had the best comment of the day, picked up by a videocamera's microphone ("Well, slow-moving Dan finally came through"). How Father Dan Riley, a Franciscan friend of ours from St. Bonaventure, had begun the ceremony with a joking reference to our rocky twelve-year courtship ("It's about time"). How Mary's father had danced with her to "More I Cannot Wish You," and how my father had looked pretty good, considering he had been hospitalized a week earlier with a bleeding ulcer that would not respond to his medicinal use of Bailey's Irish Cream. How I had danced with my proud immigrant mother to a scratchy recording of "The Galway Shawl." One two three, one two three, for what would be the last time, one two three.

> 'Twas early, early, all in the morning,
> I hit the road for old Donegal.
> She said "Goodbye sir," she cried and kissed me,
> And my heart remained with the Galway shawl.

WE RETURNED TO Rhode Island then, didn't we, Mary? We expected to buy a house, start a family, and live out our days there, watching a lawn sprinkler sweep rainbow shimmers across our own grass, ours. We knew all about that small Italian restaurant in Silver Lake with the sweet calamari, and the story behind that storefront down the street, where the Old Man had two hoods "taken out" for running a floating dice game without his sanction. We knew where to get the freshest lobster salad in Westerly; where to browse for used furniture in Warren, where to sit at the Twin Oaks restaurant in Cranston on a Friday night if you wanted to see the up-and-comers and has-beens of Rhode Island, the indicters and the indicted, sharing heaping plates of antipasto with women who were not their wives. We were up-and comers ourselves, I guess. You the high-profile advocate against domestic violence, fighting for better laws, lobbying at the State House, appearing on the six o'clock news. And me, a member of the *Journal*'s small band of investigative reporters, trying to unknot the intertwining strands of the great I Know A Guy culture.

Then what happened, Mary? Where did it go? I fear that we missed too many private Providence moments, that we should have taken one more rendezvous along the winding streets of Newport, shared one more drink at the Hot Club on a late afternoon and before the crowds, lingered one last time in the seashore cast of autumn twilight. Weren't these what I had promised in enticing you to Providence?

How did I misplace 1991? Oh, yes. An entire year dedicated to the collapse of the state's credit union system, a disaster caused by loans between friends that carried little expectation of repayment. The collapse forced the government to freeze more than $1 billion in assets, suddenly leaving a lot of retired jewelry workers, hacking in their dotage from all those years spent inhaling factory fumes, with no access to their sweat-damp money. The *Providence Journal* had to explain how this had happened, and in doing so teamed me with a breathtakingly smart reporter named John Sullivan. I wound up seeing more of him that year than of you, my new wife. Hulking about in our long dark overcoats, we were the avenging angels of journalism, knocking on the doors of credit-union officials who had things to hide. They often seemed to be expecting us, as if we had come in fulfillment of the Rhode Island maxim that sooner or later, your name gets put in the "Jernil."

And where did 1992 go? Now I remember. Lost to researching the tragicomic career of Raymond J. "Junior" Patriarca, the Old Man's inadequate heir. How, when he was four, the cops searched his mobster father's Cadillac, only to find a Tinker Toy construction set and a child's harmonica. How, when he inherited his father's crime empire, he cowered in his fortress of a suburban home, fretting about wiretaps and occasionally calling radio talk shows —Hi, this is Ray from Lincoln—to chat about the news of the day. How he presided over a secret induction ceremony that was bugged by the FBI, resulting in one of the all-time Mafia gaffes; now there are transcripts of solemn vows being administered between the sharing of prosciutto and assorted olives. Patriarca got eight years and I got seven thousand words, after which I realized that I knew more about a slump-shouldered mope of a mobster than I did about my own father.

Then came 1993, and if you were to ask where we vacationed that summer, or how we spent our third anniversary, I could not answer. What I do know is the story. My old partner Sullivan and another reporter, Dean Starkman, found corruption in the state's halls of justice, and soon the rest of the *Journal* investigative team was rooting through a court system that was being run by the Supreme Court chief justice and his top administrator like a Tammany ward. The judge was writing letters on Supreme Court stationery to get his son out of parking tickets, intervening in the traffic cases of friends, and illegally funneling legal work to his pals, while his buddy was using a secret account to pay for lavish dinners and trips to Fenway Park. The words of our stories built the gangplank and they walked it; they had no choice.

I remember only two days from 1994. The day that the *Journal*'s investigative team, led by our editor, Tom Heslin, won the Pulitzer Prize for our expose of court corruption. And the day that my detailed story about a mobbed-up Providence strip club appeared on the front page of the Sunday *Journal*. Whatever my reporting revealed about the Rhode Island nexus of politics and the mob—such as how the club enjoyed the blessing of the once and current mayor, Buddy Cianci—was lost in the uproar over the accompanying front-page photograph. If it had depicted a co-ed sunbathing in a bikini on Narragansett Beach, no one would have cared. But because it showed strippers in skimpy outfits, standing in their dressing room, readers felt violated. On a Sunday no less! Amid the angry letters and telephone calls, one response distinguishes me in the modern annals of the *Providence Journal*. A man stacked copies of that Sunday's *Journal* at the entrance to the newspaper's building and set them on fire.

We had to leave though, didn't we, Mary? Better put, *I* had to leave, and you knew it; you knew that I needed new stories to tell. After seven years at the *Journal*, I felt as though I was telling one story, over and over. No matter what I wrote about—the court system or the banking system, the legislature or the mob—the same characters seemed to surface. It was as though a small acting troupe were staging a round-the-clock production of a play called "Rhode Island," and I was the theater critic.

You knew. When *The New York Times* expressed interest, you knew.

We owned a house with a basketball hoop out back, where I had resurrected my childhood practice of communing with God between foul shots. You said that basketball hoops, like God, are everywhere.

We were working on starting a family. You said that we would have children and grandchildren and great-grandchildren and that we would die in bed holding hands, leaving only a chocolate wrapper and an empty whiskey glass on the nightstand. What could befall us? We're young; we're healthy. Send your clips to New York, Dan, and what will be will be.

The New York Times, I guess. That is what will be.

I wrote one final story for the *Providence Journal*, the last of hundreds. It was about a wiseguy, of course, a character called "The Saint" who traced his mobster lineage to an uncle named "Peanuts." The Saint was supposed to be standing trial on illegal gambling charges, but he explained to me in exquisite detail how he was unable to rise from his living room couch for any extended period—something about the need for forty-eight to fifty enemas a day. As I listened with discomfort to his words, I realized that here, then, were the sublime bookends of my eight years at the *Providence Journal*: a police dispatchers' Happy New Year chorus, and the perverse lament of a mobster. Thank you, Saint, but it is time that I go.

ONE PARTING RHODE Island memory, and it could have been 1989 or 1994, 1991 or 1993, I can't recall. I am planted in the outfield grass of the old Cranston Stadium, playing center field for the hapless Providence Grays, a team of misfits in an over-thirty baseball league. To my right squirms an outfielder who cannot throw; to my left, an outfielder who cannot run. Before me, infielders who cannot bend, catch, or complete a double play; a catcher who cannot throw to second; a pitcher who cannot throw over the plate. I thoroughly belong among them; I cannot hit.

We are playing another team of aging, balding men who possess about the same level of talent, which means that our quest to complete nine innings continues long after the sun has set and the ice cream man has

jingled his last bell. As I stand in that halo of light surrounded by darkness, with now-you're-set chatter rising from the dampening grass, I feel
fifteen again, not thirty-five. I feel as though nothing has changed in my
life, nothing at all.

I look into the deserted concrete stands, and there you sit, ready to
cheer me on for getting in the batter's box and swinging. Providence.

17

Now where was it, here—or here? No, it was right here, across from the Carter Hotel and a little closer to Eighth Avenue, and maybe someday I'll plant a votive candle at the curb. This is the spot where, one morning a dozen years earlier, I had stood perspiring in my Gene Barry getup, snapping his blue blazer as if to taunt the bulls of West 43rd Street—all because a man dizzy with drink had blessed me with malt liquor just moments before my job interview at *The New York Times*. The blazer might as well have been made of Handi Wipes, so thoroughly had its unnatural fibers absorbed the booze. And since I had never received a letter or telephone call to say that I had been rejected, I figured that the *Times* editors had forwarded my resume to the security guards in the lobby: Be on the lookout for this hack; reeks of the Bowery.

Now, many years later, I was about to enter the building at 229 West 43rd Street as a *Times* employee. I was no longer an intern at the *Daily News*. I was no longer a ditch digger with a graduate degree in journalism, watching reporters stroll into the *Newsday* building in Melville while I installed sprinklers in that newspaper's lawn. I was now a reporter for *The New York Times*, and I was terrified. Where's the malt liquor when you need it most?

A drink might have been in order, considering that trying to get hired at the *Times* had been like trying to join Delta Force. A couple of weeks after sending writing samples and a resume to a gifted journalist at the *Times* named Mike Winerip—he had once visited the *Providence Journal* to talk about the craft of storytelling—I received a telephone call from Warren Hoge, a veteran foreign correspondent who at that time was a high-ranking editor in charge of recruitment. His invitation to visit the *Times* for a series of interviews with editors caused a stir within my extended family. Mary hustled me to the mall to buy a suit; no way would she allow me to go to the interview in Gap khakis and another baggy blue blazer. Her mother asked that I pass on her compliments to the people at the *Times* for their fine product; she found the pages of the *Book Review* to be especially effective in cleaning windows. And my father—whose cluster migraine headaches had finally subsided, after twenty years— counseled me again about the importance of first impressions and firm handshakes in the Big City.

Just be yourself, he advised.

Do you think that's wise? I asked.

A typewritten sheet dictates the interview process at the *Times*, from the minute you enter the building to the minute you say good-bye— perhaps for the last time, perhaps not. It is basically a roster of everyone you are to meet during your nerve-racking visit, a roster of editors in ascending order that stops just short of the executive editor and his deputy. Winerip, a former columnist who was now an editor on the Metropolitan Desk, prepped me for my marathon over a quick cup of coffee. He advised me not to be thrown off my stride by any of the eventual questions, including "I see that you're thirty-seven; aren't you a little old to be coming here as a reporter?" and "If the *Providence Journal* is so great, why leave?" and "Since you're a big fish in a medium-sized pond, won't you have trouble being a small fish in a large pond?"

I emerged from my first pass through the *Times* gauntlet with rela- tively few psychic bruises. This time, at least, no one had asked me how many languages I spoke, nor did I feel the need to describe my hyper- borean college environment. Hoge told me that I had done well, but that I would have to wait now for the newspaper monolith to shift slightly, freeing up a position. This could take weeks or months, he said. Stay in touch.

Hoge was a gentleman's gentleman, lanky and graceful, the kind of journalist who would end a long day in the newsroom by donning a tuxedo and slipping off to some upper-crust soiree. He and I might never go to the Kozy Kabin to knock down a few Buds, but I liked him; he was straightforward, responsive, and kind. When I called him one afternoon to explain that I had just received a job offer from some very persuasive editors at the *Chicago Tribune*, he asked that I hold off for a day before giving the *Tribune* an answer.

The message he imparted was clear: At *The New York Times*, the world is your oyster.

Imagine: a newspaper that sees the world as one massive mollusk, stretching from Providence to Pyongyang. I promised Mary that if we did uproot ourselves from Rhode Island to slake my ambition, our struggle to have a family would continue unabated. Of course, she had her own career to consider. At that moment, the *Providence Journal* was preparing a long profile of Mary, who had earned acclaim for her efforts to improve the laws against domestic violence. What could I say, other than to assure her that domestic violence was not an unfamiliar issue in the city of New York. She smiled, sort of, then took a walk through a house that suddenly seemed less in need of things.

The next day, Hoge called to say that I had a last-step appointment to meet Joseph Lelyveld, the executive editor, and Gene Roberts, his deputy. Lelyveld, a New Yorker, exuded all of his city's confidence without any of its brashness; he seemed comfortable with long gaps of silence in conversation, a trait that I might have found more engaging at an occasion other than my job interview. He had worked as a reporter and editor for virtually every department in the *Times* newsroom and had won the Pulitzer Prize for a book culled from his experiences as a foreign correspondent in South Africa. He was a journalistic lion, as was his deputy, Roberts, a North Carolinian who had covered the civil rights movement for the *Times* and then gone on to become the executive editor of the

Philadelphia Inquirer, which won seventeen Pulitzers during his eighteen-year tenure.

Winerip assured me, though, that these lions had no intention of devouring me. At this point, all I had to do was to avoid being splashed with beer on my way to the interview. I managed.

Now it was a clear and warm September morning in New York, my first day as an employee of *The New York Times*. I dawdled for a while in front of the *Times* building, trying to shake off a feeling. Last time it was the wetness of beer; this time, the encroaching paralysis that fear of the future can bring. I took a step forward, and the newspaper's revolving doors flung me inside.

The *Times* building is meant to impress, even intimidate. A bronzed bust of Adolph Ochs ponders in the lobby, the portraits of many Pulitzer Prize winners adorn a corridor on the eleventh floor, and people in the cafeteria are as likely to be chatting about political strife in the Congo as they are about the latest *Seinfeld* episode. I rode the elevator to the third floor and walked through the low-ceilinged, poorly lighted newsroom, past rows of personalized landfills that were reporters' desks. Don Van Natta, who had joined the reporting staff a month earlier, and Clyde Haberman, a veteran foreign correspondent who had returned to the city to write a column, went out of their way to make me feel welcome. But most people did not even look up at the new guy intent on trying to look useful. I figured that all these grim-faced *Times* employees were too busy establishing the official record of September 5, 1995, to waste time on social niceties, a thought that unnerved me all the more.

My Barry blackness took hold, and I could not shake bizarre thoughts of failure. What if I couldn't cut it here? What if I didn't pass the six-month probation period at the *Times*? We had already put our house in Rhode Island on the market, which would mean that without jobs, Mary and I might wind up living in my parents' basement, next to that malfunctioning sump pump. There I'd be, a reporter without portfolio in Noreen and Gene's backyard fortress, where overgrown hedges insulated them from neighbors who had not stepped past the Barry house threshold in more than a decade. Watching my parents stub cigarettes in the patio's cracks. Listening to them discuss everything from my mother's b-i-t-c-h of a work colleague to my father's bitch with the phone company, the Republican Party, all the motherless bastards.

Gene, Gene, keep it light, my mother would say; Aah, the sons-of-bitches, he'd respond; and two more cans of Buds would hiss like firecracker fuses on a muggy summer's evening. Soon the backyard's only lights would be the fireflies and the tips of their glowing cigarettes; another night slipped past, with little eaten and so much said. In the complicated world of 140 West 23rd Street, my prescribed role would be as follows: go out for beer-and-smokes runs, referee quarrels, then encourage détente by opening another Entenmann's and pointing out that a good Christopher Lee horror movie was on Channel 9.

Seeking refuge from these crazed thoughts, I hustled to the bathroom and patted cold water on my face, telling myself to calm down, calm down. Just then I heard a familiar, buzzsaw-like noise. It was the sound of, the sound of—snoring! Someone was dozing in a bathroom stall at *The New York Times*, just as a *Journal Inquirer* sportswriter used to do so many years ago in that squat building back in Connecticut.

Staring at my reflection in that bathroom mirror, I had an epiphany. *The New York Times* is just another newspaper. I'm home again.

BUT EVEN THEN I heard the bog whispers of my ancestors, covered in the mud of Galway and the cow shit of Clare, conditioned not to boast, not to stand out. You know yourself, they said, we're all the same in the eyes of God, kings, and paupers, no matter. In the end, the clay covers us all; you know yourself.

A reporter, is it? For *The New York Times*.

Well. Aren't we something.

EAT DINNER WITH Mary, have a beer, and watch some sitcom's rerun on television. These were my goals for that July evening in 1996, and I felt that I deserved at least that much. I had passed my probation, during which I discovered that working for the *Times* was not much different from working for the *Providence Journal*, or the *Journal Inquirer*. Aside from obeying the newspaper's strict rules of style, such as using "Mr.," "Mrs.," and "Ms." on second references—except, of course, for sports figures and pre-eminent dead celebrities—my job had remained the same: report the news accurately, with clear and compelling writing. If there was a boilerplate *Times* way of writing a story, I avoided it.

I was now the newspaper's Long Island bureau chief, which sounded more important than it actually was, since the *Times* only had two other full-time reporters on the island, and neither answered to me. After thirteen years in journalism, I had gotten my big break with a national newspaper, only to be returned to the land of my childhood—Massapequa and Wyandanch, Patchogue and Deer Park—a land that from the *Times* newsroom seemed so foreign. Privately, I was hoping for a more exotic port of call than Rockville Centre, where Mary and I were renting a house. Publicly, I reassured my editors that they had made the right choice. I'm fluent in Buttafuoco, I told them; I know these parts. And I did. How Jones Beach in winter is better than Jones Beach in summer. How, as you travel the North Fork's truck route east to Greenport, the smell of the air turns from that of the farm to that of the sea. How my best friend, Don Seibert, beside me at St. Cyril's, St. Anthony's, and St. Bonaventure, was beside me again, in Rockville Centre. How my mother's offbeat stories and my father's oddball insights are but a half-hour's drive away. No question: I know these parts of the oyster.

But on this night, all I wanted of Long Island was again what my father had always strived for, his holy grail. Jesus Mary and Joseph, all I want is a little peace, he would say then, and what I was thinking now. Mary by my side, a beer in my hand, and a little peace.

The ring of the telephone said not tonight. It was Gerry Mullany, the night editor, sounding a little winded, telling me that I had to go—right now—to eastern Long Island. But he could not tell me where exactly, or even why. All he knew was that there were reports of an airplane vanishing from radar screens, somewhere off the South Shore.

I had just cracked open that beer, and now my well-deserved evening of relaxation was being interrupted with news of possible mayhem. How many times in my career had breathless reports of catastrophe turned out to be a fender bender with minor injuries? How many times had some police sergeant told me during one of my cop-check calls in Providence that five officers were dead and four wounded in a shootout at police headquarters? (Had you goin', Jimmy Olsen, didn't I?) Here we go again.

Jesus, Gerry, it's 9:30 at night, I whined. Isn't there anyone else to send?

But Mullany told me that everyone was being deployed and that I had to get there as fast as possible.

Where's there? I snapped.

We don't know yet. Just start driving.

I got in my car and started driving, too annoyed to think about packing clothes or toiletries. I gunned my gray Pontiac east on the nearly deserted Southern State Parkway, past the signposts of my childhood—Bellmore, Bethpage, Deer Park—pounding my palm against the steering wheel and spitting expletives into the steamy night. All the while, I twisted my radio dial back and forth between two all-news stations for the latest reports about a downed jetliner, but my annoyance at being put out prevented the words from sinking in: TWA Flight 800, out of Kennedy International Airport; bound for Paris; more than two hundred aboard; lost off the shores of the Moriches; flames in the water.

Exactly where my Damascus was along Sunrise Highway, I am not sure; somewhere near Sayville, I think. There, with the radio shouting and the car speeding at eighty miles an hour and the humid air blowing damp through the windows, I felt a sudden shame to be in my own skin. The words had seeped into my consciousness by now, waking me to the realization that at the same time the radio was telling me of 230 people likely dead, I was having a private tantrum because I had been inconvenienced. Oh my God. A jetliner filled with people had fallen from the sky? And crashed into the waters off Long Island? My Long Island? Two-hundred-and-thirty people? Holy Mother of God.

A reporter, is it? For The New York Times.

Well. Aren't we something.

Another epiphany, only the kind that strips you bare. With Long Island becoming a blur through my tears, I felt the need to ask forgiveness of the jetliner's passengers, most assuredly dead. And I pressed my foot against the gas pedal, clear-minded now and determined to tell the story of a catastrophe off my homeland's shores.

That quest led me a day or two later to the East Moriches storefronts along Montauk Highway, which led me to a liquor store, whose owner led me to the kitchen of a man named Michael O'Reilly. The liquor store owner had confided that the crash of Flight 800 had affected people all over town: Heck, a local guy named O'Reilly's been coming in here and buying vodka all of a sudden. I think he saw some things.

Now this bearish O'Reilly was acknowledging with nods that, yes, he had acquired a sudden thirst in the last two days, and yes, he had seen some things. But he was fine, just fine, he said, as he took another sip from a morning mug of vodka and cranberry juice. And no, he didn't mind sitting down with a stranger and telling his story. It would help, actually. Want some coffee?

On the night of the plane crash, he and a buddy were watching the Yankee game in his TV room when news of a plane crash flashed on the screen. They hustled down to the twenty-seven-foot fishing boat that O'Reilly kept docked at the edge of his waterfront property and headed out to sea. It was probably a small plane, and some survivors might need to be rescued; that is what they figured.

Instead, they came upon what O'Reilly called a "ring of hell": flames of burning jet fuel dancing on the black and still waters; bobbing sections of airplane silver; suitcases and ghostly white bodies floating past— including that of a child who appeared to be sleeping. The two men shouted into the fiery stillness: Hello? Anybody out there?

Only the slight slaps of waves against their hull answered back.

Finally, the two men realized that all they could do was retrieve some of what floated past; they reached for a gaff and some rope. A couple of hours later, O'Reilly's boat, *Chasin' Charlie*, slick with jet fuel and loaded down with three bodies, motored over to the Coast Guard station. They watched as others removed the bodies, and then they returned home, where they could find no rest.

Regular guy O'Reilly sat at his kitchen table, sipping some more vodka and assuring me again that he was okay. He handed me a piece of paper and asked if I could pass it on to the proper authorities. His son had found it stuck to the boat's floor a few hours earlier, a luggage tag for a woman from Bordeaux, one of the 230 victims.

Holding the damp piece of paper in my hand, I felt the singe of shame again on the back of my neck; just a little peace, that's what I had wanted. My shame soon gave way to an entirely different emotion, an emotion that so overwhelmed me I struggled to identify it. The rush of feeling, I finally decided, was a sense of humbling privilege, granted to me by this sapped man before me, this Michael O'Reilly. He had just been to that ring of hell, and now he needed to be alone with his family and his thoughts. But he knew instinctively that something larger than Michael O'Reilly had taken place, and that was why he had granted me his time. He understood my role in the societal compact perhaps better than I did. I was a conduit through which experience is shared, through which the acrid smell of burning jet fuel is inhaled, and the sight of a child, borne on the water, asleep in death, is seen. I lived these things and now so have you, he was saying; tell others.

I tucked the luggage tag from Bordeaux inside my notebook, and I told Michael O'Reilly that I would take care of it.

18

L ET ME HOLD her now. Please, it's my turn. Let me touch my
fingers like lips against her tiny chest and feel the yes-yes-yes of
that pumping heart, a heart the size of an I LUV U Valentine
candy, only real, so real. Let me feel with my fingertips that beat, steady
as a bodhran's, as she fits so snug in my arms, and let me sing to her. Let
me sing to her, soft of course, yes yes of course, no sea chanteys, no war
songs, I promise. I'll sing her one of those sweet Irish lullabies my mother
used to sing to me, there beside the Zenith's warm glow, in our third-
floor cottage in an apartment building in Queens. I can still hear my
mother's cooing as she held me for dear life. I can feel her bosom rising
and falling as she whisper-sang another one of her comforting songs,
ancient songs, songs like, like—oh that's right, my mother never sang to
me. She could not sing, oh she had the most awful singing voice, like a
cat on the rack, the neighbors would have reported her to child protection for sure. So she never sang to me, really. But if she could have carried a tune, my squirming wonder, I know that Noreen Barry, my
mother, your grandmother, would have sung one of the songs we learned
as children, comforting, sweet-dreamlike:

> *McCarthy was dead and McGuinness didn't know it.*
> *McGuinness was dead and McCarthy didn't know it.*

They both lay there in the very same bed
And neither one knew that the other was dead.

You're right, Mary, not so soothing that one. I'm sorry. But I think she liked it, she's smiling, sort of. Let me try another. This one I do remember my mother singing when I was older, off key of course, but she knew the words. Why this song of all songs, I don't know—maybe the Irish were required to sing it to get through immigration.

If you ever go across the sea to Ireland
Then maybe at the closing of your day
You will sit and watch the moon rise over Claddagh
And see the sun go down on Galway Bay.

Mary, I think she likes this song. She's smiling, and not from gas, I'm sure of it. Think she's old enough for some geopolitics?

For the strangers came and tried to teach us their way
They scorn'd us just for being what we are.
But they might as well go chasing after moonbeams
Or light a penny candle from a star.

Maybe someday we'll take you there, to Galway Bay. You'd like that, I know you would.

Nora.

Nora Mary Trinity Barry.

MARY AND I boarded the plane for San Antonio, but we had no idea where we were going. That is how it often is with adoption. We had been wounded once and fleeced once, and now were embarking on a third attempt to adopt a newborn child, our feelings protected only by scar tissue. Not the kind that Mary had developed after abdominal surgery years earlier, preventing conception, but the emotional scar tissue that comes from repeated cycles of fertility-drug treatments and two adoption attempts, bringing nothing but sobs in the night. Braced for pain in our assigned seats, we steeled ourselves further with the advice that our adoption counselors had given us: memories of all heartache and travail will evaporate the moment you cradle a baby of your own.

For now, though, we had nothing to nurse besides our wounds. I opened that day's *Times*, hoping for escape and finding not one damned story I cared about. Forgetting these dark days seemed impossible.

There was that stultifying afternoon in late June of 1997, for example, when encouraging word of a possible adoption arrived at the most awkward, wrenching time. Mary and her family had just returned from the cemetery after having buried her mother, and the Trinity house in Maplewood brimmed with friends and relatives, all waiting to have a drink to remember lovely Mary Hanlon Trinity, dead of lung cancer, just sixty-two. People in clutches repeated her many funny sayings, as if to commit them to memory while the sound of her voice was still fresh: the way she refused to leave the house until every appliance had been unplugged ("Off, off, off"), the way that every minor crisis was equated with the ever-threatening Susquehanna River of her Wilkes-Barre childhood ("My God the river!"), the way that even the clumsiest phrases flowed so naturally from her lips ("The Lord save Ireland and all that's holy").

In the midst of all the Need another beer? and Thanks so much for coming, we received word that the adoption agency had left an urgent message for us. Mary, aching to be as giving a mother as hers had been, returned the call. She hung up the phone and turned to me.

Dan, a birth mother in Texas has chosen us, she said, and I could see that my Mary was struggling to rein in all the conflicted emotions she was feeling. I took her in my arms and whispered, Your mother works fast.

Suddenly, a Pamela from Wichita Falls became an intimate part of our lives. She was twenty years old, married, the mother of a three-year-old boy, and pregnant again. She did not want a second child—she was too young, she said—and had contacted a local adoption agency despite the ambivalence of her husband and the opposition of her in-laws. After choosing the Mary-and-Dan profile from dozens of others that the agency kept on file, she and Mary had established a sweet but hesitant bond, sharing their disappointments and hopes during several long conversations. Pamela wanted a safe, loving environment for the child she planned to place, and Mary's voice cracked while assuring the young woman from Wichita Falls that this would be done, and so much more.

But Pamela, who was nearly eight months pregnant, had a request. Would Mary and I fly to Wichita Falls so that she could get to know us a little better before she gave birth? Of course, Mary said. Anything.

Two weeks after the funeral of Mary's mother, we flew to Dallas and rented a car for the three-hour drive to Wichita Falls, a city with a university on one side of town and boarded-up storefronts on the other, a city alternately thriving and wilting in the heat. When we arrived at the hotel where we had arranged to meet Pamela, a clerk handed us a note scribbled on the back of hotel scrap paper. "I am not feeling well so I am going to have to cancel. I hope I didn't ruin your weekend. . . . I will be home all day tomorrow if you would like to call, maybe I will be feeling better."

The note did not upset me; I figured that we had three more nights in the small city of Wichita Falls, plenty of time for Pamela to feel better. Mary, though, did not share my Pollyanna view of the situation. Pamela's family was pressuring her to keep the baby, she said, and that was obviously their right. It also meant that we had no choice but to wander the streets of a strange city, while a family unknown to us debated whether we were nothing more than Yankee baby snatchers.

Mary was right, of course. Whenever we swallowed our pride and summoned the nerve to telephone Pamela's home, someone would tell us that she was sleeping, or out, or not feeling well. Our hopes were raised once when a relative said that Pamela would meet us at the local mall for lunch, but we wound up skulking about the food court for hours, in vain. One night we stopped at a Dairy Queen for sweet consolation, but our ice cream cones practically exploded in the Texas heat. That told us all we needed to know; the next morning was Tuesday, time to go.

We understood what had happened, of course, but we would have preferred to suffer at home, not in Wichita Falls. While Mary sat sobbing in our rented car, I stood at a payphone outside a Winn-Dixie supermarket and, one last time, dialed a phone number that we had come to know as well as our own.

She's not available? Oh. Well, do me a favor: Just tell her that Dan and Mary wish her well. Okay? Dan and Mary really do wish her well. Take care.

And back we went to nurse the absence.

A month later, a second birth mother chose the Dan-and-Mary file. Kayla from San Antonio was twenty-two years old, had had the first of four children at fifteen, had placed two with adoption agencies, and had written on a questionnaire that "I don't want any more children and I can't parent anymore." She was nearly six months pregnant, but the adoption agency told us that she and her husband, a restaurant worker, needed financial assistance for an apartment, for food, for prenatal care.

Mary and I looked closely at the photograph of Kayla and Jimmy that the adoption agency had forwarded, and saw two young people who could have been our neighbors, our siblings. We forwarded the money for their substantial expenses, and never heard from Kayla and Jimmy again.

That happens sometimes, the agency told us. Hang in there.

By late August, Mary and I could barely function outside of work. She was now the director of the New York City Coalition of Battered Women's Advocates. I was a general-assignment reporter based in New York, mired in the case of Abner Louima, a Haitian immigrant who had been brutalized by an officer in the bathroom of a New York Police

Department precinct house. After spending our days immersed in the horrible and grotesque, we would return to the Carroll Gardens neighborhood of Brooklyn, where we now lived, to find distraction in the wacky people parade along Court and Smith Streets. When we had finally exhausted ourselves beyond the point of reflection, we would call it a night and collapse in the barrenness of our apartment.

Then came word from San Antonio. A third birth mother had chosen us as adoptive parents for her child. Sarah was thirty-one, single, taking care of a chronically ill mother, and just not ready to start a family alone. What's more, she was nearly due. We waited for the discouraging update that always seemed to follow these encouraging reports: that the birth mother has chosen another couple, that the birth mother has decided to keep the baby, that the birth mother has disappeared. But two weeks passed with no bad news, and suddenly we were on another plane bound for Texas, not sure that we could weather even one more bump of turbulence.

Early on a Tuesday morning, we met Sarah in the maternity ward of a San Antonio hospital, where her labor was being induced. Her long brown hair was offset by a touch of whimsy—a pair of Winnie the Pooh earrings—and she was sitting upright in her bed, listening with a girlfriend named Kelly to a radio blaring country-western music. An adoptive couple meeting a birth mother in the hospital just before inducement might be among the more awkward of life's moments. But Sarah made the moment seem quite normal, which was another of her gifts to us. Attached to an intravenous tube and in clear discomfort, she nevertheless became our gracious hostess. You simply have to go to the Alamo while you're in San Antonio, she said, and a visit to the Riverwalk is an absolute must. Also, this process could take a while, so you might want to go down to the Wal-Mart—just down the street—for the car seat and stroller you'll soon be needing. In a way, Sarah became our mother as well.

Two hours later, while we sat in a Burger King just outside the Wal-Mart, our cell phone rang: Time. Rushing back to the hospital, we headed to our assigned posts: Mary to the delivery room, to witness a miracle; Dan to the lobby, to stare without comprehension at that day's *Times*. Less than an hour later, Sarah's friend Kelly—a perfect stranger, truly perfect—appeared beside me to tell me that I was the father of a healthy baby girl.

A father? Mary as a mother, this I could see: her nurturing of the children at the soup kitchens and domestic violence shelters she managed, her interactions with our many nieces and nephews, her infinite patience with my puerile moments. Mary as a mother—of course. But me as a father? I had no particular insight to impart, other than to avoid splitting infinitives and to use active verb tense whenever possible. As I stumbled after Kelly toward the maternity ward, doubt, not joy, filled my mind.

It turned out that the counselors at the adoption agency were right. The moment I held that infant in my arms, my mind cleared, my fears lifted. I forgot about Wichita Falls and Pamela and Kayla and Jimmy and fertility drugs and alcoholism and UFOs and migraine headaches and baseball and Brother Noel and jump shots and journalism. I forgot, because there was nothing else but this: Mary, me, and a squirming little thing in swaddling clothes, announcing herself in belches and cries.

Nora Mary Trinity Barry.

The worst is over. Now, my girls. Now we're set.

PART THREE

The liquor scattered over Tim
Bedad, he revives, see how he rises
Timothy rising from the bed
Says, "Whirl your whiskey around like blazes
Thundering Jasus, do you think I'm dead?"
—"Finnegan's Wake"

19

S HE SAT AT the edge of that couch of hers for hours on end, refusing to lie back or lie down; that would be giving in. She would not take her Decadron; that would be submitting to the swelling in her brain. She would not take her Roxanol, her morphine, for as long as she could; it dulled her sharpness, and how she hated that. But the pain would intensify until she had no choice, and soon she would be looking about as though startled by an uninvited presence in her house. In *her* house, on *her* couch, from where she had sat in maternal sentry for so many years. Keeping that weak and wandering eye on the front door. Listening for quarrels in the bedrooms upstairs. Attuned to the soft sighs of three sleeping dogs in the hallway, to the humming rhythms of the dryer in the family room, to the rumbling cycles of the washing machine in the kitchen, forever on the verge of swirling into imbalance. The wink of a car's headlights: one of hers was finally home. The banging on an upstairs wall: another headache, he'll need some ice. The smell of rain: the whites on the clothesline have to come in.

Gone. It was the winter of 1999, and my mother was dying of lung cancer.

She would not eat, which drove the family mad with alarm. We clung to this almost primal belief that if *only* she would eat—An egg, Mom, how about an egg and a piece of toast?—her strength would return. That she would overcome this sickness, as though it were simply a really, really bad cold, and life in the house would be restored to its approximation of normal. But the days of London broil on the barbecue were gone, of hearty beef stew ladled over a bed of noodles, of spaghetti and meat-balls—their masterpiece together, Gene rolling the balls of seasoned meat to uniform perfection, Noreen standing at the stove, stirring a sauce whose ingredients an Italian neighbor had confided to her when first she came to Brooklyn. Their cigarettes weaving smoky braids, their glasses full, the radio playing Irish music from the station up at Fordham, the children moved out, the kitchen windows fogged by the steam of their togetherness, Gene and Noreen. Gone.

Now boxes of Entenmann's covered the kitchen counter, just in case she asked for something sweet, and cases of a dietary supplement that tasted like a pasty milk shake blocked our path to the clothes dryer. We placed glass after glass of this gunk before her, and we dumped glass after glass of it down the kitchen drain, in streams of chocolate, vanilla, and strawberry, the rainbow of our despair. A half glass of ginger ale, that's all she ever wanted, to nurse long after the carbonated bubble dance had ended.

She would cup her bare head in her hands, as though to prevent upset-ting thoughts from escaping; she never talked of death, never. Those were strong hands of hers, hands that had clipped hedges and pushed a mower, cleaned dishes and painted walls, built this house in her image, shampooed us, one, two, three, four, hard enough to rock our heads back and forth, and then, after, stroked our sweet-smelling hair until we slept. They were the hands of a farmer's daughter, and they looked large to me in those last days, as though impervious to the diminution of death. With fingernails painted the color of lilac and veins like taut cords, those hands seemed determined still to squeeze the best from a life of toil.

Downstairs on the dining room table sat a stack of get-well cards from coworkers who refused to accept that their Noreen was not coming back. In that grimy office on Route 110, where rows of women hunched before early-generation computers, typing numbers onto spreadsheets for a few dollars an hour and longing for the salvation of their fifteen-minute break, my mother was their Cool Hand Luke. For years she had struggled with a despised superior, but she had won that battle with humor, diligent work habits, and the resolve never to let anyone think she cared what that superior thought of her. She had earned that trifling lima bean of a gold pin for her twenty years of service after all, but she'd be damned if she ever wore it.

Noreen, come back, called the cards on the table. Please, Noreen. Come back.

They stayed in a pile on a dish, most of them unopened. My mother could not bear to read beckoning notes from a world that was behind her; it had been that way with Ireland too. Her desktop now was a glass-ringed coffee table bought cheap at a garage sale, upon which her things were laid out: her glass of flat ginger ale, her pack of Parliaments, her plastic lighter, a few unlucky lottery tickets, and a couple of those hand-sized, beep-beep video poker games designed to waste time. Now and then my mother would look at this odd collection and then at her strong hands. She would close her eyes. Okay, she would whisper. Okay.

Once in a while, during a fleeting lapse, she would let slip an Oh God, but then another Okay would quickly follow.

Okay.

Okay.

Of course, it was not.

The anchor that kept the house on West 23rd Street moored to the neighborhood, to the fringes of functioning society, really, had given way, leaving my father to cast about in uncertain seas. He could not accept that his life's companion—his wife, his love, his friend, his mother, never abandoning him, always there no matter what—was receding wraithlike before him. Every morning seemed to bring a little less of her. Searching for peace all his life, searching for security, searching for a time when both would be retired, with no concerns beyond what beach to visit and when to start defrosting that Tupperware bowl of spaghetti sauce. Now? Now, just when both had scrapped and fought their way to make it to their sixties? And it had to be Noreen first, not Gene? All those stories of the paranormal he used to tell, like the one about the farmer who disappears in a field, then calls out for years after from the other side of a dimensional fold. Now this: a story of the normal, only so much more unsettling. Gene in one dimension, and Noreen slipping into another.

Often he sat beside her, through the afternoon and into the night, smoking cigarettes, drinking beer, fretting that the Gene-and-Noreen dialogue of forty-five years was at an end.

Please, honey, please eat, he would say.

Maybe later, she would say.

And that would be that. Perhaps they were too stunned to talk, or maybe they were afraid that the mention of some shared word—Woochin, their pet nickname for each other—would cause them to crumple.

He could not bear it after a while; he had to hide. He would trudge heavy-footed back up to his bedroom, close the door, pull the shades, and place a pillow over his head as if to suffocate himself. You knew, you just knew, that he was seeking to strike another bargain with that God whose existence he had always questioned. Curse me with another twenty years of cluster migraines, You Almighty Bastard, only save her. Save her.

I'll NEED A bowl of water, Danny, and my toothbrush and some toothpaste. And some liquid soap to wash my scalp because they use this oil at the radiation place.

My mother was calling to me from her couch, directing me, an hour before another radiation treatment and a couple of weeks before the end.

There are some beige pants in the closet, she said, as she tried to summon the strength to sit up. And find a top that matches. And the socks.

How's this? I asked from the top of the stairs, holding the pants, top, and socks together like some dress shop's attentive clerk.

Fine.

After she allowed her son to half-carry her to the car, and who knows how many neighbors were looking; after she swallowed her nausea for the twenty-minute ride to the clinic; after she wheeled through the doors and smiled to everyone as though she were there for nothing more serious than a pesky cough; after she endured the illusion of treatment with a two-minute beep of radiation; after her son, now the *Times*'s City Hall bureau chief, tried to distract her with some dopey political gossip (Giuliani lived on Long Island when he was a kid, but you wouldn't know it . . .); after her son half-carried, half-escorted her to the bottom of the stairs, where the last seven feet to the couch might as well be seventy— this is what she did. She went that last seven feet. She made it to her couch. And she gazed up at her son, decided not to read the heartbreak in his face, and she said, Danny, I need a drink.

I fixed her a vodka and 7 UP, gave her some pain medication, and turned on *Judge Judy*. The 7 UP fizzed away, and so did my mother, as I jotted notes in the spiral-bound notebook that my siblings and I used to record what medication my mother took, how much liquid she drank, and when she seemed in prolonged distress. There were Brian's scribbled notes, and Brenda's, and Elizabeth's, and mine—four examples of how the Sisters of St. Joseph at Sts. Cyril and Methodius had failed to ease the hard press of the Barry nub against paper. It was the written attempt by a disorderly family to impose order on a situation beyond control. It was a guest registry of sorrow. It was the Book of Noreen.

No one wanted to say "hospice." We were, after all, Noreen's children; to say "hospice" was to acknowledge that she was dying, and we refused. Mom's lost the use of her legs? Fine. Brian and I will carry our mother to the car for her radiation treatments. Buckle up, Mom. Got your cigarettes? Your lighter?

One day we arrived twenty minutes early for her appointment at the back end of Good Samaritan Hospital in West Islip, so I drove down a side street to park at the edge of the Great South Bay. We watched the angry slams of the bay against the dock; the water was slush gray, the color of February. In the distance, we could make out the great pencil-like tower that looms over Robert Moses State Park, and the bridge leading to Captree Beach, where my parents once walked the shore, drinking beer and considering the infinite sands. Seagulls arced and dangled before us, suspended in air.

I envy their freedom, sighed my mother from the back.

The car crawled toward the hospital for one of the last of her useless radiation treatments. She exhaled some smoke and, for the first and only time to any of her children, addressed the subject of her approaching death. She was talking about how the drugs made her feel so stupid when she stopped abruptly in midsentence to watch a few people walk out of the hospital's back entrance. Suddenly, she began to lament how she had treated others during her lifetime.

I've learned something from this experience, my mother said.

What's that? said Elizabeth, sitting beside her but unable to look at her, for fear of the tears that would surely come.

That I've been too critical.

It was Noreen Barry's last confession, given through a Parliament curtain in the backseat of a Saturn. With the grace of silence, Elizabeth and I absolved our mother of all sins.

I parked the car and, with Elizabeth's help, got my mother settled in a wheelchair. I wheeled her, so light, past the automatic doors that hushed open, past the healthy clerks and nurses. The treatment was so brief that I wondered whether they had even turned on the machine. Then, as I wheeled my mother away, she gave a regal nod and wave to the nurses at the front desk.

Good-bye, ladies, she said.

Good-bye, Mrs. Barry, they called out.

I LAY ON the floor at the foot of my mother's couch, wrapped in bed sheets that I had dug out of the back of the linen closet. They were sheets that she had washed and folded many months before, but they still had her smell to them, of fabric softener and last fall's crisp air and Noreen.

Now she was on the couch above, wasting, and I was down here, fidgeting, on the living room carpet that hadn't been vacuumed in months, that had absorbed many years of smoke and spills and words of anger, words of joy. Valentine's Day cards from her husband and children lay scattered on a table downstairs, each one containing love notes never to be read by their intended. It was too late by Valentine's Day; hallucinations were trumping coherence. The late-night winter winds rapped against the window like an impatient tax collector. The clock clucked its tongue. Her slow breathing missed the beat of sleep's metronome. I feared each pause, welcomed each breath.

Pull me up, Danny! Pull me up!

Suddenly my mother was wide awake, agitated, frightened, shouting into the night because of the awful sensation that she was falling. I leapt to her side and told her, No, no—gently as though talking to an infant— No, no, you're not falling. It's all right. It's all right now.

Pull me up, Danny!

She locked her hands around my neck, hands that never failed to beat me in arm-wrestling matches on the picnic table, hands held open always for me. Okay, okay, she whispered, in ever-softening brogue. Okay, okay. I rocked her in my arms, saying, Now, now, it's all right, but her imagined descent continued into early morning, down, down.

Pull me up, Danny! Pull me up!

It's okay, Mom. I've got you.

Oh, Danny, pull me up!

I am, Mom. It's okay. I love you.

Danny, Danny! Pull me up! Oh pull me up.

20

ASH WEDNESDAY BEGAN and ended unacknowledged at 140 West 23rd Street. With our mother and wife dying in the living room, we didn't need a priest's greasy thumbprint on the forehead to remind us of the ash heap of mortality. It was just as well; Barrys tend to believe that the thumbs of priests are aimed for the eyes.

Because the Barry children had almost no experience in the matter of mourning, we prepared in the only way that we knew. We had enough beer in the house—that was rarely an issue—but had exhausted our supply of another essential, Entenmann's. My father, who had stopped drinking, was now craving sweets. Brian and I, who were beginning to drink, were craving distraction, so we volunteered to go on an Entenmann's run. My father requested two specific Entenmann's: the chocolate cake with the chocolate-pudding center, and the Danish that we have always called the "raspberry drizzle." He also gave authorization for the purchase of a third cake of our own choosing.

Brian and I spent the short drive to the King Kullen supermarket amusing each other with imitations of our father. How he makes a certain hand motion in describing his beloved "raspberry drizzle," as if to mimic the factory flow of white frosting upon cake. How he toils over a simple shopping list as though it were classified CIA code. Any departure from the written script, after all, might result in a revolution in Central America—or, worse, the purchase of unsalted butter when lightly salted butter was required.

By the time we returned with our milk and cake, a hospice nurse with an ash-smudged forehead and a proper air of maternal efficiency had arrived to begin watch over our mother. It was unsettling to have a stranger in our midst, to be observed with our defenses down and hands unclenched. But we relaxed a little when this stranger said that she had the same kind of Irish bric-a-brac on display in her own house. Her name, by the way, was Mary.

We reached for our cans of Budweiser, loaded our plates with the dinner prepared by Brenda and Elizabeth—a Noreen favorite of spaghetti and clam sauce, bread and salad—and headed to the living room. This is what we always did when we were happy together: settle into the living room to watch a Marx Brothers movie, play Scrabble, or, most often, tell stories made jagged by sharp observations and pointed asides. Usually my mother led the storytelling with drawn-out, hysterical reports from life in the factory on Route 110. The nasty executive who looked like Ernest Borgnine in a dress, her ham-hock legs taxing her panty hose so much that you could hear her walking in from the parking lot, sounding like ripping linens, *shht, shht, shht*. The coworker who was nice enough, but a "weak reed," as they say, ready to agree with the boss no matter how ridiculous the comment (The sky is green today, he'd say; And a lovely green too, she'd say). The supervisor who began mimicking everything my mother did, including dyeing her hair red-brown (Maybe I'll wear a clown's nose to work, just to see what happens).

On this night, though, with beers cold and plates full, we gathered about our storyteller, lying now on a portable hospital bed in the center of the room, her eyes closed and her breathing labored. With Mary the nurse as our guest and audience, we paid tribute to Noreen Barry by doing what she had always done so well. We told stories, all featuring the same heroine, each one flowing seamlessly into the next, without pause for reflection, as though we were trying to filibuster her death somehow. Empty red-and-white beer cans piled up on end tables.

Tea was made, the obligatory Entenmann's came out, the stories continued. How she had held the house together with an Old World practicality: when the bathroom tiles became worn and discolored, she just painted over them; when her husband and children punched through doors and walls in fits of rage, she simply hung pictures over the gaping holes.

How, during her final stay at Good Samaritan Hospital, we wheeled her outside to a small smoker's shed, where nurses and aides huddled for hurried drags from their cigarettes before returning to care for people weakened by cancer—people like my mother. When the talk turned to party plans for the upcoming Super Bowl between the Denver Broncos and the Atlanta Falcons, my gaunt mother drew on her own cigarette before saying, with a haughty touch in her brogue, We don't watch the Super Bowl at our house, we're a baseball family.

The filibustering ended at midnight, at the close of Mary's shift. She pressed her hand against our mother's leg and told us that edema was setting in; the body was shutting down. Then the nurse with ashes on her forehead wished us all well and bade good night.

Brian and Elizabeth asked to sleep in the living room. Brenda slept in the old boys' bedroom and I lay down on the floor in the old girls' bedroom, where there was no bed, only an ironing board draped with my mother's clothing. Around one, Brian came in to tell me about something strange that had just happened: our father had come out of his bedroom and down the stairs, blanched and shaken. He said that he had been thumped five times on the arm, and then felt a great pressure on his chest. Of course, he interpreted this to mean that his wife was trying to tell him something. As Brian told me this, our mother became agitated. All four children gathered around to soothe her. Then back to our own fitful sleep.

THE MORNING DAWNED with a cold rain and the realization that Noreen Barry was dead. There was nothing else, just her death. My weeping father asked us to gather in the living room to pray, something that the family had never done beyond some hurried mumbling over holiday spreads. We did as he asked, reciting the Hail Mary and the Our Father, but for me these prayers did little to erase the distressing math that we were six, and now we were five.

A young nurse with talons for nails came to confirm the death. She collected all the controlled substances, telephoned the funeral home, and, with the keening of my father echoing through the house, said, Okay, I'm outta heah. Then came two representatives from a funeral home on Deer Park Avenue to remove the body and go over funeral details that any other family would have tended to weeks earlier. We children elected to handle the details ourselves, allowing our father to continue mourning in his bedroom sanctuary.

Open casket? One of the visitors asked, her pencil poised over a form on the kitchen table, her face a studied expression of concern.

Closed, I said, to the nods of my siblings.

Do you mind my asking why?

Because this is not how we want to remember her.

Well, a lot of families provide photographs of their loved one, she said. And with cosmetics we are able to re-create the loved one.

Re-create the loved one. Elizabeth's snort sent cigarette smoke out her nostrils. The Barry family's profound distrust of strangers was front and center now. The thoughts of Noreen's four children shouted in chorus: Our mother's body is in the living room, and you are quarreling with our request because it might reduce your profit margin? You are in the Barry lair, lady. Tread lightly.

Closed casket, I said, locking her with the inherited Barry glower that said, Move on; let's keep it to one dead body.

With raindrops coursing down the front door's window, I watched the black hearse pull away from our house and drive slowly down West 23rd Street. I could see Carl Down the Street, who lost his wife Celeste a decade ago, watching from an upstairs window. He looked back at our house, and I thought I saw him nod before he disappeared.

My gaze settled on our rain-soaked front yard, which never looked more like a miniature golf course in the off-season. Discarded knick-knacks from the lawns of others, bought for spare change at garage sales, dotted the lawn, her lawn: ceramic trolls, plastic frogs, wooden geese with pinwheel wings spinning in the wet wind. The insulating hedges were high and squared off, just the way she had shaped them when last she wielded her trusty Black & Decker clipper like a suburban Joan of Arc, a cigarette in her mouth, mortality on her mind. And sprinkled around the sprawling rhododendrons and budless rose bushes were the rocks and seashells that my mother had pilfered from state beaches. The rain beat harder against the front door.

The funeral Mass, of course, was at Sts. Cyril and Methodius, where the February sun scattered stained-glass shards of light upon my mother's casket. We had spent so much time crowded in these pews, my siblings and I; we had received the sacraments of First Holy Communion and Holy Confirmation here; we had squirmed through dozens of First Friday Masses, the girls in their St. Cyril's green-plaid skirts, the boys in their St. Cyril's green pants and gold shirts. So many celebrations, so many Masses, so many people. Now the church was all but deserted, save for two-dozen mourners: a few friends and neighbors from Deer Park; a few colleagues from my mother's factory; some friends from the *Times*; Mary's family; us. My father once seemed so massive in this church, all Sunday scowl and ready to flick the backs of our heads for giggling. But standing beside me this day in the pew, his hands gripping the wooden support in front of him, he seemed diminished, not so much by the church as by the death that had returned him to its hold.

The organist played none of the songs we requested. The boy of a priest had trouble with English. The mourning Barrys in the first pew stood and knelt at the wrong times. No matter, all is forgiven in grief. The priest swung his lantern-like censer over the casket, a signal for the paid pallbearers, who just moments earlier had been smoking cigarettes outside, to step forward. Out we went, to the strains of a hymn we had not asked for.

The final Noreen Barry caravan traveled east along the Long Island Expressway for nearly an hour before turning north for Calverton National Cemetery, that great and humbling necropolis, with more than 150,000 gravesites spread over a thousand acres, their white tombstones standing at attention, as if ready to salute. This is where soldiers and their spouses are afforded internment, headstones and "perpetual care" for free, as a kind of final thanks from a grateful government. And this is where the government gave final thanks to an Irish farm girl for having married a smart-ass army corporal.

We muttered a final prayer above her casket, the Our Father or something like it, something about being reunited after the Second Coming. We could not linger in the open-air chapel because this place does some fifty internments a day. There was another hearse with engine idling, waiting its turn, and another after that.

We returned west without Noreen.

That afternoon we gathered with some friends in the back room at the John Thomas Inn, just off Sunrise Highway, for a ziti buffet and some pitchers of beer, while a portable tape player blasted Clancy Brothers songs about fighting, forever fighting, against the pull of the tide:

Now the storm is raging
And we are far from shore
The good old ship is tossing about
And the rigging is all tore
But the secret of my mind, my love,
You're the girl I do adore
For soon we live in hopes to see
The Holy Ground once more.
Fine girl you are

NEARLY FOUR YEARS would pass before I could summon the will to visit her grave. One brisk morning in November, her birthday month, it just seemed the right thing to do. But once I made it to Calverton National Cemetery, its vastness nearly swallowed me up. I feared that if I did not ask for assistance, I risked never returning to the land of the living.

The man behind the counter in the administration building had a thatch of gray hair and teeth the color of vanilla pudding, and he appeared to be much older than my mother, who had been only sixty-one. He sucked on a piece of Halloween candy while listening to my question. Though he had heard the same inquiry thousands of times before—Can you tell me where my mother is buried?—he flashed a warm pudding smile and settled down before a computer.

What's her name and when did she die?

Tap, tap, tap, and there it appeared, my mother's name, along with the date of her death and the coordinates of her grave. The man pulled a sheet from a stack of Xeroxed maps and used a yellow marker to draw a path from the administration building to the section where my mother is buried.

She's in Section 19, he said. Section 19, Grave 1023.

Thanks very much, I said, folding the map into my pocket.

Now be careful, 'cause it's confusing, he called out after me. You can go down one long path, then discover that the grave you're looking for is at the other end of another row, he said. I know. I worked out there.

Got it. Thanks again.

I drove past acres of white tombstones, all exactly twenty-four inches high, one side the veteran, the other the spouse. Thousands and thousands of tombstones, set aglow by the sun and marching on and on, stopping, it seems, only for the occasional stand of trees. This was a long way from the cemetery in Shanaglish, where her parents were buried, and Aunt Nora, and the rest, farmers here and IRA martyrs there, all among the lichen-blotched Celtic cross tombstones jutting from the lumpy ground. But she belonged in Calverton, didn't she, surrounded by the other toilers and strivers of Long Island, all looking for that elusive little peace and quiet. The men and women of Levittown, and North Babylon, and Deer Park; the men and women of our neighborhood, of my child-hood: serve your country, get a job, get married, leave the city, buy a house, grow grass, have kids, drink your Schmidt's, eat your burgers, retire, watch the sweep of sprinklers, die—and be carried away to Calver-ton, where a stone like Ivory soap, like a mah-jongg tile, will bear your name.

Where, though, was my mother's?

I walked down the wrong row in Section 19, of course, just as the pud-ding man had predicted, but only because I was secretly hoping that she was buried near a grove of trees. She would have liked that, I thought, which was immediately followed by a second thought, What the hell am I thinking? Down the other way, toward the anonymous swallow of a cemetery's center, and there she was: NOREEN E. wife of CPL. EUGENE F. BARRY.

Well, Mom.

Well.

It was no use. I am Noreen Barry's son, which means that I cannot talk to a stone. She would have laughed at the thought. In tribute to her view of a world where the shells and stones belong to us all, I placed a pebble on the top of the twenty-four-inch tombstone she will someday share. Fine girl you were.

21

A CHERRY STAIN. A lipstick kiss. A melted gumdrop. A rose petal. If only.

It was another muggy June afternoon in the journalistic squalor of Room 9, the storied pressroom in City Hall. On the drab walls hung dusty and barely noticed mementoes of New York mayors past: the photograph of William Jay Gaynor in shock after being shot; the hat and cane of John Lindsay, his sly gift to the press corps; the outrageous caricatures of munchkin-sized Beame, of how'd-he-do Koch. Beneath their cartoon gazes, one reporter struggled to focus after another liquid lunch, while another reporter—a superb journalist who hadn't filed a story in years—shuffled papers, tidied up. Press releases never to be read blanketed desks like oversized confetti, and the smell of someone's curried chicken take-out occupied the air.

All around me, reporters from the *Daily News* and the *Post*, *Newsday* and *El Diario*, the Associated Press and the *Staten Island Advance* tapped away on the "Giuliani Attacks (Fill in the Blank)" story of the day, while I sat bent before my own computer in the corner, not typing, just coughing. I didn't want to disturb my colleagues, but I seemed unable to dislodge this feathery sensation in my throat. It had been there for days, weeks even, and now, finally, I felt movement.

Cough cough cough. Tap tap tap. Cough tap cough tap cough.

Something came up into my mouth. I bent down at my metal desk, seeking cover behind the ramparts of city documents piled high around me—the mayor's glowing reports of his own management, the sunny budget forecasts—and I spat hard into a paper napkin. I folded the napkin like a tiny newspaper and opened it again to see what it would tell me.

A rose petal? A lipstick kiss? No. A clot of blood, as dark as the darkest red, looking like a spent bullet as it rested there in the bed of my napkin. My interest in the City Hall story of the day vanished; the clack of typing around me grew distant. My private little newspaper was reporting my own life's story with a single mark of punctuation, an exclamation point the color of scarlet. Read all about it.

BY THE LATE spring of 1999, I had been the City Hall bureau chief for the *Times* for nearly eighteen months, which meant that for eighteen months I had written almost exclusively about one man, Mayor Rudolph W. Giuliani. It was the year after the start of his second term, the year before the public collapse of his marriage and diagnosis of his prostate cancer, and more than two years before the World Trade Center terrorist attacks that would beatify him. He was in all his jaw-jutting glory at this point, reigning as king of the city he proclaimed "the capital of the world," flirting with a run for the Senate or, wink-wink, even the presidency. I was among the many reporters who tagged after Giuliani, fascinated by the behavior of a man who seemed intent on willing the metropolis into civility. Without question he had revitalized the city through his crackdown on "quality of life" crimes and his unabashed pride for all things New York. But he could also be an insufferable scold, a short-tempered father, glaring through the rearview mirror at the eight million New Yorkers in the back of his station wagon. Don't you dare question his pivotal role in the lowering crime rate, the soaring dot-com economy, or the latest Yankees world championship; he just might pull over.

Nearly every day, Giuliani held a news conference in the Blue Room of City Hall that, depending on his mood, could be either a forum for informing the public or a vehicle to mock the press corps. Like a headmaster harboring contempt for his doltish students, he would filibuster, intimidate, and ridicule, eliciting mirthless chortles from his coterie of sycophantic aides leaning against the walls. I never asked questions in these settings, in part because I feared that if he publicly ridiculed me, I might involuntarily blurt out a choice Gene Barry epithet.

When I returned to City Hall after my mother's burial, I struggled to catch up with all of Giuliani's concurrent piques and squabbles. With the city in renaissance, the mayor had more than enough time to indulge in one of his preferred methods of effecting change, which was to antagonize. At the moment he was quarreling with Governor George Pataki, his fellow Republican, and school chancellor Rudy Crew, his former friend. In addition, the recent shooting death of Amadou Diallo, an unarmed African immigrant, by four white police officers in the Bronx had not only raised questions about aggressive police tactics in minority neighborhoods, it had exposed Giuliani's stunning lack of communication with any of the city's black leaders. Under intense pressure to build bridges in the wake of the Diallo shooting, he reluctantly agreed to meet with the Manhattan borough president, a black woman, for the first time in a year. In any other multicultural city, the meeting would have been routine; in the New York City of Rudolph Giuliani, the session took on the significance of a Botha-Mandela sitdown.

Although I dutifully recorded the mayor's every accomplishment and rant, I began to sense a sameness to the Giuliani story. There were only so many times that I could have his aides tell me he was the best mayor in the history of the city; there were only so many times that I could write a different lead to "Giuliani Attacks (Fill in the Blank)." Besides, I had other matters to write—and think—about. For one thing, human remains kept surfacing in the loam just outside the doors of City Hall.

Seeking air from the stifling confines of City Hall one afternoon, I stepped outside to watch construction workers churn up the grounds as part of an extensive renovation of City Hall Park, a nine-acre patch of land that had once been center stage for Lower Manhattan's epic evolution from meadowland to metropolis. Here, in the 1730s, the Common Council built the first almshouse as living and working quarters for "disorderly persons, parents of bastard children, beggars, servants running away or otherwise misbehaving themselves, trespassers, rogues and vagabonds." Here, many were buried, the poor, the criminal, the disease-ridden. Here, the average New Yorker first heard the stirring text of the Declaration of Independence.

I noticed that some of the people working in the park were kneeling in trenches with sifting screens. Between furtive glances back to City Hall, they explained that they were archeologists, quietly hired by the city to salvage every musket ball and bottle shard that surfaces during the construction work—as well as to ensure the dignity of any unearthed human remains. It may not be something that the Giuliani administration wants trumpeted, they whispered, but they have found many skulls and femurs that were scattered like rocks and twigs by the great construction projects of the past, including the building of that nineteenth-century monument to Tammany corruption, the Tweed Courthouse. They have come across and protected many intact skeletal remains as well, they said—those of soldiers and criminals, hanged or shot; of paupers; of babies buried in the arms of mothers.

The mayor and his attendants hustled out of City Hall and toward his glass-tinted Suburban, and I couldn't give a damn where they were going. I turned back toward the dig, staring into the grass and earth, and began wondering about Giuliani's place in the continuum of time, and mine. Standing there in the park, plotting how to write this story about the bodies in City Hall Park, I began to think about my mother. I wondered whether she was watching over me, whether her spirit was one with the spirits of all the colonists buried around me, the paupers and patriots and children. It was sophomoric, but I could not help but imagine a scene that mirrored an old Abbott and Costello movie, *The Time of Their Lives*: Noreen Barry with ghosts in tricornered hats and big-buckled shoes, all of them sipping mulled cider and watching Danny muddle along toward the Answer they already knew.

Did they know why I had lost my voice? And why I was having trouble breathing?

For several months now, I had been whispering through life. My regular appearances on the *This Week Close-Up* television program—in which *Times* journalists discuss New York politics—had become exercises in public humiliation, as my performance anxiety seemed to further constrict what was left of my vocal abilities. Repeated examinations and two biopsies led a pulmonary specialist at Mount Sinai Medical Center to conclude that I probably had sarcoidosis, a fairly rare disease that causes scarring in certain vital organs. Still, he admitted that he had never seen X-rays quite like mine, with what appeared to be an inflamed lymph node crushing the nerve of one of my vocal cords and most likely contributing to my hoarseness. He prescribed Prednisone, a strong steroid, and told me to come back for monthly checkups.

But it wasn't just my voice. I normally jogged several times a week, carving a three-mile loop through the narrow streets of Brooklyn that began in our neighborhood of Carroll Gardens and included a view of the majestic Manhattan skyline from the promenade in Brooklyn Heights. Now I could barely make it to Atlantic Avenue, a few blocks from my home, without stopping to gasp for air. Even climbing subway stairs became a challenge; after a few steps I would have to rest against the handrail, while the young and the old brushed past me on their way up and out.

I rationalized these symptoms away, thinking to myself that I had a cold or was simply getting older. Mary and I put our trust in Prednisone. But the impact of my diminished air capacity continued to reveal itself in unsettling ways, especially during my time with Nora, who was now eighteen months old. I would pick up one of her books—*Goodnight Gorilla*, say, or *Jamberry*—and not be able to read even a short sentence aloud without pausing for a breath. I would want to sing to her on long rides in the car or at night while she was preparing for bed, and find that

I could not summon the air. Oh, the songs that I had wanted to sing to my child, inch by inch and row by row, and now just "Good night" and "I love you" would have to suffice. "Too-rah-loo-rah-loo-rah" was out of the question.

Archeologists were on their knees in City Hall Park, searching the soil. And the City Hall bureau chief for *The New York Times* was standing beside them, searching too. Then revelation came in a spit of scarlet.

AT FIRST THE blood would come for a day and subside for two, just long enough to trick me into thinking that it was all a mechanical fluke in this wondrous, complex machine known as the human body. Then it would come for two days and subside for one. Then it would be with me all the time, ready to spill, it seemed, at the slightest head move, the gentlest cough. Despite Mary's efforts to calm me, I became frightened of my own body. I worried that if I made a sudden move, or talked too loudly, or took too deep a breath, I would shatter the fragile dam at the back of my throat, unleashing a Johnstown Flood of blood.

I was terrified, and I met with as many doctors as would see me. I drew comfort from what they had to say: either I had an extremely bad case of bronchitis, or a blood vessel had ruptured toward the back of my nasal passage (that would explain the post-nasal-drip sensation, thought the patient who had nearly failed high school biology). The Pulmonary Specialist put me on antibiotics. The Voice Specialist was more concerned with my damaged vocal cord—it was apparently paralyzed—but he cauterized one or two irritated blood vessels. There, I thought. That should take care of the problem. And Mary, Nora, and I flew to Cleveland to spend the Fourth of July weekend with my college roommate, Tom Conlon, and his family. At this point my close friend—with whom I had shot so much pool, drank so much beer, talked so much politics—represented more than just good fellowship to me. I saw him as providing calm Ohio refuge from New York, which I now equated with blood and doctors and deadlines. We can swim in the local pool, drink evening gin and tonics, admire fireworks from our picnic blankets. I'll just keep my head up as though I had a nosebleed, I figured, and let the antibiotics spin their magic.

Cleveland killed these delusions. I spent the afternoons sitting rock-still on a lawn chair in the stultifying Midwest heat, trying to control the spasms of coughs; now and then I'd spit blood flecks on the lawn. The nights were even more frightening, with the blood flowing freely, unnaturally, into my mouth. The last night there I spat for nearly two hours, painting my friend's nice suburban sink an abattoir red with my blood while trying not to waken Nora. In the short windows between the passing of one spasm and the onset of another, I'd stare at the frightened, sallow man hunched before the mirror, and then at the woman beside him, rubbing his back, unable to mask her own terror. By the time my tears of pity blinked into view, it was back to retching the life flow out of me.

A few days later I was sitting in the examining room of the Voice Specialist, telling him of my nightmare weekend in Cleveland, when I began to illustrate my story by spitting up blood. He peered down my throat, and his affable, sure-sure demeanor changed to alarm. The blood isn't flowing down from your nose, he said, reaching for the telephone. It's coming up from deep in your throat.

THE SURGEON'S OFFICE was decorated with surgical collectibles, fragile sculptures, and, for the moment, an illuminated display of my chest X-rays. I sat before him, a supplicant searching for reassurance in his averted eyes, while Nora—a bundle of toddling curiosity, dressed in OshKosh overalls—squirmed and squirreled in my lap. The Surgeon and I had slightly more than a passing acquaintance; twice in the last several months he had operated on me, and twice he had found no evidence of cancer. This time, though, he said, in a tone as flat as a test pattern, he was all but certain that the dark mass glowing like a lunar eclipse on my X-rays—There. See it? Alongside the trachea?—*was* cancer. At this point Nora freed herself from her stunned father's arms and toddled off in the direction of the doctor's precious surgical collectibles. Now with a personal stake in this discussion, the Surgeon raised his voice in alarm. Hey!

The next afternoon, I was anesthetized so that I would not gag on the many fingers and utensils being shoved down my throat during the bronchoscopy. When my eyes opened and adjusted to the false recovery room brightness, I saw the Surgeon looming over me. He reached for my limp hand and shook it.

It was malignant. Tough luck.

That was all he said, and then he was gone.

Okay, I mumbled to his absence. Thank you.

AFTER THE ANESTHESIA had worn off, after I had buttoned up my shirt as though I had been through just another checkup, after other doctors had materialized to say what needed to be said—including the utterance of the word "inoperable"—Mary took my hand. We walked in silence, almost in apology, through the cool and antiseptic corridors of the Mount Sinai Medical Center, into a late Friday afternoon in July, with temperatures in the high nineties. The stink of cigarette smoke and human sweat greeted us as the doors opened out onto Madison Avenue.

The bridge? Mary asked, as she clicked her seat belt.

I answered with a whatever shrug. The George Washington Bridge, the Lincoln Tunnel, a helicopter, astral traveling, I didn't care; I just wanted to get the hell away. I locked my own seat belt, then wondered why.

Before we could deal with matters of life and death, though, we first had to deal with weekend rush-hour traffic to Maplewood, New Jersey, where we were now living. After getting stuck in the northbound traffic leading to the bridge, we turned around, only to inch along for an hour in a line snaking toward the Lincoln Tunnel. I sipped from a can of warm Pepsi and squirmed against my seat belt, resenting the restraints.

Creeping, stopping, creeping, stopping. It was all so maddening that I slammed the dashboard with my hand. Mary barely flinched. She had been waiting for an outburst.

Haven't we just gone through this? I shouted. First your mother! Then my mother! Christ, we just buried her five months ago!

I glowered at the people in the cars that surrounded us, people so perfect and healthy. People with sunglasses, people flicking cigarette ashes, people listening to radio music, people eager to get home, take a swim in a backyard pool, get lost in a ballgame, eat a hot dog, breathe clearly, live. Outside, people with a future; inside, me with inoperable cancer—at forty-one.

I can't get a fucking break even now! Even now! I moaned.

It was a familiar theme in our relationship: the shit-always-happens-to-Danny theme. Only this time, there was no context that Mary could summon to prove me wrong. This time, I was right.

Creeping, stopping, my anger subsided, my fear set in.

Shouldn't they have a special lane for people like me? I asked, my voice breaking. Shouldn't they have a special lane for people who have just been diagnosed with cancer?

Mary and I spent the weekend stumbling about. One minute we were psyching each other up like football underdogs preparing for the Big Game—Yeah! Yeah! Yeah!—and the next we were in our own private comas, staring out the window at the summer rain. It was reminiscent of our experiences with adoption, only so much worse; this time, no one was assuring us that our pains would vanish with an infant's magic touch. We found a baby-sitter to watch Nora for a couple of hours and walked to Maplewood village for an ice cream distraction, but wound up sitting on a bench, snapping at each other as the ice cream tears of our melting cones dripped onto our hands.

Mary took charge, as I knew she would. She telephoned friends to share the news, only to wind up consoling them as they wept. She jotted down the advice that came pouring forth from friends who did not know what else to say. Eat a lot of almonds. Got it. Embrace antioxidants. Got it.

Mary, I asked. What's an antioxidant?

We went to a chic supermarket to buy grains, fresh produce, almonds, and whatever food we could think of as healthful and cancer combative, fully prepared to adopt an after-the-fact diet. We bought books on the relationship between cancer and lifestyle. One night, while Mary rocked Nora to sleep, I flipped through the pages to the sections addressing cancers of the throat, only to be lectured by the authors for having put myself in this dire situation by smoking cigarettes—which, of course, had not been the case. Every book included statistics regarding the chances of survival beyond a year, two years, five years. After my eyes happened to linger on one figure for a specific kind of upper-body cancer (fewer than ten percent survive a year), I closed the book and never looked at another cancer-related book again.

The Surgeon had scooped out about seventy-five percent of the lemon-sized tumor, which had grown so large that it was invading my trachea, causing hemorrhaging and cutting off nearly four-fifths of my wind capacity. Physically, I was breathing easier; emotionally and mentally, I was suffocating. The rest of the world was riveted on whether John F. Kennedy Jr. was alive or dead; his plane had disappeared somewhere off the foggy coast of Nantucket, just a few hours after I had received my diagnosis. But I could only focus on my story. Another Kennedy tragedy, but what about me?

Whenever my thoughts wandered off in such poisonous, destructive directions, I would reach for Nora's favorite book and call her to my side. Come, I would say, patting the seat beside me. Then, with my baby snuggled in the hold of my arm, I would read *We're Going on a Bear Hunt* aloud while privately applying its fantastic lines to my life:

Oh-oh! A cave!
A narrow, gloomy cave.

We can't go over it.
We can't go under it.
Oh, no!
We've got to go through it!

M A R Y A N D I tiptoed through the next two days, frantically trying to choose which cave to enter. The wrenching choice of treatment—radiation or chemotherapy—was made all the more difficult by the mysterious nature of my tumor. This was my formal diagnosis: "squamous cell carcinoma of the thoracic region, primary undetermined, lung versus esophagus." I did not know what all this meant, other than that I was in extremely dangerous terrain—upper respiratory cancers—the minefield that had claimed my mother just a few months earlier. The memory of Noreen not quite Noreen was vivid in my mind as we tiptoed. Fresh too were other memories, of unopened Ensure cans, of pull-me-up sensations, of strangers coming into our house to take away my mother, dead and so very light.

We're not scared. Oh, no!

The weekend passed, and now it was Monday again, when matters of commerce and medicine resume. Mary and I met with Dr. Lynda Mandell, a radiation oncologist at Mount Sinai Medical Center, in a basement office whose lounge was crowded with people reading old magazines and drinking coffee from small Styrofoam cups. It had the high-traffic feel of a muffler shop's waiting room, except that all the customers were wearing cheap cotton bathrobes. And they, not their cars, would be the ones soon raised on lifts, while technicians addressed their faulty parts.

Blond and youthful, Dr. Mandell exuded a can-do confidence in her hunch that she could eradicate the tumor with radiation. But she could tell that her encouraging pitch was failing to calm this white-knuckled clench of a man in her office who refused to make eye contact, who obviously felt as if he were the butt of some cosmic joke. She said that she

understood my anger—at the months of misdiagnoses, at the cancer, at
the surgeon looking down on me and saying tough luck. But she argued
that I didn't have the resources to waste on anger; all my energies had to
be directed toward getting better. She was right, of course, and her words
stirred in me the faintest hope. I nodded, and stumbled out of the building toward Central Park, exhausted by a meeting that lasted less than
an hour.

A few hours later, Mary and I carried my X-rays and medical files to
the Memorial Sloan-Kettering Cancer Center, where Dr. David Pfister, a
medical oncologist with an expertise in cancers of the head and neck,
had agreed to review my case. We sat in an examining room for nearly
two hours while he read the files, examined the charts, and consulted
with other doctors. Finally, the doorknob turned and he walked in, tall,
lean, and clearly deep in troubled thought. When he began to speak, I
understood why: interspersed among all the technical terms flowing
from his mouth were phrases like "very serious," "very, very serious," and
"not good."

I begged him to tell me something that *was* good, something that I
could aim for. I play a lot of sports, I said, including basketball and softball. Give me a basket that I can see; give me a base to run toward.

Dr. Pfister remained quiet for a moment. Then, as if to adhere to some
stipulation in the Hippocratic oath, he explained that he was not a hug-
your-dog-and-everything-will-be-all-right kind of oncologist. It is what
it is, and what it is is very bad. But let's hold off judgment on the best
course of treatment, he added, until I present your case to the Tumor
Board at Sloan-Kettering.

The old Dan Barry would have joked that the Tumor Board sounded
like some kind of trade organization. Was there a Tumor Board softball
league? A Tumor Board seal of approval? But the changed Dan Barry
could not find it in him.

Tumor Board?

A panel of experts, he explained, who gather regularly to review cases
and offer advice on the treatment of life-threatening tumors. His

description conjured in my mind a group of men and women who had not laughed in a very long time, huddled around a long conference table and crossing out name after name as they worked their way down a printout of the week's cases. Next? Next? Next? These, I imagined, were the best and the brightest at Sloan-Kettering, the best and the brightest cancer hospital in the world. Maybe they would recognize that I didn't belong here; maybe they would discover the clerical error that had led to this misunderstanding, this misdiagnosis of cancer. Maybe the joy of finding some good news for a change would send them clambering onto the conference table to dance and shout, the Marx Brothers, the Ritz Brothers, the Andrews Sisters, the Dionne Quintuplets, the Tumor Board, all jitterbugging and shouting the nonsense song, "Not a Tumor, Only a Rumor."

I'll call you when the board reports back, Dr. Pfister said.

And it was back to afternoon rush-hour traffic, with no lane reserved for the terrified.

DR. PFISTER KEPT his promise and called on a Friday night, one week after my diagnosis. As Mary and I listened on separate extensions, he explained that after reviewing the case of a forty-one-year-old non-smoker with squamous cell carcinoma of the trachea, the Tumor Board could not reach consensus on treatment—mostly because the cancer's root had yet to be determined. Almost everyone on the panel agreed that the tumor was inoperable because it was positioned deep in my throat and too close to some delicate wiring. Some said radiation; others said chemotherapy. There was a collective shrug of the shoulders, and the panel moved on to the next disturbing case. No dancing on the table for Danny.

What are we going to do? I asked, the crack in my voice betraying panic to a man I barely knew. I had no sense of him other than that he was candid, almost too candid, about the bleakness of my situation.

Dr. Pfister emphasized that the first shot at treatment was my best shot. He said that he had no strong sense about which drastic course was better, radiation or chemotherapy, although he was inclined to recommend his own specialty, chemotherapy. And if I chose that route, he said, he would be inclined to use a cover-all-bases regimen designed to address a cancer whose nature had not been determined. It would be good, for example, if I turned out to have testicular cancer, because chemotherapy is very effective in many cases of testicular cancer. Other kinds of cancer, though—well, he said, think about it over the weekend.

Mary and I dedicated that weekend to mind-clearing distraction. We played hide-and-seek with Nora. We took an aimless drive through the western Jersey hills. We watched hot-air balloons float across the evening skies like a fleet of weightless Easter eggs bound for a mission of joy. Sunday night came, and our minds were no clearer, no less panicked.

I returned to Sloan-Kettering that Monday for yet another test, then called Dr. Mandell from a phone bank in the building to tell her of my conversation with Dr. Pfister. She strongly, *strongly*, recommended that I choose radiation. I hung up and immediately telephoned Dr. Pfister, who by now was strongly, *strongly* recommending that I choose chemotherapy. The two doctors were in agreement, it seemed, on only one point: time was not on my side.

I felt like the protagonist in Frank R. Stockton's story *The Lady, or the Tiger?* Behind one of these two doors was the faint possibility of life. Choose the right one and you might—*might*—live. Choose the wrong one and you will die. I was on my knees before a phone bank in a public lobby, weeping like a sinner at an automated confessional. Oh Father, please, only say the word and I shall be healed. Let's make a deal, just tell me. Door Number One or Door Number Two.

I wandered through the Midtown streets to the *Times* building on West 43rd Street, into the newsroom, past oblivious friends and colleagues. I found my way to the glass-enclosed office in the corner, where Joe Lelyveld, the executive editor, was talking with another editor about something. It could have been anything from the next day's front page to the travails of a reporter in Afghanistan, to the latest complaint from the White House. When Lelyveld saw me, though, he dismissed the subordinate and waved me in.

The day after my diagnosis he had called me at home, his voice quavering; I remember vaguely telling him, We'll figure it out—my pat response to any crisis, large or small. Now it was my turn. I looked around the office before training my eyes on the large framed poster of the Three Stooges on safari that he had on display. I tried to say something smart-ass, but it just wouldn't come. I choked up instead.

Between my spasms of sobs, I tried to explain the terror I felt, the anger. I said "fuck" a lot.

Lelyveld was in his early sixties, a compact and dignified man with piercing eyes that seemed to nail you into place. Some at the *Times* thought that he was distant and almost too erudite for the newsroom's rough-and-tumble atmosphere. But he had always been kind and supportive to me, before—and after—my diagnosis. I revered him.

I'm so fucking mad, I finally said.

I know, he responded.

He said that he understood all too well, and I knew this was true. A member of his family had been battling cancer for years. But he did not pat me on the back, or cry with me, or tell me everything will be all right. Instead, he said, Your body has betrayed you. And now you have to fight back.

Hearing these words from Joe Lelyveld helped me to focus. I thanked him, promised to keep him apprised, and found a corner in the newsroom to gather my thoughts. I telephoned Mary, and then Dr. Pfister. I told him that I—we—had chosen the chemotherapy regimen, but that if there were a radiation component, I wanted it to be administered by Dr. Mandell at Mount Sinai. He said that he would call her, and that I should come to Sloan-Kettering in the morning for an ultrasound of my abdomen and testes. There was that slim hope of testicular cancer, he said, which would be much easier to treat than the more likely culprits of lung cancer and esophageal cancer.

When I got home, Nora was outside holding a bouquet of sorts: a small plastic bucket of oversized color chalk. I spent the next hour drawing happy face after happy face—one in red, one in blue, one in green—on the sidewalk and the driveway. Nora delighted in this bubbling sea of happiness, while I offered up the perverse prayer that I had testicular cancer.

Nora, I thought. Wouldn't it be great if Daddy only had testicular cancer?

22

W E CAUGHT AN early-morning train out of Maplewood that was crowded with people so white-collar crisp,
all reading newspapers, sipping coffee, and preparing to
conquer the day. Mary and I sat in uneasy contrast, dressed as though
bound for a late July vacation—she in her summer dress and sandals, I
in a golf shirt and khakis. I even had an overnight bag nestled between
my feet on the floor, containing clothes, a few books, toiletries, and whatever else I could think of to bring for my first extended stay at Hotel
Sloan-Kettering.

As the train ground its way toward Manhattan, I looked out upon the
ordinary scene whirring past: the lush trees of South Orange, the spent
streets of Newark, the muck of the Meadowlands. I searched for one of
the snow-white swans that grace the swampy mire, as if the sight of one
would signal the presence of a reassuring spiritual force—the Holy
Spirit, perhaps. Spotting a bird as white as a Communion dress, I felt a
brief lift of hope before the ensuing crush of shame. The Holy Spirit of
the Meadowlands, come to save me from cancer. How absurd.

I yearned for the mundane. I wished that I too were a commuter on
his way to another routine day at work, able to afford the fleeting anger
over a missed A train, or a story in *Newsday* that I should have broken.
Now I could barely bring myself to read the *Times*. An article by another
reporter about the city's last Checker cab had recently appeared on the

front page; I had been assigned to that story weeks earlier. And on this morning, there appeared a story about Mayor Giuliani visiting Arkansas for the express purpose of taunting his would-be Democratic rival for the Senate, Hillary Rodham Clinton. I should be in Arkansas, I thought, writing about another odd political moment with Rudy Giuliani. I would have welcomed even that.

I was aware of how irrational these thoughts were as soon as they entered my head, but this was how I felt. I wanted to be a loving husband and father who earned his living by writing about New York City's mayor for *The New York Times*. Now I was perhaps the only commuter on this train who was carrying underwear for a hospital stay, who saw the Holy Spirit in the Meadowlands. I was a body of text appended to the wrong story; I was out of context.

The cabdriver drove us to Sloan-Kettering by way of Central Park. It was turning out to be the kind of summer morning that, even before my diagnosis, would give me joyful pause, with that coolness before the heat, that fresh promise of another day. I wanted so many more of these. I squeezed Mary's hand, and she squeezed back.

The corner of East 68th Street and York Avenue, the location of the nation's foremost cancer hospital, was enveloped in what I came to learn was a constant shroud of cigarette smoke. On the East 68th Street side, nurses, orderlies, and other hospital employees hurried to squeeze in two cigarettes before the end of their break. On the York Avenue side, patients dragged on cigarettes with a blithe manner that suggested their IV poles were mere fashion accessories. I tried to block out thoughts of my mother outside Good Samaritan Hospital on Long Island: wheelchair-bound, dying, freezing in the winter air, and luxuriating in one of her very last cigarettes, leaving it to others to cluck at the link between her addiction and her condition.

I signed in at the admissions desk and we found seats in a room already crowded with patients-in-waiting of different ages and sizes and stages in the disease. My eyes came to rest on a man about my age who was wearing shorts and a 1996 Yankees World Championship T-shirt. His hair was gone, and he had the intravenous plumbing already inserted into his arm. Clearly a Sloan-Kettering veteran, I thought. He looked at me several times before I realized why. I was staring at him, trying to imagine myself in his place. I fumbled to find distraction in my *Daily News*.

An older woman wearing a broad smile and a powder-blue blazer called my name; she would be our volunteer escort. I reached for my suitcase, and Mary and I followed her into an elevator. The woman hummed as the elevator rose, hummed as it opened onto the eighth floor, hummed as she led us along a brightly lit corridor, hummed as a low, begging-for-mercy moan escaped from one of the rooms we passed. Oh Jesus God, I thought. Oh Fuck. The escort kept humming what sounded to me like a melding of "I Feel Pretty" and "Streets of Laredo."

The escort brought us to the threshold of a semiprivate room and stopped just short of telling me to enjoy my stay. Within five minutes, the bald, pallid patient in the other bed had pulled back the curtain, introduced himself as Arthur, and launched into a detailed soliloquy on his illness, peppered throughout with tips about hospital service. He spoke so hurriedly that his words collided to create a kind of breathless cancer-ward prose poem: advanced prostate cancer, renal failure, kidney failure, preparing to die, dialysis, Tracy the nurse is very nice, you should get cable right away, now they're giving me a chemo regimen that can treat but not cure, but I'll take it, so what are you in for?

I'm sorry?

What are you in for?

I had always imagined that if I were ever asked that question, I would answer with "Crimes against the state." I let the urge pass and decided to level with my partner in cancer.

There's a malignant tumor in my trachea.

But what kind of cancer is it?

They thought it might be testicular cancer, but now they don't think so. They're still trying to figure it out.

Arthur studied me with eyes set so deep in dark sockets that he looked more than a little like Uncle Fester. I could tell that he was sizing me up: determining my place in the cancer spectrum, calculating my chances of survival, and measuring accordingly how much empathy I deserved.

Oh, he said. But I could not tell whether his Oh meant Oh, you're one of us, or Oh, you're fucked, or just Oh. Even though I had just met him, I considered Arthur to be a battle-wise grunt who knew all the angles, who had crunched the life expectancy statistics on every conceivable form of the disease. All he had said was Oh, but I knew so little about my own cancer—and was so frightened by it—that I began to deconstruct his Oh as though it were scriptural text.

Arthur remained suspicious. I sensed that he thought I might be a cancer fraud—a cancer wannabe.

Well, is it operable? he asked, not bothering to conceal a note of impatience. I mean, are you here for chemo? How come they don't know what it is?

As I pondered his question, a question that was already foremost in my mind, I remembered the advice of Joyce Wadler, a *Times* reporter who had once written a book about her own struggle with cancer. After word of my diagnosis spread through the newsroom, she telephoned me and, though she barely knew me, called me "my poor baby"—a blessing. She then advised me on how to survive my hospital stays. Ignore the comments of nurses, friends, and other patients, and listen to only what the doctor tells you. Carve out time for quiet reflection, time to prepare yourself as if girding for battle. And get a private room; the extra money you spend is worth the sanity you save.

This is the worst time of your life, she said. Take care of yourself. Cut out the sources of confusion and pain—sources, I imagined, like Arthur, who was now filling the void created by my silence with more cancer musings: For testicular cancer, they slit you from stem to stern and then examine every single lymph node, cutting the bad ones, leaving the good ones. It takes about twenty hours. The soup is pretty good here, by the way.

I thanked Arthur for his insights, pulled Mary aside, and asked her to go to the nurse's desk and inquire about the availability of private rooms. She returned to give me a discreet nod.

It looks like I've been transferred to another room, Arthur, I said.

Oh, he said again.

I decided not to parse this Oh, and instead shook his hand and wished him the best of luck.

Good luck, he answered, with a hesitant handshake signaling that he still suspected me of being one of those cancer wannabes.

A few minutes later we were escorted to a recently vacated private room. I tried not to think about the circumstances behind its availability. Then a nurse practitioner appeared to help me get acclimated. She pointed to a dresser drawer where my hospital-issue green pajamas were stored, but I told her that I would not be wearing pajamas, or a bathrobe, or slippers—just street clothes during the day and sweatpants at night. I had already decided that if I wore pajamas, especially during the day, I would be ceding psychological ground to the disease. I considered myself to be in battle mode, and soldiers in battle mode do not wear green pajamas and paper slippers.

Fuck you, I was telling cancer. The pants stay on.

The nurse practitioner was not happy with my sartorial decision, but she moved on. She invited me to avail myself of some of the amenities, including an arts-and-crafts room upstairs and a nice patients' lounge at the end of the hall. I winced. Mary and I had already peeked into the lounge to see members of the cleaning staff taking a break, watching the fuzzy television and chatting in Spanish, while an elderly woman rocked in a chair and wept into cupped hands.

The scene jarred me. The lack of interaction between the cleaning staff and the crying woman meant, at least to me, that moments of public anguish in this ward were so common that employees had become accustomed to them. It made sense, I supposed. If the maintenance workers focused on every sobbing person to appear in their workplace—if they noticed every child attached to an IV pole—they would be unable to work; they would go mad. And the only way that I could keep from going mad was to wisecrack that the lounge looked like hell's waiting room.

The joke took the nurse practitioner aback. She nodded, looked away, released an ahem or two, then sort of backed out of the room. She seemed genuinely surprised, even offended, that I was not happy to be in the cancer ward.

Moments later, a smiling young woman exuding an air of commitment to healthful diet and exercise—all bouncy brown hair and even white teeth—walked into the room. When she introduced herself as a hospital counselor, I realized immediately that she had been alerted by the nurse practitioner to a "situation": a new admission with immersion problems; one of those patients who will focus on the sobs and moans rather than the encouraging words.

The counselor gave me a firm handshake, her way of reaching across an invisible but distinct divide to the land of the unwell.

You're angry, aren't you? she asked.

I looked to Mary, who signaled without so much as raising an eyebrow that I should remain calm because this nice young woman was not responsible for my disease. I did the best I could.

I'm forty-one years old, I said evenly. I've never smoked. I have a baby girl who's not yet two years old, and I'm in a goddamned cancer hospital. Now. Wouldn't *you* be angry?

The counselor nodded, less in agreement and more in confirmation that yep, we have a "situation" here. She explained that her office was just down the hall—If you ever need to talk—and then, like her colleague before her, backed away and out, as if to avoid any sudden movement in my presence.

A few minutes later, Dr. Pfister appeared, a furrowed brow in hospital white. In his mid-forties and very tall, he tended to stand at a slight forward angle, permanently poised, it seemed, to listen to the complaints and breathing patterns of his patients. So far I had found him to be thorough, candid almost to a fault, and determined not to raise false hopes.

He laid out every option and every potential outcome in painstaking detail, reflecting a rock-solid belief that science and the mysterious workings of the body—not hugs and the lighting of votive candles—will determine the future. He seemed obsessed with anticipating his nemesis's every possible move, as though he and cancer were decades deep in the same game of chess.

This did not, however, mean that Dr. Pfister was oblivious to the needs and worries of his patients. Several times in the short time that Mary and I had known him, he had started his hospital rounds at seven in the morning, spent the day meeting with dozens of other cancer patients, worked his way through the typical office politics of a major hospital, and then sometime after eight in the evening, telephoned to share what little more he had gleaned about my case. One of the nurses later told me that while she barely knew Dr. Pfister—He was hardly chatty, she said—she had caught a glimpse of his essence one quiet evening on the hospital's eighth floor.

He had asked a dying patient a perfunctory question: Is there anything at all that you need: more juice maybe, or another pillow? The patient looked toward the window and whispered something about just wanting a little fresh air.

Instead of changing the subject or calling for an orderly, she said, Dr. Pfister carefully bundled the patient up, eased him into a wheelchair, and pushed him slowly, leisurely, around the block. Doctors just don't do that, the nurse said.

Now Dr. Pfister was trying to protect another one of his pawns in that endless chess match: me.

He explained that I was about to embark on a chemotherapy marathon: round-the-clock chemo, drip by drip, from Wednesday morning until Sunday afternoon. This round was just the first of six five-day, inpatient treatments that would begin every four weeks. He said some other things that made me again wish that God had blessed me with testicular cancer, then confided that the nurse practitioner and the counselor had expressed concern about where I was "with all this."

I turned again toward Mary, seeking and finding once more that imperceptible signal: stay calm, take a deep breath, everything will be all right. But I could not understand why everyone seemed to think that I should treat my hospital stay as nothing more than a few days at a bad Holiday Inn.

Look, I said, with a touch more exasperation than I had intended to reveal. This is your world—your environment—so maybe you don't see it to be as intimidating as I do. But if I plopped you into the middle of a newsroom and started asking you questions on the record, wouldn't you be a little rattled?

He nodded.

And this is about my life! I said, body and voice trembling now. I'm not crying, I'm not yelling, I'm not banging my head against the wall. But that doesn't mean I'm glad to be here. I'm very, very angry, and what you're seeing is my game face. My attitude is, this sucks, so bring it on.

I could see in his face that he understood. It was worthy of every epithet I ever learned under the streetlamps of Deer Park, on the Phelan Bus, in the sweat of deadline journalism—and yet, even combined, they still fell far short. And who could I blame? The doctors, who missed that mass growing to the size of a lemon as they pondered my X-rays, so many X-rays, in September and October and March and April? My parents, for smoking in my presence for all those years, filling my baby pink lungs with secondhand smoke? God? Was I going to blame God? Oh God if You do exist, then why this, why now? And oh my Sisters of St. Joseph, oh my Franciscan brothers and fathers, enough with that working in mysterious ways bullshit. We die; what's the mystery? But why me now?

In the name of almighty fuck, I thought, why fucking me? Why fuck me? Fuck.

Okay, my doctor said.

And that was that.

Mary stacked my folded clothes in a couple of drawers, set my books down by the night table, and wedged a few snapshots of Nora in the nooks and crannies of my small room. We thought these little touches would lend a homey feel to my temporary situation, as if we could not smell the disinfectant, or notice the jug that was meant to measure my urine, or hear the prattle of doctors and nurses and orderlies just outside the door.

While the sunny promise of a July afternoon streamed through the blinds, a nurse shoved a needle into my right arm. I watched the first drip fall like a raindrop from the clear bag at the top of my IV pole, slither down a transparent tube, and disappear into my being. It was official: I was on chemo.

Mary went down to a delicatessen on First Avenue to buy me a turkey-and-Swiss sandwich, not too much mayo, for dinner. We unfolded its wax wrapping on the bed, as though laying out a blanket for a picnic. I ate everything, including the pickle, figuring that I might as well store energy while I still had an appetite. Before I knew it, the sunlight had gone from the window, and Mary was rising to leave; she had to get back to Nora. She kissed me, told me everything would be all right, and closed the door behind her.

I sat for a few minutes in the encroaching dusk. Okay, I said to no one but myself, Okay. Realizing that my mother used to say the same thing when she was ill, I stood up and took my IV pole for a walk.

The IV pole had wheels that squeaked, like one of those damaged shopping carts that drives you mad before you've even reached the produce section. That pole would become my evil twin, my steel shadow, my toxin-seeping savior. And, in the days to come, it would mark me as a cancer patient wherever I went. Between bouts of nausea, I would escort my pole around the eighth-floor ward a few times, trying not to notice the emaciated conditions and worried expressions that were all about me. I would study the leaflets stapled to the bulletin board next to the elevator bank: the schedules for counseling sessions, the time for the screening of *The Sting*, the announcements of support-group meetings for the families of dying loved ones, the hours of operation for the arts-and-crafts room upstairs.

I went up to the arts-and-crafts room a couple of times, mostly to step out onto a sun deck for some fresh air, but also to satisfy my curiosity. It seemed all very nice and necessary, with patients losing themselves in watercolors and pottery and tile design. Considering all the IV poles in the room, I would have fit right in. But I could not do arts and crafts for the same reason that I could not wear pajamas: I refused to succumb to the culture of the sick. No hospital johnnies, and no hospital aide cooing over my vibrant use of the color red. With all due respect, I'm just passing through. Yessir, back on the streets in no time.

In the morning, if the desire to retch had subsided for a while, I would take the elevator down to the first floor to buy the *Times*, the *Post*, the *News*, a cup of coffee, and a cheese Danish. Then I would find a corner in the visitor's lounge and try to blend in among the well, as though I were waiting for someone else who was sick. It was an absurd pretension, of course. I was tethered to that IV pole, the giveaway that I was on the other side, that I was only posing to be healthy. I could feel the furtive glances in the elevator, hear the minds whirring to take in all the clues and figure out what kind of cancer I had. I could sense the wide berth given to my pole and me as we glided down drab corridors, a sickly Fred and a ghostly Ginger, her squeaky wheels keeping the beat to my song:

Soon
We'll be without the moon,
Humming a diff'rent tune
And then,
There may be teardrops to shed.
So while there's music and moonlight,
And love and romance,
Let's face the music and dance.

Any lingering thoughts of "This ain't so bad" evaporated on the second day of chemotherapy, as the clear and caustic fluid coursed through my body, killing blood cells, searing veins, and—conceivably at least—attacking my tumor. My head throbbed, and even the act of breathing nauseated me. I had a headset and a portable CD player, but I could not bear the music. I had several books, but I could not keep focused. I lined the windowsill with the fruit that came with every meal, but I could never summon the appetite, or fully suppress the sensation that I was about to vomit. I ate crackers, forced down water, pissed in a jug, and got tangled in my IV accessories.

People came to visit. Kevin Davitt, City Hall habitué and professional political adviser, presented me with a pint of rotgut called Mad Dog 20-20, saying it had cost him nearly two bucks; what's more, he had to walk ten blocks to find a liquor store that stocked it. The very next day, Kevin McCabe, a former City Council chief of staff who truly knows where the bodies are buried—he used to work in the morgue—presented me with an open quart container of beer that he had somehow smuggled into the hospital. The smell of it made me gag, and when I complained about the IV pole impeding my way to the bathroom, McCabe called out the traditional Irish blessing: Want some cheese with that whine? Instead of vomiting, I laughed. And when I returned, he slipped me a prayer card that Mother Teresa had given to him years earlier.

Keep it pressed against your throat, he confided. Only give it back to me when you're done.

Joe Lelyveld arrived one night with two *Times* reporters, my close friends Matt Purdy and Joe Sexton. They were both about my age, with young children of their own. They knew the gravity of my situation, but they also understood what Davitt and McCabe had understood: no clucking, no keening, no acknowledgment that they were standing and healthy and I was in bed with cancer. It was as though my three *Times* colleagues had come to wish me well on my trip, with the understanding that we'd all get together when I returned. Lelyveld presented me with a cancer-hospital comfort bag. There were some hard candies for when the medicine parches the throat, a pillow designed for neck support, and some CDs meant to transport listeners to another place.

Thanks for stopping by, I called out as they left. See ya.

One afternoon, my father and my sister Brenda appeared with Mary

at my door, carrying three bags of goodies from the King Kullen supermarket on Deer Park Avenue. There were Oreos and Fig Newtons and
pieces of fruit, and, of course, some Entenmann's. I ate none of it, not
even the Entenmann's, which prompted my father and sister to exchange
worried glances that said, Too sick for Entenmann's?

I tried to mask how poorly I felt by teasing my father. I said I could
just picture him driving Brenda mad by the time they reached Exit 48 on
the Long Island Expressway, filling her car with cigarette smoke, fidgeting, commanding the sun to cease its annoying glare. Watching him pace
about the room, looking in vain for some corner of comfort—No ashtray?—I realized how hard all this was for him. He had traveled to his city
of bad memories to visit his oldest child in a cancer ward, just a few
months after his beloved Noreen had died of cancer. How could he see
me in my bed and not think of her? He paced some more.

Now and then he slipped behind a mask of his own, making a big production about the hospital's amenities. Hey Danny, at least you've got
cable, he said at one point. You can watch the Yankees.

He picked at my untouched cafeteria lunch before finally excusing
himself to get something to eat from a delicatessen. I need to keep up my
strength, he said. He needed some food, but he also needed some time to
himself: cigarette smoldering in tight-lipped mouth, smoke curling back
into narrowed eyes, thinking how can there be a God, what with his son
like this and his wife dead, and not a sign from her since.

He came back a half hour later with an aluminum tray of fettucine
alfredo and chicken and peppers and a few other items that had caught
his eye at the deli's steam table. He ate and joked and ate some more,
keeping up his strength to be with me, and I loved him for that.

Eventually all hospital guests must leave. My father came to my bed as
I had come to his so many times when he was sick with headaches. He
shook my hand, extra firm for extra love, and said good-bye. Mary kissed
me and promised to call when she got home. Of course she would hug
Nora for me, I didn't even have to ask. And there I was again, alone in the
enveloping darkness, with the only light a sliver escaping through the

crack of the closed door. Beyond that door came the muffled conversations of the night shift, punctuated by an occasional, mirthless laugh.

Maybe they were laughing about the time I was being guided through the CT scan doughnut at another hospital, scared out of my mind and obeying the recorded announcement—Breathe in; hold your breath—when I noticed that the technician watching from behind the glass partition was shucking and eating peanuts. Or maybe they had heard about my recent encounter with a surgeon who, while reviewing my scans, had noticed what appeared to be a small bump on the side of my esophagus, separate from the tumor that had already been discovered. He sat me in a room, reached for a pad and paper, and quickly sketched a few lines to represent my trachea, esophagus, and voice box. If a biopsy of that bump indicated malignancy, he said, then he would have to remove all this. Using his pen as an imaginary scalpel, he drew a circle around most of what he had just sketched.

I stared at the childlike sketch, and then at him. You'd remove my voice box, I said.

Yes, the voice box would have to go, he said.

Would there be a way for me to talk again?

Oh yes, he said. There are all sorts of things we can do now.

Perhaps. But all that I could think of was holding a Norelco electric razor against my throat while reading *Goodnight Moon* to Nora. It would be like the Frankenstein monster singing her a lullaby; she'd need therapy by the age of four. Still, my voice box for my life seemed like a fair trade.

They wheeled me through the corridors the way that workers in the garment district wheel bolts of fabric, turning this way and that, through door after door. I muttered fractured Hail Marys all the way—Hail Mary, full of grace—never forgetting how it had been my mother's favorite prayer, and look what good it did her. It was the same prayer I had whispered before the bronchoscopy that led to my diagnosis, and look what—Oh never mind, oh Hail Mary. If the bump proved to be malignant, then I had esophageal cancer. In medical terms, it meant that I had less than a ten percent chance of surviving a year; in Deer Park terms, it meant that I was fucked. The surgeon fed a fiber-optic wire topped with a minuscule camera down my esophagus to locate the bump before snipping a piece for a biopsy. But he couldn't find it; the bump had disappeared. Glory be to God, I said when I regained consciousness. But how could a bump simply disappear?

Might have been a piece of bagel, I was told.

A piece of bagel, I imagined the laughing people saying, just outside my door. *A piece of bagel. Ain't that a scream?*

Hail Mary, full of grace, the Lord is with thee.

TIME AT SLOAN-KETTERING drips, as from an IV bag. Attached to my IV-pole companion was a beeping device that regulated the flow of the chemical cocktail being pumped into my bloodstream. If the chemicals flowed too slowly or too quickly, or if the IV line jammed somehow—if I scratched my nose with the wrong hand, if I rolled over in bed—the device's metronomic beep would change into a mechanical call of distress, similar to the warning sound of a truck in reverse. The only way to stop the beeping was to summon a nurse, who would fiddle with the line as though trying to align a rabbit-ear antenna for the best reception on an old Philco.

I found myself equating the beeps of the machine with the drips of the toxins, seep, seep, seeping into me. If the sound wasn't hypnotizing me into head-throbbing semiconsciousness, it was contributing to the overwhelming nausea brought on by the chemo, by the hospital's latest attempt at international cuisine—paella?—by the mere waft of a nurse's particular perfume. But in my better moments, I imagined those beeps and grinds to be the actual sound of the curing process: the sound of specially prepared fluids going directly to the tumor and wearing it away, like drips of boiling water on an ice cube. They were the sounds of chemically altered holy water, washing away the sin of my cancer.

In those dark hours of night, the sounds from beyond my door came as escaped sighs, death rattles. And I would obsess about the doctors on their evening rounds, pausing outside my room to study my charts, then appearing at my bedside like befuddled angels in lab coats. Their names and faces kept changing, but the questions they asked remained the same (And when exactly did you begin spitting up blood?). After resurrecting every painful moment in the matter of *Daniel F. Barry v. Cancer*—So the cancer has not been classified yet?—they would vanish behind the cloth curtains that surrounded my bed. And I would hear them whispering again at the threshold of my door.

Are they talking about my prognosis? Are they calculating my chances, like those of some pony in the fifth race at Aqueduct? Is the tumor shrinking, is it growing, will I see Nora graduate, will I waste away as my mother did, slipping in and out of coherence, staring at *Judge Judy* while a glorious afternoon's light glances over the television? Will Mary have to carry me to the bathroom? Oh Christ oh Christ, I have to stop.

I reached for the switch by the side of the bed and turned on the small television that dangled before me from a retractable arm. Oh good. The Yankees are on. Who's pitching?

Baseball has that amazing ability to transport. Its rhythms are so mesmerizing, its present so intertwined with its past, that you can pause to catch half an inning, begin an interior riff on all things baseball, and then turn around to find that your wife has left you and that you have somehow misplaced September. I came to treasure baseball as a narcotic. The Venetian blinds would be drawn to block the taunt of sunset; the oranges from lunches and dinners not eaten would rest along a ledge; my head would pound, my stomach would churn, my bladder would fill with the waste of toxins—all with the beep of that blasted machine reminding me in three-second increments that I have cancer . . . I have cancer . . . I have cancer.

And then Paul O'Neill would step into the batter's box and squint so intensely that I half expected his eyes to bleed. Soon I would be lost in every twitch and half swing he made, remembering that sensation I knew so well, of *battus interruptus*, when a left-hander's curveball could make me swing as though I were trying to swat a shuttlecock. And then the camera would follow the arc of a foul ball into the crowd, and I would remember the feel of a beer's foam caressing my hand as it spilled from those cheap wax-plastic cups. Then the Yankees dugout would come into view, showing Joe Torre and his trusty sidekick, Don Zimmer, the Ed McMahon of baseball. And I would remember that Zimmer was once knocked unconscious for a week by a pitched ball, and that in a shoebox at home I have a baseball card of Torre when he was a catcher for the Milwaukee Braves, and it was a toss-up as to who looked tougher, his mug or his mitt. And thoughts of home would remind me of Mary, and how she has always calmed me in the unrest of deep night—even before I was diagnosed—when I would wake her to ask, Am I going to be all right?

Imagine you're playing baseball, and you're in the outfield again, she would say, stroking my back. *Centerfield. And it's a night game. Everything is lit up, the way you like it, aglow. And the grass is soft and lush and just a little damp, because it is a late summer's night. You call out to your friend the pitcher, your friend the catcher, your friend the shortstop, just to let them know you're there for them. You'll back them up. The batter hits a fly ball, a beautiful fly ball. And you run to where it is falling, falling like a star. And you catch it, on the run.*

Later tonight, alone in my dark hospital room, I would smell at the surface of sleep the perfume that makes me gag. I would open my eyes to see a nurse looming over me, ready to take my temperature, check my pulse, and jab me for more blood. For now, though, I feel Mary's conjured fingertips drawing curlicues of comfort on my back, I hear her soft play-by-play, and I remember nights spent alert in dew-wet cleats, waiting for the distant meeting of bat and ball, anticipating the thwock of that encounter, then running, running across grass to end this one baseball poem with the period landing in my glove. Then into the dugout to be slapped on the back by teammates from so many teams, wearing the uniforms of the Ducks and the Friars and the Providence Grays. I reach for my bat and walk to the plate, familiar words of encouragement trailing after me: *Wait for your pitch, Danny; Come on, Danny, just a little bingle.* Oh did I want to hit a bingle for my teammates, those boys and men; oh did I want to reach base, safe. The good wishes of a thousand summer nights would drown out the beep and bop of my IV machine, and sleep would come, for a little while.

23

JULY INTO AUGUST, back in the hospital. August into September, back in. September into October, back. October into November, back. Three weeks out, one week in; three weeks out, one week in. This was the cycle of my seasons, spinning inexorably toward an answer to the most elemental of questions: life or death?

I would return home from Sloan-Kettering, recuperate for a few days, then wobble off to the *Times* until the start of my next treatment. For the first few weeks I reported to Room 9 in City Hall, where cancer had announced itself with blood on a take-out napkin, then after that to a desk in the distant corner of the third-floor newsroom on West 43rd Street, there beside the snack room. My decision to continue writing for the *Times* had nothing to do with professional dedication or journalistic swagger, and everything to do with the need to declare myself alive, in newsprint and ink.

I kept in mind the advice that Bob McFadden, the Pulitzer Prize–winning master of evocative, even mournful prose, had once shared with me. I like *The New York Times*, the veteran reporter had said. But I don't love it.

His words reflected no disrespect for the *Times*, but instead offered sly comment on the tendency of some reporters and editors to lose themselves entirely to the fast pace and raw ambition at the paper of record, where one's worth is measured each day at deadline. Ever so gently,

McFadden was signaling that this is a very good job, perhaps the best in journalism—but only a job. He was right, of course: Mary and Nora first, then our families, and then *The New York Times*.

After my diagnosis, though, I began to see the *Times* as something more than a great newspaper. I saw it as a vehicle to remind everyone about me, as a way to write formal, impersonal letters to friends and acquaintances around the country. The letters may have been about the most incremental City Hall development, but the byline would carry my name, marking my existence, saying that I had made it to here at least. To affirm my life, it seemed, I needed to tell stories. I needed to report.

A few days after completing my first round of chemotherapy, I dug out a brief newspaper clip I had saved about a baseball player named Mark Lemke. Once the second baseman for the Atlanta Braves team that won four National League pennants and a World Series during the 1990s, he was now playing for a team called the Jackals, in a bandbox ballpark in Little Falls, New Jersey. At thirty-four, he had lost a half step in his game, more than enough to make him expendable at the major-league level, and so he had decided to become a knight errant of baseball: a knuckleball pitcher.

Success as a knuckleballer takes more than just learning how to grip the ball. It also requires a mystical understanding of the game, the counterintuitive ability to entrust the baseball to the fickle air. Lemke had not yet achieved that level of trust, that Zen-like ability to let go. "You can't make a knuckleball happen," Jim Bouton, a former major-league knuckleball pitcher, told me. "There is nothing you do with your hands except release it and leave it up to the wind and the air and the gods."

Now, in the press box at tiny Yogi Berrra Stadium, I rooted for Lemke as though for myself, and began drafting the sentences to a story that would appear on the front page of Sunday's *Times*. I noticed his level of concentration. How he seemed oblivious to the cavorting of the mascot, Jack the Jackal; to the Cajun music being played to promote "Mardi Gras Night"; to the Little Leaguers clutching baseball cards that depicted a younger, more successful him.

My story began: *The first pitch moved through the night like a butterfly drunk on tequila, floating blithely past the catcher. The second pitch sailed about like a party balloon sputtering helium. The sixth pitch tripped and fell somewhere near home plate, bouncing off a batter's shin.*

And it ended: *According to the game's official scorer, Lemke had given up two earned runs and only three hits in five innings, a success by any measure. But there was also the unrecorded gift that he had presented to those fans paying attention: knuckleball after knuckleball, dancing summertime waltzes on a muggy night in New Jersey.*

Mesmerized by those knuckleballs, I forgot about cancer, and chemo, and death. Then I scratched my scalp, and strands of chemo-killed hair fluttered down by the dozens upon my reporter's notebook.

A FEW DAYS after my diagnosis, my friend the Franciscan, Dan Riley, had called to comfort me. He is the St. Bonaventure priest who performed our wedding ceremony, a man who brings refreshing vigor to the cliché of living one's faith, my trusted spiritual guide. Yet I had shouted at him that I didn't want to hear any more about the crosses we must bear, or that God gave me this burden because He knew I could handle it, or that I should prepare for the possibility of meeting my maker before Nora graduates from kindergarten. Not that Riley had said any of these things. I had simply used him as a foil for God.

I love your anger, Riley had said through his tears. That's what makes you *you*.

Interpreting this to be a priest's blessing of my anger, I raged on through the days and weeks. Gradually, though, fear displaced rage. I found that during my weekday walk from Penn Station to the *Times* building, my whispered mutterings of God, oh God, became the softest notes among the street shouts and horn bleats and gear shifts that are synthesized daily to create the Eighth Avenue Morning Symphony.

I began these walks of fearful prayer, always, by looking up at a

twenty-story advertisement that loomed over the intersection of 34th
Street and Eighth Avenue. It depicted a woman in dark sunglasses gazing
heavenward, and included the Amtrak slogan: "Return your mind to its
upright position."

Got it; mind upright.

Then would come the Lord's Prayer. I tried for the first time in my life
to pry each word from the hoary prayer-block and think about its meaning, reflect on how many times it had been uttered by how many billions
of people over how many centuries, at births and executions, before battle and after. I knew that I had uttered this prayer thousands of times,
during classroom rosaries chanted under nun glares, during Masses at St.
Cyril's, at St. Anthony's, at St. Bonaventure, and I had recited it always in
a kind of street-corner singsong. Now I would parse the words for meaning. My predicament required it.

Our Father. Got it.

Who art in heaven. Got that too.

Hallowed be thy name. Check.

Up Eighth Avenue I'd walk. *Thy kingdom come. Thy will be done, On
earth as it is in heaven.* Ambling past storefronts that had been there for
a week or forever. Habib Fabrics. Papillon Fashions. Gem Pawnbrokers.
Praying all the while, or trying to. *Give us this day our daily bread.* Bread!
Yes, the bread of life. Life! Yes! Weaving through the clutches of weary
garment workers, sidestepping the fishtailing carts weighed down with
bolts of cloth. *And forgive us our trespasses.* Please, God, forgive me my
many trespasses.

As we forgive—Jesus Christ! Another damn taxi lurching into a crowd
when the walk sign is OBVIOUSLY on! Hey! Don't give me that shrug!
You know you're wrong! Almost killed me, you stupid ass!—*those who
trespass against us.*

And lead us not into temptation, But deliver us from evil. Amen.

Amen.

A quick Hail Mary, and then I would be standing at 40th Street,
where some fifteen years earlier I had been baptized by beer while on

my way to be interviewed for that clerk's job. How unlucky I had felt back then; imagine. I had three blocks to go, plenty of time to forget about cancer by thinking about my *Times* story of the day. Often it was about Giuliani: Giuliani cutting city funds to the Brooklyn Museum because an exhibit offended him, or Giuliani arranging a patronage job far from City Hall for his controlling assistant because their personal relationship had ended. But other days would bring assignments that were blessedly free of Giuliani, from a profile of an advocate for the homeless to a rewrite job on the crash of a jetliner off the coast of New England. Writing these stories both sustained me and allowed me to send out the cryptic three-word message of continued existence: By Dan Barry.

There were other stories, though, that I fully reported but did not write. They were vignettes, really, all belonging to a single story that followed an age-old plot: a man goes on a journey.

Sixty-eighth and York, I said.

Sloan-Kettering, huh, said the driver.

He stole glimpses of my bald scalp through his rearview mirror while his taxi hurtled uptown, cutting through a muggy late August mist. All I could make of this man were his broad shoulders, large ears, and those eyes in the mirror, inquisitive but kind.

Yep, I said, my yep clearly signaling that I didn't want to talk about it.

Yeah, he said. There was silence. Then he said, Yeah. I been there.

Really? I said, giving in a bit. What for?

Prostrate, he said. It was too pat, a cab driver saying that, but he said it. Prostrate, a word that in the context of cancer seemed appropriate.

N'you? he asked. I told him what little I knew. He nodded.

We sat in quiet awe of our connection. As the cab sliced east through the Central Park green, I studied the back of his head and what little I could make of his face in the mirror. He looked fine, healthy, beyond it.

So, I said finally. How you doing?

Good, good, thank God, he said. But hey—you never know. Know what I mean?

Yeah, I said.

The cab pulled up to the smoke-choked threshold of Sloan-Kettering. As I reached for the door handle, I gave the driver a tip that matched the fare.

Take care of yourself, I said.

He turned around without looking at the money I had placed in his hand. Hey buddy, he said, holding my gaze. Good luck now. All right?

All right.

SMALL MOMENTS LIKE this—even small things—grew large in meaning. I watched with childlike surprise as fireflies floated around me like undying sparks of energy upon the warm breath of summer evening. I obsessed over the thought of eating a simple olive, whose mouth-watering explosions of saltiness seemed, in my chronic state of nausea, to be an impossible experience. And, of course, there was that small wonder called Nora, just turned two.

After slogging through another day, I would collapse on the couch and wait for her to toddle over and assure me, Nice haircut, as the bristle patches jutting from my scalp tickled her tiny palms. Then she would plop a copy of *The Runaway Bunny* onto my chest and say, Read. Each time I read, The End, she would say, Again.

She loved all kinds of music, from Ray Charles to Raffi. One of Raffi's albums, a collection of folk songs, included an old spiritual that had become my anthem. Driving through suburban New Jersey streets in a Saturn cluttered with Cheerio bits and empty juice boxes, I would sing with all the conviction once summoned by those from another time and place. I too wanted Almighty intervention. I too wanted freedom.

Daniel in the lion's den
Daniel in the lion's den
Daniel in the lion's den

Daddy, play something else.
Just a minute, honey. Daddy wants to hear this.

God, He sent an angel down
God, He sent an angel down
God, He sent an ang—

Da-a-ddy!
Just a minute. One more minute.
I want "Five Little Ducks"!
Just a second.

Angel locked the lion's jaw
Angel locked the lion's jaw
Angel locked the—

Five. Little. Ducks!

Five little ducks went out one day
Over the hills and far away
Mother duck said "Quack, quack, quack"
But only four little ducks came back

I would squeeze the steering wheel in frustration, unnerved by the thought of five ducklings lost and worried that not finishing my prayer-song would jinx me. Soon, though, I would be singing along, finding comfort in ducks found. Me singing, Mary's hand resting lightly on my neck, and the sight of Nora in the rearview mirror, waving her hands as she sang her—our—song.

Sad mother duck went out one day
Over the hills and far away
Mother duck said "Quack, quack, quack"
And all of her five little ducks came back

I DRANK WATER, but it tasted like liquid lead. I shaved, but there was scant need. I had the same blue eyes, the same teeth, the same hint of a cleft in my chin, but I bore little resemblance to Dan Barry. I looked more like Arthur, my ten-minute roommate at Sloan-Kettering, which meant that now we both looked like Uncle Fester. Once chemo-rinsed, we cancer-struck become like one another and different from the rest. That is why, when my friend Jon Elsen and his fiancée, Ellen, asked me to be in their wedding party, I tried to dodge the offer, saying that if I put on a tuxedo I'd look like Daddy Warbucks on crack.

I'll screw up your wedding album, I said.

Jon persisted because he knew that he could. The two of us had grown up in journalism together, first at the *Journal Inquirer* and now in Manhattan, where he was the business editor for the *New York Post*. Although I cringed at the thought of parading before a hundred wedding guests—a harbinger of mortality in a rented tux—I consented. They could always have their photos retouched.

The evening before the rehearsal dinner, Dr. Pfister stood before me in one of the examining rooms at Sloan-Ketttering and shared some encouraging news: according to my latest CT scan, the tumor seemed to be shrinking. He did not smile, he did not shake my hand. He only said that while shrinkage is better than growth, my prognosis remained uncertain. Oh, and one other thing: my red blood cell count was so low that I needed an immediate blood transfusion, for which there was at least a two-hour wait.

By this point I would have licked a subway platform clean rather than spend another second in a hospital, so I decided to breathe in the fresh autumn air and find a place to eat. But exhaustion took me by my knees within a block, and I had to rest for a while on a soot-covered stoop on First Avenue. I felt frightened and embarrassed by my weakness, as the young and old hustled past me on an evening alive with New York possibility. A few looked at me for a beat too long, and I answered their thoughts—And so young too!—with narrowed eyes that suggested they kiss my Irish ass. I resented what I represented: an intrusion upon thoughts of where to get a drink and what movie to see, a reminder of what awaits us all, and on such a gorgeous night. Most people looked through me, though, which bothered me even more. It seemed that without hair and a rosy complexion—without good health—I wasn't there. In fact, I took insult whether people noticed me or not.

I tried to rationalize my hurt away. The reactions of the people passing by were perfectly understandable, I thought. The metropolis knows full well that Chemoboy needs to conserve his energy to fight the forces of evil.

A misunderstanding over destiny has left our hero, a mild-mannered reporter at a major metropolitan newspaper, battling a grave disease. To save his life, doctors have pumped gallons of toxic chemicals into his bloodstream, rendering him powerless and invisible. Still, our hero is determined to live: to use active verb tense in his writing, to rail against injustice and inconsiderate drivers, to hug his beautiful wife and young child.

Join him now for the next installment of "The Amazing Adventures of Chemoboy."

Chemoboy, in fact, was just one of my superhero identities; I had become my own Justice League of America. There were times when I morphed into Detached Man and talked about my cancer the way others might discuss lawn care (It's in the trachea, but there's no sign yet of spread). Other times I was Magnanimo, taking no offense when people refused to accept my true, medical-chart identity (forty-one-year-old nonsmoker), or when one person quickly segued from the matter of my health to possible job openings at the *Times* and could I help her. And who could forget the Jokester, with my arsenal of disarming one-liners about the underrated benefits of chemotherapy. (Hey, it's lowered my cholesterol!) Ba-dum-bum.

I continued trudging along First Avenue at twilight, until a diner's neon glow filled me with a craving for true comfort food, a meatloaf platter. Feeling as though I barely warranted a table for one, I took a seat in the back, where the waitress handed me a menu as thick as a hymnal.

Somethin' to drink, dear?

She had dyed-black hair twirled like boardwalk custard, and a way about her that said she truly cared whether I chose peas or carrots. Given that she worked in a diner around the corner from Sloan-Kettering, I figured that she had seen plenty of superheroes in her day. I ordered the meatloaf and a Coke.

Okay, hon, she said.

The meat and gravy were of uncertain provenance, the potatoes were instant, and the beans were green logs of mush: just the way I like my diner food. But my ambitions surpassed my abilities, and so I picked—a green log here, a scoop of white stuff there—and stared into the fluorescent nothingness. The loud conversation of a man and woman sitting two booths away revealed that they were resident doctors at Sloan-Kettering. They were passionately sharing a plate of mozzarella-drenched French fries while gossiping about colleagues and patients. Suddenly, the woman whirled around, as though to catch someone creeping up on her. And there I sat, a person from the other side of the bedpan. She flashed a cosmetic-counter smile, turned back to her companion, and began talking in that stage whisper I had heard so often from my hospital bed.

My waitress seemed to intuit what was going through my mind, and rushed over to ease my pain with that glutinous salve known as rice pudding. Returning a few minutes later, she placed an eleven-dollar check on the table.

Take care, hon, she said.

———

THE NURSE IN the transfusion unit released the cinch, sending dark red tears inching down the transparent IV line. The drops fell every three seconds at first, I was counting, but soon the trickle slowed to every six seconds, or just ten drops a minute. Just what I needed at midnight, I thought: a malfunctioning IV. The nurse finger-flicked the bag to no avail. When she pulled the apparatus apart to find the problem, a single drop of blood fell onto my khaki pants.

Being a Barry, and given my horror-movie surroundings, I naturally thought of Bela Lugosi, which conjured memories of Boris Karloff, and Lon Chaney Jr., and Maria Ouspenskaya, the great character actress who, as the gypsy woman in *The Wolf Man*, knew the meaning of the mark of the pentagram. In an instant I was back in my childhood living room, surrounded by parents and siblings, watching old Universal horror movies, my father doing a dead-on impression of Ouspenskaya. And then I was back in the present, in a recliner, being pumped with someone else's blood. My throat was parched, my head was throbbing, my doctor had just leveled with me—I'm not going to bullshit you; this is still a very serious problem—and all I could do was take silly pride in knowing who Maria Ouspenskaya was. And Colin Clive, as Dr. Frankenstein. And Una O'Connor, the great screamer. And Glenn Strange, who played the monster in *Abbott and Costello Meet Frankenstein*.

Could the world afford to lose such knowledge? Do you want me to recite the names of twenty Abbott and Costello movies right now? I will!

If you let me live.

One o'clock in the morning, and the first bag had yet to empty.

Three o'clock, and I was the only patient left. The second bag was still plump with blood, dangling like some overripe tomato from an IV vine. I don't know why it's so slow tonight, said a new nurse, who had replaced the old nurse. Sometimes they're fast, dear, and sometimes they're slow.

Four o'clock, and the drips came in five-second intervals. Tonight I would be at a rehearsal dinner for Jon and Ellen. Tomorrow, Mary and I would dance in defiance as much as joy, stepping lightly one two three, one two three, in and around the happy. But for now there was no one two three, only drip, drip, drip. God Almighty, I thought, get me the hell out of here.

The nurse, anonymous in white, came in to check the bag.

Five more minutes, she said.

THE WAITING ROOM at Sloan-Kettering's satellite offices in Mid-town Manhattan had everything you could want, short of a nurse rush-ing in to say you can go home now, it's all been a clerical mix-up. Effort had been made to create a serene, new-age atmosphere for patients awaiting consultations and treatment. A small waterfall in the center of the room whispered whatever karma you wished to hear. There was even a coffee machine that made moccachino. Such were the amenities avail-able to you for the price of admission, which was to have cancer.

And when the time came to talk with a doctor about your latest CT scan or blood test, a young and vital assistant would stroll through the room and softly call your name: Mr. Barry? Daniel Barry? Mr. Barry?

I knew the drill. I was a regular. I would put down the grapefruit juice that I imagined was somehow making me stronger and follow the young and vital person through a door that would close with a hush. Then, after a while, I would emerge. Whatever the news—good, bad, stable—I would flee like some fugitive being chased by the one-armed man of reality. Outside this place, I wanted life to be extended like pulled taffy, so that I could slow down and savor the moments of my existence. But inside this well-appointed waiting room, I wanted life to speed up. I wanted to see the doctor now and get the hell out, even if it meant standing on a crowded E train stuck between stations—because even that was life, and better than waiting. Others might embrace these waits beside an artificial waterfall as perfect for reflection, but I simply was not evolved enough to find bliss in the quiet of chaos.

So I had sat there, racing in place as time inched along: with a large tumor, and then a smaller one; with hair, and then none; in the short sleeves of summer, and now the fleece jackets of fall.

Bald, blanched, wasted by a chemo regimen that stopped just short of including Drano, I wanted to be glad again; I wanted to be happy in the moment without having to think about how lucky I was to *have* the moment. I glanced up at one of the young and vital assistants walking past, thinking that she might be looking for me. But I returned to my private session of self-pity when the name she called was not mine.

Mr. Klemperer? Werner Klemperer? Mr. Klemperer?

Slowly, the name worked its way through my mental fog. Klemperer? Werner Klemperer? There's only one Werner Klemperer: Colonel Klink.

Just then I looked up to see the character actor shuffle past me, a nurse guiding him by the arm. He had won two Emmy Awards for his portrayal as the befuddled commandant of a Nazi prisoner-of-war camp on *Hogan's Heroes*, but he was always so much more than a character in that '60s sitcom. And now here he was before me, so much more than Colonel Klink.

The pulled taffy of time stretched back, and again I was a boy, watching afternoon reruns of the program with my brother and sisters. Then I was a teenager, standing in the outfield of a baseball park on a late summer's night, shagging fly balls as a junior high school band practiced the *Hogan's Heroes* theme over and over. Now, thirty years later, here I was with Werner Klemperer, two POWs sharing a waiting room equipped with everything but a laugh track.

It was all so absurd, even funny—as funny as the time that a fussy nurse accidentally squirted me in the face with a chemotherapy solution, as if in homage to an old Three Stooges routine. For hours after seeing Klemperer, I could not get the theme song out of my mind. I wanted to march, I wanted to shag flies, I wanted to laugh. Klemperer would die the following year, but the mere sight of him had buoyed my spirits, filling me with a determination to linger a while, like all those black-and-white sitcoms that lasted long enough to reach color.

I WAS NOT rising so much as I was being raised up, hallelujah. Flat on my back, my arms stretched behind my head, my cotton robe opened at the chest. Filled with dread, yet strangely excited about the experience that awaited me. In the distance, the soaring strains of Gershwin's *Rhapsody in Blue*. Was this how it felt to die?

All set? the technician asked.

I guess so, I said.

You'll be fine, he said.

He was from the Bronx. He had a paunch and a neatly trimmed beard. And right now he was the most important person in my life. During his short breaks he would trot outside to his car and shove quarters into a meter on Fifth Avenue. I was the fifth of thirty radiation patients he would see that day, but he knew that this was my first time. He reassured me with his words and with the music emanating from his boom box sitting in the corner. He had tapes of everything from Mozart to Motown.

Just keep still.

Immediately above me dangled a laser, its eye calibrated to send a beam of radiation directly at a tattooed dot at the base of my throat, marking where the tumor resided within me. The dot was about the size of one of those white candied balls imbedded in a nonpareil. At Christmastime, Mary and I would always share a box of nonpareils. We'd open a bottle of red wine, make sure the blaze in the fireplace was just so, and . . .

Just remember not to move, the technician said. He checked me one more time, tucking the sheet tighter around the raised plastic cot that supported me. Then, as he walked to the door, he said it again. Remember: Don't move.

Being stuck with that needle for my first round of chemotherapy had been a Moment, of course, but this, my first of thirty treatments of radiotherapy, seemed so much more theatrical. Here was Daniel Francis Barry, being raised several feet from the ground and presented to the heavens, as if to say, And what about him?

Frozen in place and staring at the dropped white ceiling, I noticed the rough pattern of a cross among the random holes peppered across its surface. The lights flickered, and then a grinding sound—the sound of radiation, I supposed—found its cue in Gershwin's rhapsody. The slight taste of metal came to the back of my throat, and I prayed to the pockmark cross on the ceiling.

24

T ELL ME, DOCTOR, tell me oh tell. Tell me for the Love of
God tell me. Tell me what comes next in my story.

Tell me what happens to this Daniel, in this Lion's Den. You
tell me what you know, and I'll tell you what I know. They called me
Danny. Born in the time of Eisenhower, the first child of Gene and
Noreen; grandchild of farmers and drinkers; descendant of singers of
songs and tellers of tales; of scrappers, Doctor, bounce-back scrappers
who just wanted some peace and quiet, that's all, goddammit, but who
seemed to find peace only in beds of clay. Born in Gotham and raised in
a park with no deer; drank the milk of ShopRite and ate the bread of
raspberry drizzle; learned the Gaelic songs of love and war but could not
sing them; chased white balls through fields and down sewers; flinched
from the hands of others, some in robes; got paid to tell tales; loved, lost,
and loved again; heard the cries of a newborn, the moans of parents, the
reassuring whispers of a wife. Cursed with cancer in a midparagraph of
life and forced to endure altered waters and beams of fire in hopes
of hope.

Tell me now, Doctor, tell me the rest of that paragraph, just don't tell
me it's the last. I know that my story is no different from any other story,
that I am everybody, anybody, but it is my story, the only one I have. Tell
me the story, Doctor. Tell me my story only please.

Please tell me there's more.

THE TREATMENT ENDED. Dr. Pfister told Mary and me that it would take several weeks before the inflammation would subside and a CT scan could be taken of the battlefield that was my chest. He urged us to *really enjoy* this Christmas. He said it twice, in fact, using the same heavy emphasis: *Really enjoy.* When I pushed him a little, he leveled with me, as always. If the tumor is still evident in the next scan, he said, that would be *very bad.* He said that twice too: Very bad.

Really enjoy. Very bad. Really enjoy. Very bad.

We traveled home by train, a woman and her whisper of a man, her hello-can-anyone-hear-me-of-a-man, tucked beside her in the seat like a thing of wax. After five months of kitchen-sink therapy and thirty days of radiation, I felt sapped of me. I trained my eyes to look past the scary reflection in the window and out into a December night in New Jersey. I saw no snow-white swans of hope, only the strands of Christmas lights strung across the houses of strangers. O Holy Night my ass, I thought, so cold and forbidding and uncertain was this Advent of mine.

Mary's father was baby-sitting Nora at his house, where she was toddling about the living room when we walked in, clutching her copy of *Goodnight Moon.* Mary did her best to make believe that everything was fine, sidestepping that nagging matter of life and death by asking whether I had a hankering for dinner. Whatever, I answered. Exhausted from the after-effects of my treatment and our meeting with Pfister, I collapsed into the folds of the couch to stare without comprehension at the television.

The hell with this, I thought. I have to shoot.

I slipped into a St. Bonaventure sweatshirt that swallowed me up, dug out a basketball from the hall closet, and went out into the cold and dark for another solitary encounter with a basketball hoop. How many years now had I presented myself before the basket, seeing in its eighteen-inch diameter the magical ring between what is and what could be. Then, in my childhood backyard in Deer Park, shooting at a backboardless basket bolted to a crooked pole, there by the light streaming through the kitchen door window; now, in my wife's childhood backyard in Maplewood, peering into the night at a basket secured above her father's garage door. Suddenly, light. Mary had flicked the switch for the backyard floodlights. On stage at center court: me, a ball, and cancer.

I dribbled a few times, testing the ball's obedience. The ping of inflated ball on asphalt echoed off the surrounding houses, where people ate their dinners, unwound, talked of Christmas approaching or not. In the distance, the New Jersey Transit train to Dover—an eon removed, it seemed, from the Long Island Rail Road train to Ronkonkoma—clattered past. The wind brushed against leafless trees. A dog barked, as all dogs must.

Bonnie, Pixie, Gypsy! Good girls.

My chemo-numb fingertips searched again for the Braille of the ball, the slight black indentation that you feel more than you hold. The seam. There.

The first few shots clanked off the front of the rim. It was as though the treatment had affected my depth perception. More likely, I was just weak. Slowly, though, the hand-eye coordination, the instinctive adjustment to the late-fall winds—it all came back to me. I inhaled the cold air as deep as I could, then imagined the puffs of my exhalations to be the release of fetid, disease-ridden, hospital air.

I hit a short jump shot, and God did that feel nice. I felt again that intense desire for competition, the kind that makes diving on asphalt for a loose ball in a pickup game seem logical.

Fuck, I thought. And I shot.

Fuck you, I thought. And shot again.

No way, you bastard. No way. Another shot.

I prepared myself for what lay ahead by engaging in my game, my mental-physical-spiritual game. Ten consecutive foul shots, wasn't it? To beat whom? Cancer? Was my disease wearing a black basketball jersey, leaning over to rebound my miss? Was death prepared to block my foul shot with his scythe? It's supposed to be a free throw, but then again, death is death. It cheats. Was I going mad?

I could not help myself. No matter how absurd, I needed to view my predicament as a competition. One. Two. Three. Four. Five. Six. Seven.

Eight. Nine. Ten. Ten, you fucker, ten. You—what were my father's words of fist-waving rage? Oh yeah. Ten, you motherless bastard.

When I wanted to make the high school basketball team, I shot baskets. When I wanted a date to the prom, I shot baskets. When I wanted my parents to stop arguing, stop suffering, stop, I shot baskets. When I didn't know what to do with my life, when I was about to be married, when we went through nearly seven years of infertility treatments and adoption travails, I shot baskets. When we were blessed with Nora, I shot and shot until I made twenty consecutive baskets—not ten—to seal the agreement that God would help us always to do what was best for our beautiful daughter. And when my mother was dying, I shot baskets, thinking—what a fool—that each foul shot I made would somehow ease her pain and provide graceful passage into the next life. This foul shot is for my mother, I would say to myself, this foul shot is for her.

Now it was time to resurrect my basketball dialogue with God. Vespers, in the chapel of a backyard court, before a choir of dogs and trains, in the cold month of Your son's birth, when Christmas lights blink and wink from naked trees.

In the name of the Father and the Son and the Holy Spirit, Amen. Okay, God, I'm back. Fuck this. Not fuck You, for that would be sacrilege. But fuck this, this cancer. You know what I'm saying, don't you, God. Fuck this. No it is done; *it* ain't over. Okay God, gather round me. Yeah, yeah, I know You are all around me, You are everywhere, but the hell with that catechism shit. Gather round me and listen up. Here's the bet: if I make ten consecutive foul shots, I get to live. Okay? God?

I searched for the seam. I arced the ball into blackness.

One.

THE DISEMBODIED VOICE told me what to do: Breathe in. Hold your breath. Breathe.

Once again: Breathe in. Hold your breath. Breathe.

That was it, the telltale CT scan. I stepped off the cot and turned to look for a hint of my fate in the faces of the technicians behind the glass. Nothing. But that did not stop me from interpreting their lack of expression to mean that the scan had revealed an oil slick across my chest. So I called from the payphone outside the office, for no other reason than to say it, and to hear it.

I'm scared, I said.

I know you're scared, Mary said, again. But I also know that it's going to be all right. I know it.

How can you know?

I know.

I found enough comfort in just this to make my way through chaotic and vibrant streets, back to my newsroom refuge.

A week later, in that new-age waiting room, a young and vital assistant appeared from nowhere to call out above the soothing ripple of the artificial waterfall.

Daniel Barry? Mr. Barry? Daniel Barry?

She led Mary and me down a hall to an examining room, said that the doctor would be right with us, and closed the door. My wife and I looked at each other. This was it. Everything—*Everything!*—rested on what we were about to be told about my latest scan. I sat down and muttered a few disjointed Hail Mary fragments: Blessed art thou among women and—and—oh Mary, please take care of me please. Amen.

We skimmed over sections of that day's *Times*, but the drama of its news seemed to pale beside our own unfolding news event. It was February, the paper said, the month of my birth; February, so cold. We paced. We sat down. We held hands, then released the hold because my palm was damp with panic sweat. We stared at the silvery doorknob, waiting for it to turn.

A half hour passed. Then an hour.

This is bad, Mary, I said. If it were good news, he would have come in by now and we'd be out of here. He's probably taking so long because he has to get psyched up to tell us the bad news.

Dan, he has dozens of other patients. For all you know, he's taking so long because he has to give someone else bad news. Trust me: it's going to be all right.

Aah, Mary. I'm losing my mind.

I know.

An hour and a half. Two hours. Then, finally, the doorknob turned, and in came the long white coat, the file held in one hand, the stethoscope around the neck. Dr. Pfister, we meet again. Tall, angular, leaning forward to hear the patient's every word. Would he wheel me around the block if I wanted fresh air in my dying days? The door clicked behind him.

Well, he said. Your scan was clean.

Mary cried, oh Mary cried, for the first time in my presence in nearly a year, through all the bad news she had never, and now she was, Mary crying for joy. And Pfister smiled, for the first time since I had known him, flashing a grin so foreign to me that it was like seeing a bishop in street clothes. But I am a reporter, a skeptic, a professional doubter: Dan Barry.

But what does this mean?

It means the regimen that we cobbled together for you worked, as far as we can tell. There was no sign of the tumor.

But is this good?

Of course, he said. Yes.

No—?

No.

I wanted something more definitive from him, maybe a written promise that the cancer would not come back, that it could not come back, that it was medically impossible for me to be diagnosed with cancer ever again. Say it, Pfister, say it.

But what does it mean for me? I asked. What next?

We'll monitor you with a scan every three months, for now. And if it stays clean, then we'll do the scans less frequently. And if you're still clean after five years, then you and I are going to a Yankees game together.

You keep saying "if."

Nothing is definite, especially since we never determined the root of your cancer.

Is that bad, though?

Look. Just be glad that the scan was clean.

I was still not convinced.

I'm not trying to be difficult, I said slowly. It's just that—Is this good?

You don't understand, my doctor said. I thought you'd be in a hospice by Christmas.

The image stunned me. My doctor had been considering what I had most feared: hospice. I would be my mother: Mary, Mary. Pull me up. There in the living room of my house, family members gathered round, telling stories over plates of spaghetti and cans of beer. Pull me up, Mary, pull me up.

Dan, he said, locking me with a stare. This. Is. Good.

Finally, I understood. This was good.

EPILOGUE

And now the storm is over
And we are safe and well
We will go into a Public House
And we'll sit and drink like hell
We will drink strong ale and porter
And we'll make the rafters roar
Until our money is all spent
Then we'll go to sea once more

—"The Holy Ground"

A<small>ND THERE WE WERE</small>. Nora like a chick in her yellow slicker, Mary wrapped in a sweater matching her serene blue eyes, and me in that tattered tweed blazer of a dead merchant marine. Down we went along Ireland's western back roads, under Galway skies pregnant with rain. Past the stone Celtic crosses jutting from the unmade beds of graveyards, past the swans of Coole, past.

We stayed in the farmhouse of my mother's sister, Chrissie, and her husband, Sonny, in the hamlet known as Laughtyshaughnessy, down a boreen from where my mother was born and just beyond the town of Gort. Chrissie and Sonny's children are grown and gone now, as far away as Dublin and as close as the house next door, except for their youngest, Brendan. Struck and killed many years ago while walking home from school, he was just fourteen. Into town and back, into town and back, two-dozen times a week Chrissie and Sonny must pass the memorial stone that marks the spot. And each time they do, worn fingertips tap worn brows in hurried signs of the cross.

Sonny is now in his eighties. He wears a dark-blue suit most every day, sometimes with a Christmas tie that can play "Jingle Bells." He pelts rocks at the birds nesting in his shed's roof, then takes long, solitary walks in the fields, gathering sticks to burn in the hearth. He closely follows current events, by television, newspaper, and radio. Before going to bed each night he has a bottle of Guinness, a piece of chocolate, and a banana. And if you coax him enough, and if the moment suits him, he will close his eyes and sing like a lark.

> *You may travel far far from your own native home*
> *Far away o'er the mountains, away o'er the foam*
> *But of all the fine places that I've ever been*
> *Sure there's none to compare with the Cliffs of Dooneen*

In the lined face of Chrissie, I saw my mother. Wasn't it like Noreen, she said, not to tell us that she was sick; I could have flown and been to see her one last time. I nodded, though I knew my mother never would have allowed it. A visit from her sister or a visit from the Pope, it didn't matter; my mother would have imagined the pity in the eyes. Chrissie's own eyes welled, and she was off to boil more water, for cups of tea must always be in the hand, if only for the warmth of it. And then she was back in her chair, positioned between the window and the hearth so that she could flick her cigarette ash into the fire while looking out the window for the odd car that might come down the boreen. The radio that sat high upon a shelf rattled with the broadcasts of a station that follows a traditional reel with Jim Morrison moaning for baby to light his fire.

With a cracked cup of tea firm in her hand, Chrissie began to weave one of her stories, bits of different-colored yarn that her tongue somehow laces together into something fine and complete. It may begin with the dear price of land now that the country is doing better than it was, segue into the tip that any cloudiness in the jar tells you the poteen is no good, and then reach back to the time, say, when my mother was just eleven, and one of the nuns in town slapped her for just being, and a beloved aunt marched back into the school to find the offending nun and—here Chrissie's eyes narrow as she zeroes in on the punchline—told her: If you ever strike any of the Minogue children ever again you'll get the back of my hand yourself, you magpie!

Magpie! How does the rhyme go?

One for sorrow, two for joy. Three for a girl, and four for a boy. Five for silver, six for gold. And seven for a secret that's never been told.

I liked that, I liked that a lot. I liked it so much that I began hunting through the cabinet for one of Sonny's bottles of silky black beer.

WE LINGERED A while in Gort, where years ago one of the few phones in town was to be found among the bins of potatoes and boxes of corn flakes at Gallagher's market. Its rare ring would summon the proprietor, and over the line he would detect a distant yet familiar voice, straining to be heard above an ocean's muffle. A call from the States, young Nora Minogue wanting to pass on a message to her family: It's a boy! It's another boy! It's a girl this time! And now she has a sister, God love her! *Three for a girl, and four for a boy.* Hurried conversations, these; the cost was dear, so dear, back then.

We spent hours with my mother's brother, Joe, his white mane combed back, his eyes locking me in, his hands rough from a lifetime of hard labor. He has to take it easy now, only Heineken, no Guinness. But he remains proud of his legendary stamina: having gambled and drank but mostly having worked, the measure of a man as defined by the code of another time and place. He too can spin the stories, some in agreement with Chrissie's, some in contradiction, all echoing my mother. When he recalls racing his father, Dan Minogue, through the long-grass fields on a Sunday morning to the church in Shanaglish, you can hear my grandfather's heavy breathing, sense the dying man's pride in seeing his blond boy scamper ahead, all legs and elbows and life.

On one of our last days in Ireland, we joined Chrissie in her Sunday ritual of dancing at the Archway in Gort. Sunday night was once when farmers came into town, maybe with their wives, maybe to find a bride, often to dance. Now it is mostly the older people, the ones set in their ways, who come: the men at the bar, faces lined and hair pomaded, softly talking about this one and that one between sips of stout; the women around the small tables, sweaters pulled over their shoulders, whispering about that one and this one between sips of ginger ale that may have a drop of something more. On this night their whispers sounded like the trickles of a spring-fed brook.

At the front of the room, a farmer from the nearby crossroads of Peterswell removed an accordion from its black case, with all the care of a mother lifting an infant from a cradle. As he set the instrument on his knee, two men beside him faced the crowd in silence, one holding a flute, the other a guitar. Men and women gathered on the worn wooden dance floor, silent as if in a shared hypnotic state. A burst of ceili music shook the room, and then they began to whirl, arms interlocked, bleats of glee escaping their lips.

As I watched Chrissie spin about, her eyes closed in seeming rapture, I realized that I could not identify the reel she danced to, yet I had often heard it in the distance, flowing from joyous to mournful and back again, from present to past. I could feel the pull of its ancient call, as black shoes banged in cadence on a scuffed floor, as if in defiant exclamation to every challenge ever faced by the Irish. Stomp to them all—stomp, stomp, stomp!

Sitting, watching, I let the timeless music carry me a while. I pounded my feet hard against the floor, stomping in rhythmic confirmation of my joys and losses, my relief, my continuance. The music ended, and the people returned to their places, shirts as damp as if they had jigged and reeled in a spring rain. A moment. They reached for their glasses; I reached for my pen.

We packed our things, our Paddy's whiskey and Barry's tea, our pens and paper, and prepared to return to a colonial-style home in New Jersey, where basketball hoops beckon from backyards, and a newsroom in New York, where the focus could shift to the stories of others. Why had I chosen Ireland as the place to celebrate a life tenuously extended, I could not say. I harbored no desire to determine whether I was descended from rebels or traitors, peasants or kings. My instincts told me that mine had eaten the famine grass to survive. Maybe that had been the pull.

Before saying good-bye to Ireland, though, we traveled the narrow back roads to Kinvara, a village nestled to Galway Bay the way sleeping Nora was nuzzled this night against Mary's chest. We stood together, my wife and I, beside the pier's wall of stone, accepting the seawater's applause for having made it this far. We felt at home. I gazed down into wild waters as dark as the stout that awaited me, and realized that I knew now what it was like to nearly drown. Then there came the sting of a salt-water blessing upon my face.

ACKNOWLEDGMENTS

LTHOUGH I ACCEPT entire responsibility and blame for this book, it has many authors. They share this story, having been there with me, and for me.

From my Deer Park days, I thank the nurturing and patient residents of West 23rd Street, especially those who put up with the Barrys for all those years; the Hornik and McShane families; Jim Sutton and John Morris; and Deer Park—just Deer Park—often forgotten except when heroes are needed, as on one September Tuesday.

From my St. Anthony's days, I thank the Franciscan Brothers, especially Benilde Montgomery and Cletus Burke, who teach me still; and my bicentennial classmates, especially Brian McShane and Dave Kreinsen, who for three decades now have helped me to sort it all out. And from my St. Bonaventure days, I thank the Fede family; a certain Acra Manor ecdysiast; my professors at the university, especially Jean Trevarton Ehman, Jim Martine, and Rick Simpson; the Rev. Dan Riley; Carol Palumbo; and that core of friends who have stuck by me. They know who they are.

From my Connecticut days, I thank those who taught me news: Elizabeth Ellis, Chris Powell, Bob Boone, and Ralph Williams; those who sat beside me in the newsroom; and Nancy Duffy. From my Rhode Island days, I thank Brian Andrews, Terry Burgess, and Brendan Doherty of the state police; the Patriarca crime family, who provided material so unselfishly; Joe Cavanagh; and all those in the *Providence Journal* newsroom, whom I now consider family.

And now, in my New York days, I thank so many at *The New York Times*: Joe Lelyveld, Howell Raines, and Bill Keller; Mike Oreskes, Joyce Purnick, Jon Landman, and Susan Edgerley; Andy Rosenthal, Mike Winerip, and Jack Kadden; Angel Franco, Fred Conrad, and the photographers, editors, researchers, and support staff who always improve the story. Thanks also to the Wesleyan Cinema Archives; the *Times*, the *Journal*, and the *Journal Inquirer* for allowing me to revisit previously published material; and Holly McIntyre, for helping me to relocate a bit of Bonaventure lore that I had misplaced. In addition, I want to acknowledge the use of a few books for reference: *Deer Park Through the Years*, by Anthony F. Cesare; the dedication book for the opening of Sts. Cyril and Methodius Church in 1963; and *Recollections: Deer Park, 1900–1950*, by a creative writing and illustrative design class at Deer Park High School.

I can never thank enough the extraordinary people at Memorial Sloan-Kettering Cancer Center; Dr. Lynda Mandell; and, of course, Dr. David Pfister, who is nothing less than heroic.

I also want to thank those who help me to find my moorings, including Mary Ellen and Tom Barrett, Bob Barry, Betsy Causey, Susan Chira, Gail Collins, Tom and Viv Conlon, Rev. Dennis Corrado, Dave Crombie, Kevin Davitt, Barb Durr, Jim Dwyer, Jon Elsen, Tom Fay, Rick Funaro, Terry Golway, Abby Goodnough, Mike Gray, Mike Hefferan, Paul Hendrie, Tom Heslin, John and Kathy Hill, Jan Hoffman, Margo Jefferson, Leith and Maria Johnson, Mary Jordan and Kevin Sullivan, Bill Keveney, Rev. Mark Lane, Bill Malinowski and Mary Murphy, Kevin McCabe, Patty McQueen, Mark Pazniokas, Kate Phillips, Matt Purdy, Peter Quinn, Willie Rashbaum, Joe Sexton, Dan Shea, David Shipley, Debbie Sontag, Rhonda Stearley, John Sullivan, Don Van Natta—and Don and Tina Seibert, who are always there.

I thank all the Trinitys, especially Joseph Trinity, the loving patriarch.

I thank my friends in Kinvara: P. J. Mara, Maureen Heffernan, and all the Brogans. I especially thank my Hartigan-Minogue relatives in Ireland— Chrissie and Sonny Nestor, Joe and Mary Minogue, and all my cousins— who have never begrudged me my questions, my befuddlement, my need for another cup of tea.

The stories in this book would have remained in old notebooks and bar napkins if Todd Shuster, my agent, had not called one day to challenge me; if he and his partner, Lane Zachary, had not pushed me; and if the people at W. W. Norton had not supported me at every turn. Among them: Jeannie Luciano, the director of publishing; Bill Rusin, the sales director; and so many others: Louise Brockett, Abigail Cleaves, Felice Mello, Amanda Morrison, Debra Morton Hoyt, Nancy Palmquist, Elizabeth Riley, Gina Webster—and the ever-patient Brendan Curry. Above all, there is Bob Weil, my tireless and gifted editor; his sense of language and storytelling so permeates this book that he deserves to share the byline.

None of this would have been possible without the Barrys, and those who dare to love them. My brother, Brian, and my sisters, Brenda and Elizabeth, who make me proud of my surname. My father, Gene, who, among other gifts, even proofread this book. And my mother, Noreen, so dearly missed. Finally, I'd like to thank my daughters, Nora and Grace. And Mary. That is how this acknowledgment should end: Mary.

ABOUT THE AUTHOR

DAN BARRY IS the "About New York" columnist for *The New York Times*. He has been a reporter for the *Times* since September 1995, and has served as the newspaper's City Hall bureau chief, Long Island bureau chief, and general-assignment reporter. He has written extensively about many issues and events, including city politics, police brutality, and the World Trade Center catastrophe and its aftermath.

Born in 1958, Barry grew up in Deer Park, New York, where he played a lot of baseball and basketball without ever learning to hit for power or dribble with his right hand. He dug ditches, manned the counters at several Long Island delicatessens, and earned degrees in journalism from St. Bonaventure University and New York University. Before joining the *Times*, he worked for four years at the *Journal Inquirer* in Manchester, Connecticut, and for nearly eight years at the *Providence Journal* in Rhode Island.

He has won several journalism honors, including a George Polk Award that he shared with two other *Providence Journal* reporters in 1992; a Pulitzer Prize for Investigative Reporting that he shared with other members of the *Journal*'s investigative team in 1994; and the American Society of Newspaper Editors award for deadline reporting in 2003.

Barry lives in Maplewood, New Jersey, with his wife and two daughters.